OFFERT LIVRE EN LIGNE

L'intégralité de votre livre et du corrigé correspondant* accessible en ligne

avec une simple connexion Internet !

+ Des outils utiles et intuitifs :

- sommaire interactif
- surlignage en couleurs
- notes personnelles et marque-page.

Pour ACTIVER votre livre en ligne

- Rendez-vous sur www.nathan.fr/livre-en-ligne .
- Créez un compte **Nathan** en suivant les indications en ligne
- Cliquez sur « Activer un livre », saisissez votre clé d'activation personnelle puis le mot du livre qui vous sera demandé.

Votre clé d'activation personnelle :

ODKZD5-CS4-B24G

Pour toute CONNEXION ULTÉRIEURE

Connectez-vous sur www.nathan.fr/livre-en-ligne avec vos identifiants **Nathan**

IMPORTANT

Votre clé d'activation est unique et personnelle : une fois utilisée, elle ne sera plus valide. Elle offre un accès de 24 mois à compter de la date d'activation. Elle est réservée à un seul utilisateur et ne peut être partagée.

Configuration minimale requise : Internet Explorer 8, Mozilla Firefox 3.4, Chrome, Safari, Opera toutes versions.
Retrouvez les conditions générales d'utilisation sur www.nathan.fr/livre-en-ligne.

Nathan

*Service disponible à partir du 31 août 2020, pour l'intégralité du manuel et de son corrigé.

DCG 12 Anglais appliqué aux affaires 978-2-09-167153-6

ÉPREUVE

DCG 12

Anglais appliqué aux affaires

Manuel & Applications

Dominique Daugeras

Claire Cornet

Groupe Revue Fiduciaire

Nathan

Édition : Samuel Briand-Favard

Conception maquette : Anne-Danielle Naname

Conception couverture : Vincent Rioult

Fabrication : Christine Aubert

Mise en pages : JOUVE

ISBN 978-2-09-167153-6

Sommaire

FICHES MÉTHODE

ANNEXES

Programme : UE 12
Anglais appliqué aux affaires

Programme du diplôme de comptabilité et gestion (DCG)
***BO* n° 25 du 20 juin 2019.**

Niveau L : 150 heures – 14 ECTS

LES COMPÉTENCES ATTENDUES :

- Comprendre et commenter, en anglais, des documents de la vie des affaires tels que des textes, graphiques, et tableaux tirés de revues ou d'un rapport annuel d'entreprise ;
- Rédiger une note de synthèse en français ou en anglais, à partir de documents en anglais concernant les thèmes ci-dessous ;
- Rédiger en anglais un document de travail.

LES THÈMES :

1. L'entreprise
L'organisation d'une entreprise
La révolution numérique
L'entreprise citoyenne
Stratégie et compétitivité d'une entreprise
L'économie sociale et solidaire
Conditions de travail et dialogue social
Communication et culture d'entreprise
2. Questions d'économie
Les énergies
La concurrence et la loi
La mondialisation
Les principaux espaces économiques régionaux
Les pays émergents
La protection sociale, l'évolution de la démographie

CHAPITRE

1

Company organisation

L'organisation de l'entreprise

The great secret of success

In an increasingly complex and volatile world, the key to a company's success is a high-performance organisation: this brings it an enormous competitive advantage.

What makes for[1] a high-performance organisation?

A company should normally have a clear, well-adapted organisation chart, or flow chart[2] showing who does what and who reports to whom. Organisation charts graphically show the firm's formal structure concerning authority, functions and relations. There are several types or organisations: the most common ones are hierarchical, but there are also matrix and linear structures (see page 8), etc. Organisational structures define staff members' positions, tasks and duties, so as to avoid overlapping[3].

The best organisation will be efficient only if it has the right person in the right place. The quality of the workforce is essential: in addition to[4] being motivated, competent and hard-working at all levels of the hierarchy, they must also be dynamic and able to work well with other people, possibly in teams.

Coordination and integration

The real power of any organisation arises from its capacity to coordinate and integrate people, activities and systems. The various departments or business units should communicate and work closely[5] with one another: for example, Sales with Accountancy, Manufacturing with Information Technology, Marketing with R&D (Research and Development), not to mention Human Resources, which plays an essential role. They have to work together in order to achieve the company's goals and values. The organisation should also help to encourage and integrate innovations which are essential to growth, and combine them with a global approach in the case of multinationals. The hierarchy must therefore be flexible and open to new, creative and even revolutionary ideas. Moreover, nowadays firms must take into account new laws imposing gender parity and try to provide a sensible work-life balance, especially for young parents and ageing workers.

Agility

This new concept for organisations is spreading: it means the ability to adapt quickly to innovations and market changes in an increasingly fast-changing environment.

Management's role

Managers should encourage coordination, integration, and innovation, which are essential in today's highly competitive world. They therefore must develop a strategy, encourage feedback, and conduct an analysis of the major activities (selling, marketing and advertising, order taking, invoicing[6], product development and manufacturing, project management, purchasing[7], maintenance, customer service, shipping[8]) in order to identify ways to make them more efficient and creative, cheaper and faster. They also have to define functions and responsibilities, supervise recruitment, decide on lay-offs[9] when necessary (even if they often do so reluctantly[10]), improve the company's social policy to motivate the staff, and control quality and prices to keep customers happy. They should also be charismatic leaders.

Making decisions

Leadership consists of making decisions, which is a difficult art: designing the organisation and the strategy, assigning the right tasks[11] to the right people clearly, making them accountable[12], as well as checking and tracking[13] the impact of the decisions made. As seen above, agility can also be helpful to good leadership.

Research shows that only 15% of companies have an organisation good enough to help them outperform[14] others. That is why many firms seek help from business organisation consultants, such as the well-known American (and international) ones, McKinsey, Bain or the Boston Consulting Group (BCG).

Various types of organisation charts

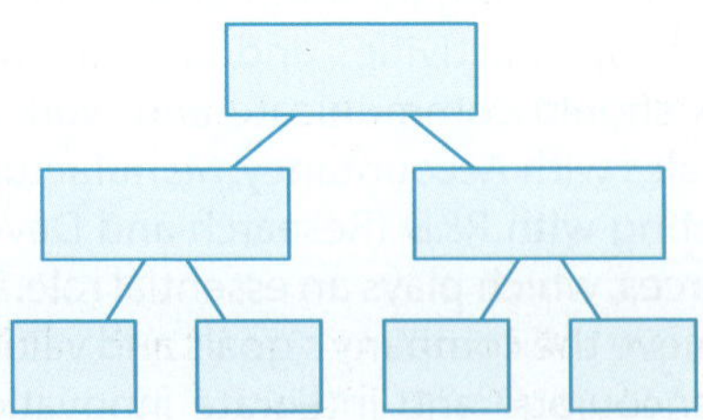

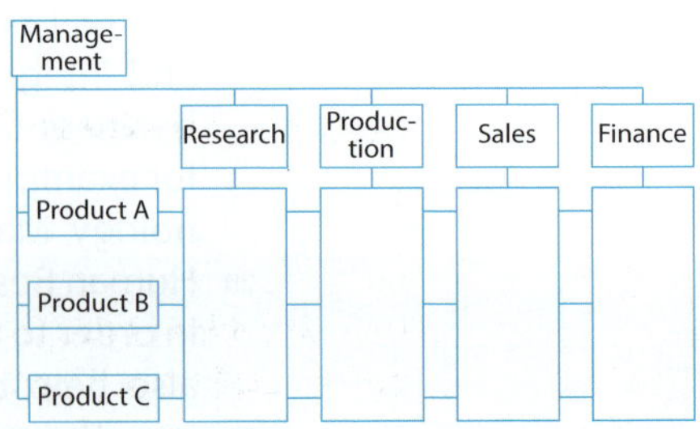

– **The hierarchical chart** (left) is the most classical and widespread one.

– **The matrix pattern**[15] (right) combines functional and product areas within[16] the organisation to obtain the advantages of each. Teams of functional personnel (e.g.[17] research, finance, technology, sales and marketing) report to a manager with project responsibility. Functional personnel also report to their functional bosses, who are responsible for maintaining the quality of functional performance. Within[17] the matrix, functional personnel report to two bosses, which requires on their part a lot of understanding and co-operation.

– **Linear or flat organisation** has few or no middle managers between employees and top management, because well-trained workers are supposed to be more productive when they are involved in the decision-making process, rather than supervised by several layers[18] of management. This is possible essentially in small firms or in units within big ones. Feedback is often quicker than in other organisations.

– Other structures can also be found, depending on schools of management, fashions, organisational specialists and consultants, etc.

1. to make for: *contribuer à.*
2. organisation / flow chart: *organigramme.*
3. overlapping: *chevauchement.*
4. in addition to: *en plus de.*
5. closely: *étroitement.*
6. invoicing: *facturation.*
7. purchasing : *service achats.*
8. shipping: *transport de fret.*
9. lay-off: *licenciement.*
10. reluctantly: *avec reticence.*
11. to assign a task: *assigner une tâche.*
12. to make sb accountable: *rendre qqn responsable (de ses actes).*
13. to track: *suivre à la trace.*
14. to outperform: *faire mieux que.*
15. matrix pattern: *modèle matriciel.*
16. within: *à l'intérieur de.*
17. eg: *par ex.*
18. layer: *couche, niveau.*

Repérer les notions essentielles

Answer the following questions.

a. Why is a good organisation essential?
b. Name six different company departments mentioned above.
c. What is an organisation or flow chart and what are the three main types?
d. What role does the manager play in the organisation of a company?
e. Describe the qualities of a good organisation.

Résumer le texte en français.

Résumez ce texte en français, *en 150 mots environ.*

Approfondir

Using the Internet, find information about the organisation of a successful company you know. Then give an oral report about it.

Lexical work

• acc**ou**ntancy	comptabilité, expertise comptable
• acc**ou**nting contr**o**l	contrôle de la comptabilité
• acc**ou**nts dep**a**rtment	service comptabilité
• to acqu**i**re / buy out / p**ur**chase	acheter, acquérir
• to app**oi**nt / assign to a position	nommer à un poste
• app**oi**ntment	nomination; rendez-vous
• to be on the p**ay**roll / staff	faire partie du personnel salarié
• board of d**i**rectors	conseil d'administration
• br**ai**nstorming s**e**ssion	réunion de réflexion informelle
• b**uy**out / acquis**i**tion	rachat d'entreprise
• CEO (chief ex**e**cutive **o**fficer) / m**a**naging d**i**rector	directeur général
• CFO (chief fin**a**ncial **o**fficer)	directeur financier
• to chair a comm**i**ttee / m**ee**ting	présider un comité / une réunion
• d**e**puty m**a**nager / ass**i**stant-m**a**nager	directeur adjoint
• div**e**stment	scission
• d**ow**nsizing	réduction d'effectifs
• eff**e**ctive / succ**e**ssful / eff**i**cient	performant
• eff**i**ciency / comp**e**titiveness	efficacité, compétitivité
• fac**i**lities	outils de production
• head **o**ffice	siège social
• to h**ea**dquarter a c**o**mpany	établir le siège social d'une société
• h**u**man res**ou**rces (HR) dep**a**rtment	direction des ressources humaines (DRH)
• lean str**u**cture	structure allégée
• m**a**nagement acc**ou**ntant	contrôleur de gestion
• m**a**nagement **au**dit	contrôle de gestion
• m**a**nagement **o**perating s**y**stem	système intégré de gestion
• to manuf**a**cture / to prod**u**ce	fabriquer, produire
• m**a**rketing (dep**a**rtment/**u**nit) m**a**nager	chef du service marketing
• to merge	fusionner
• mergers and acquis**i**tions / M&A	fusions-acquisitions
• m**i**ddle / j**u**nior m**a**nager	cadre moyen / débutant
• non-ex**e**cutive dir**e**ctor	membre du conseil d'administration
• PR (P**u**blic Rel**a**tions) dep**a**rtment	service de la communication
• pr**e**mises	locaux (de la société)
• to prom**o**te	promouvoir
• p**ur**chasing m**a**nager	directeur du service achats
• rank and file	personnel de base
• to res**i**gn, resign**a**tion	démissionner, démission
• restr**u**cturing	restructuration, réorganisation

• rules and regulations	règles, règlement
• to sell out	revendre, vendre en totalité
• senior / executive manager	cadre supérieur
• senior staff	ensemble des cadres supérieurs
• society	association, société philanthropique
• subsidiary	filiale
• team leader / spirit	chef / esprit d'équipe
• to temp	travailler en intérim
• temporary worker	travailleur intérimaire
• top management / manager	cadre(s) dirigeant(s)
• trainee	stagiaire
• turnover of capital / staff	rotation des capitaux / du personnel
• to upgrade	revaloriser, améliorer
• vice-president (US)	chef / directeur d'un service
• warehouse	entrepôt
• workshop	atelier
• to write off an operation	passer une opération par pertes et profits

Use the list

1 Complete the lists below with the corresponding verb or noun.

Verb	Noun	Verb	Noun
a. to acquire	▸ acquisition	d. to …	▸ temporary worker
b. to …	▸ appointment	e. to train	▸ …
c. to resign	▸ …	f. to merge	▸ …

2 Complete these sentences, making the necessary changes, and translate them.

subsidiary – facilities – efficient – mergers and acquisitions – vice-president – appoint – temporary worker – write off – Human Resources – premises – resign – trainee – position (x2)

a. Companies can grow externally thanks to … .
b. Mrs Watson has just been … to the … of … manager.
c. Finn and Co Ltd has just opened a … in Singapore.
d. Bill Graves, one of the …, has just … because he completely disagrees with the manager's reorganisation of the firm.
e. Our … really need to be modernised.
f. Jane, our …, is so efficient that we should offer her a permanent … .
g. … do not always want permanent jobs because they wish to remain free.

Grammar work

Articles indéfinis *a / an / Ø / some / any*

› Aide-mémoire grammatical, p. 163

Analysez, puis traduisez ces exemples en mettant (ou pas) l'article qui convient en français :

1. Ms Fox works as a manager at MTV Networks, a division of Viacom, an American media group.
2. She must find Ø new ways of doing Ø things.
3. This chain of shops sells some expensive clothes, and Ø others that are quite cheap.
4. That company knows how to save Ø time and Ø money.
5. A firm cannot operate without an accountant.
6. Can I ask you some questions?
7. Have you designed any marketable innovations?

Remarque

Some et *any* dans une phrase interrogative sont des déterminants qui peuvent correspondre à des indéfinis en français.

1 Ajoutez *a, an, some* ou Ø selon le cas, puis traduisez. Vous avez parfois le choix, mais la traduction sera différente.

a. B&A, … well-known company, is … tough competitor for us.
b. It sells … top quality material.
c. They have … excellent international strategy and even … bilingual managers.
d. … people do all their shopping there.
e. Our firm flies … goods to America, and ships … others by boat.
f. As … accountant he is very efficient, but as … colleague he is … very unpleasant man.
g. You cannot enter the USA without … passport and … visa.
h. This shop sells … new designs twice … month.
i. We made … big profit last year.
j. Have you got … change, please?
k. Are there still … workers in this factory?

2 Traduisez les phrases suivantes en anglais.

a. Nous avons des clients très fidèles.
b. Et nous avons aussi quelques clients très riches.
c. Mais certains clients ne sont jamais contents.
d. On ne peut pas gérer une entreprise sans stratégie.
e. Avez-vous une idée sur la façon d'améliorer l'organisation de notre service ?
f. Cette entreprise a des salariés très efficaces, mais certains veulent partir.
g. Une cliente est venue sans carte de crédit et sans argent, et n'a évidemment pas pu acheter les articles qu'elle avait sélectionnés avant.

La forme en *-ing* après les prépositions et certaines expressions

› Aide-mémoire grammatical, p. 185

Analysez et traduisez les exemples suivants :

1. This company makes a lot of profit while keeping prices low.
2. That firm fell behind despite launching innovations.
3. We look forward to meeting the new manager.
4. The Chairman was exhausted after chairing the committee for four hours.
5. The CEO may have a lot of difficulty (in) restructuring the firm.
6. It is not worth restructuring it in fact.
7. In addition to being motivated the staff must be good at speaking foreign languages.

Remarque

To have a lot of difficulty (in) doing peut être remplacé par *to find it difficult to*, ou *to struggle to*, moins lourds, et suivis d'une base verbale.

3 Complétez les phrases ci-dessous avec les verbes mis à la forme voulue :

resign – work – understand – start – take – make – spend – be – listen – renovate.

a. We will outperform our competitors by … better organised than them.
b. The employee put an end to his troubles by … .
c. They find it difficult … the whole issue.
d. How can they … while … to music?
e. Is it worth … a lot of money on … our premises?
f. I look forward to … work soon with that company.
g. One can rarely earn a lot of money without … risks.
h. He often has difficulty … decisions, which is bad for leadership.

4 Traduisez les phrases suivantes en anglais.

a. En plus de rénover les bureaux, cela vaut la peine de restructurer notre service Recherche et Développement.
b. Il faut prendre un rendez-vous avant de venir voir le directeur du marketing.
c. Vous ne pouvez pas entrer dans nos locaux sans porter de badge.
d. Dans les entreprises, les salariés qui n'ont pas l'esprit d'équipe ont bien du mal à être performants.
e. En plus de fabriquer des produits de qualité, notre société doit être agile.
f. La direction de cette unité de fabrication a eu du mal à la réorganiser.
g. Notre stagiaire aimerait continuer à travailler dans notre service.

Exam work

Document 1

How Telecom New Zealand, a small declining state-owned monopoly, was turned around[1]

The Human Resources Director Joe McCollum and the Customer Director Jolie Hodson explain how their company became agile.

Joe McCollum: In our pre-agile world, we would have had seven or eight layers between the top and bottom of the company. Now, across[2] much of the company, we have three. The result is that things are massively faster. When you talk to people, you hear things like, "We're getting stuff[3] done now in two weeks that used to take us three months." Emails have dropped off significantly, because when the developers lived in one part of the building, and the marketing people lived over there, and the product people were in another part of the building, just to organise a meeting was 27 emails. All of that has gone. Now, there's ten of us sitting around a table. In fact—and not surprisingly—there's been a big drop-off in the use of our designated meeting rooms because of this. When you have a multidisciplinary team already working together around a table, why bother[4] getting up and decamping to a meeting room in another part of the building when they could simply stay where they are and solve the problem in real time?

The decision making is also a lot richer now, and transparency improved immeasurably. I can't stress this enough. Otherwise, you're in a world where people come in to work, they do their little bit, they go home, but they may have no idea where that fits into the big scheme of things. Agile puts direct ownership and real-time accountability[5] with the squad[6] so that they have absolute clarity about where it all fits now. That's where the engagement comes from—employee engagement goes off the chart because people have richer jobs, they've got a broader[7] perspective, and they're focused on solving problems. (...)

Jolie Hodson: If you think about getting a product to market the old way, it could be quite slow, involving an idea working its way through multiple groups. In an agile setting, you're starting with having all the people in the squad who can largely give you an end-to-end[8] capability. We even have customers work with us on some of these squads, too, which exponentially speeds up the time from idea to design to commercialization.

For example, we've partnered with Network for Learning to provide the fiber broadband[9] and security layers to 2,500 New Zealand schools. In the past, the design process alone would take many months with lots of documents flowing back and forth[10] before testing or any migration of schools even started. Whereas in an agile model, we've already designed the new solution, rolled out the proofs of concept[11] for different-sized schools, and migrated half of the schools in eight months. This would never have happened at that pace[12] in the past. (...).

www.mackinsey.com

1. to turn around: *remettre à flot, redresser*. **2.** across: *à travers*. **3.** stuff: *des trucs*. **4.** to bother: *se donner la peine de*. **5.** accountability: *responsabilité financière*. **6.** squad: *équipe, groupe*. **7.** broad: *large*. **8.** end-to-end: *de bout en bout*. **9.** broadband: *à large bande*. **10.** to flow back and forth: *faire des allées et venues*. **11.** proof of concept: *démonstration de faisabilité*. **12.** pace: *rythme*.

1 ***Compréhension.*** Présentez les moyens utilisés pour rendre cette entreprise « agile », et le résultat de cette réorganisation. *(Environ 150 mots, en français.)*

Document 2

"Brainwriting"

According to decades of research, you get more and better ideas if people are working alone in separate rooms than if they're brainstorming in a group. When people generate ideas together, many of the best ones never get shared. Some members dominate the conversation, others hold back[1] to avoid looking foolish, and the whole group tends to conform to the majority's taste.

Evidence[2] shows that these problems can be managed through "brainwriting." All that's required is asking individuals to think up ideas on their own before the group evaluates them, to get all the possibilities on the table. For instance, at the eyewear retailer[3] Warby Parker, named the world's most innovative company by *Fast Company* in 2015, employees spend a few minutes a week writing down innovation ideas for colleagues to read and comment on. The company also maintains a Google doc where employees can submit requests for new technology to be built, which yields[4] about 400 new ideas in a typical quarter[5]. One major innovation was a revamped[6] retail point of sale, which grew out of an app that allowed customers to bookmark[7] their favorite frames[8] in the store and receive an e-mail about them later.

(...) Suggestion boxes can be quite useful, precisely because they provide a large number of ideas. In one study, psychologist Michael Frese and his colleagues visited a Dutch steel company (now part of Tata Steel) that had been using a suggestion program for 70 years. The company had 11,000 employees and collected between 7,000 and 12,000 suggestions a year. (...) For the Dutch steelmaker (...) the suggestion box regularly led to improvements—saving more than $750,000 in one year alone.

The major benefit of suggestion boxes is that they multiply and diversify the ideas on the horizon, opening up new avenues for innovation. The biggest hurdle[9] is that they create a larger haystack[10] of ideas, making it more difficult to find the needle. You need a system for culling[11] contributions—and rewarding[12] and pursuing the best ones—so that people don't feel their suggestions are falling on deaf ears.

Adam Grant, *Harvard Business Review*, March 2016.

1. to hold back: *se retenir.* **2.** evidence: *signes.* **3.** eyewear retailer: *opticien.* **4.** to yield: *rapporter, produire.* **5.** quarter: *trimestre.* **6.** to revamp: *réaménager.* **7.** to bookmark: *noter, consigner.* **8.** frame: *monture.* **9.** hurdle: *obstacle.* **10.** haystack: *botte de foin.* **11.** to cull: *éliminer.* **12.** to reward: *récompenser.*

2 ***Compréhension.*** Explain the title. What are the three ways in which the organisation of a company can stimulate innovation, according to this text? *(About 150 words in English.)*

3 ***Expression.*** Do you think the organisation described here contradicts the one described in document 1? *(About 150 words in English.)*

Document 3

Is Google's model of the creative workplace the future of the office?

When it comes to keeping employees happy and productive, companies such as Google lead the way. The brand is as famous for its staff perks[1] – pool tables[2] and bowling alleys, free food and gym memberships – as it is for its technology, and even employs a chief happiness officer whose sole job is to keep employees happy and maintain productivity.

Now other companies are catching on fast, boosting engagement and motivation by involving employees in creative activities and offering incentives that help them enjoy their jobs and feel good about themselves.

Workplaces all over the UK are creating breakout[3] zones and gaming areas, where staff can chill out[4], chat, and stimulate their creative juices, or offering classes that equip staff with creative skills, such as languages, painting and drawing, and learning musical instruments.

Why? Because organisations that foster[5] a workplace culture of creativity are likely to[6] have happy, motivated employees who are more loyal and more productive.

Mark Rhodes, director of marketing at recruitment firm Reed, says: "All employers stand to[6] gain by promoting creativity at work. The most successful businesses are those that engender creative thinking and develop environments where everyone generates ideas, has a voice, asks questions and challenges the norm. Some ideas will stick[7], some won't, but what's certain is you'll learn a lot from the process along the way."

Lateral thinking[8] and the ability to communicate are crucial skills in any organisation. Some employers are actively encouraging creative collaborations between teams. Every year, Manchester Metropolitan University (MMU) runs an event called Engage Week, where staff host[9] events for other members of staff who want to learn something new. These range from[10] sporting events to craft[11] activities, such as metalwork, sausage making, chocolate making, picture framing[12], and learning basic sign language.

Alison Coleman, *The Guardian*, 11 February 2016.

1. perk: *avantage en nature.* **2.** pool table: *table de billard.* **3.** breakout: *recréation.* **4.** to chill out: *décompresser.* **5.** to foster: *encourager.* **6.** to be likely to / to stand to: *avoir des chances de.* **7.** to stick: *perdurer.* **8.** lateral thinking: *pensée latérale (technique pour encourager la créativité).* **9.** to host: *accueillir.* **10.** to range from... to: *aller de … à.* **11.** craft: *artisanat.* **12.** picture framing: *encadrement.*

4 ***Compréhension.*** What firms are described here? Analyse how and why their organisation enables them to maximise the core qualities of their businesses: employees' innovation and creativity. *(About 100 words, in English.)*

5 ***Expression.*** You work in one of these high-tech Californian companies or corporations. Send an email to a friend who works in a more traditional organisation, giving him/her your opinion about yours. *(About 150 words, in English.)*

Document 4

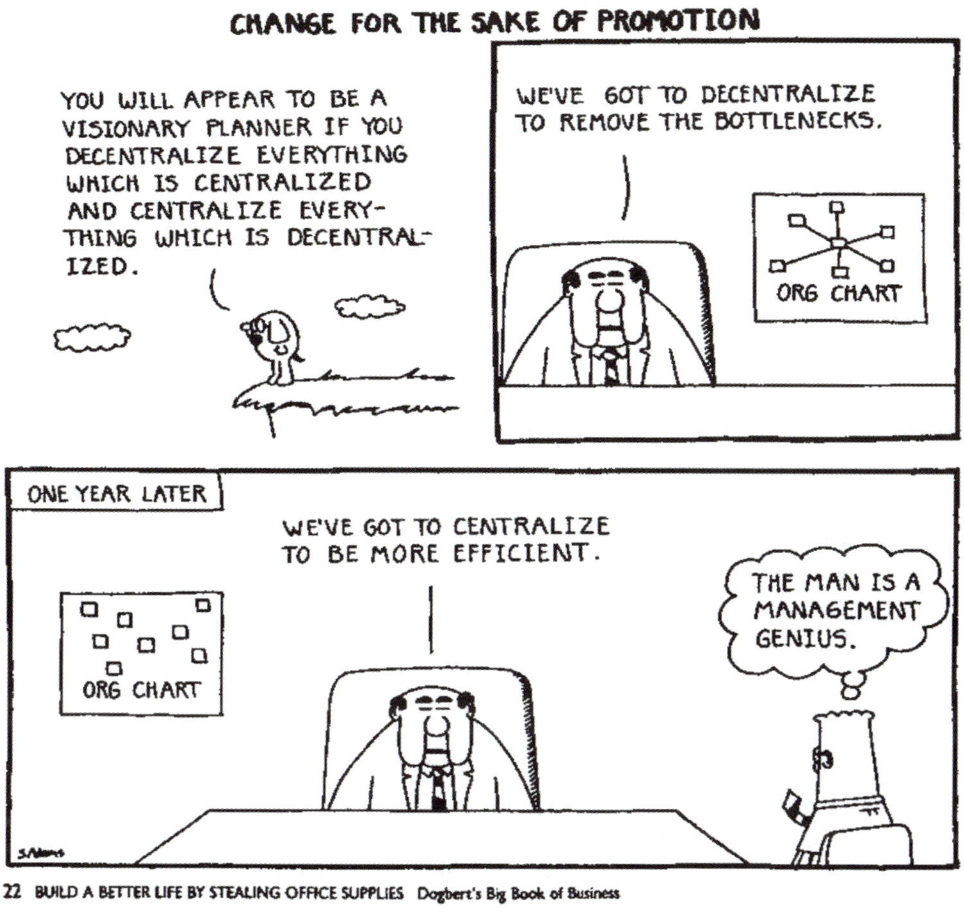

Scott Adams, *The Dilbert Principle*,

*bottleneck: *goulot d'étranglement.*

6 ***Compréhension.*** Quelle conclusion peut-on tirer de cette caricature ?
(Environ 100 mots, en français.)

7 ***Synthèse.*** Montrez comment l'idée exprimée par cette caricature peut s'appliquer à l'ensemble des documents précédents sur l'organisation des entreprises. En conclusion, quel est à votre avis le meilleur type d'organisation ?
(Environ 250 mots, en français.)

8 *Expression*. **Travail professionnel.** Rédaction de courriel en anglais.

Vous êtes Peter Taylor, directeur commercial de M&D, chaîne de magasins de vêtements en Grande-Bretagne.
Vous envoyez un e-mail de réclamation en anglais à votre fournisseur chinois Han Jun car vous n'avez reçue votre livraison prévue pour le 15 septembre que le 15 octobre, soit avec un mois de retard.
De plus, il manquait à l'arrivée les 10 manteaux de femmes (réf : AX 256 à 266) que vous attendiez.
Vous lui demandez de résoudre tous ces problèmes d'urgence et éventuellement de réorganiser son service production et/ou son service expédition, afin que cela ne se reproduise pas. Vous attendez ses explications.
Date et salutations d'usage.

CHAPITRE

2

The Digital Revolution

La révolution numérique

Everyone, from companies to states to individuals, is concerned by the Digital Revolution. The upheavals[1] due to the transition of modern technology from mechanical or analog electronic computers to digital tools and computers (based on digits or figures, 0 or 1) are countless. This Fourth Revolution follows the First Industrial Revolution caused by the steam machine, the Second by oil, and the Third by computers.

The Fourth Revolution

Digital systems revolutionise the way billions of people work, live, and relate. They carry out extremely fast calculations combining physical, digital, and biological technologies. The digital shift[2] is accelerating and disrupts[3] almost every human activity, thanks to breakthroughs[4] that bring in almost limitless communication, Artificial Intelligence, robotics, the Internet of Things (IoT), 3-D printing, biotechnologies, medical treatments, software that translates or invests, etc. Computers are becoming ever smaller and more powerful. There is more technology and computing capacity in an ordinary smartphone today than there was in NASA's giant computers that helped put the first man on the moon in 1969.

The World Wide Web and the Internet

Created in the 1990s, and at the heart of the Digital Revolution, the acronym "www" (World Wide Web) refers to a worldwide network that links all kinds of data sets[5]. Being often free, open and universally accessible, the Web and the Net are egalitarian and unrivalled. They have boosted exchanges and activities in trade, manufacturing, healthcare, transport, financial transactions, offices, education, leisure and culture for all. By abolishing frontiers they have stimulated globalisation and cooperation (people can have instantaneous access to nearly all the knowledge, products and services they want), but the Web and the Net have also enabled illegal activities.

Big Data

More efficient than traditional data processing software, digital systems combine many huge data sets from mobile devices[6], cameras, connected objects, social networks in parallel computers to find new correlations. By combining volume, velocity and variety, they detect patterns[7] and process data through analytics and algorithms in order to detect meaningful information. This created value can be used in business (through better aimed advertising and marketing), healthcare, etc. It is also a tool for machine learning. "Cookies" are for transferring users' data to the services, companies, etc. they deal with. However, the question remains: who does this data belong to? A highly controversial issue...

Artificial Intelligence

All the above is facilitated by complex algorithms, so people are now talking about Artificial Intelligence. However, supercomputers and digital machines cannot entirely rival human intelligence or replace people. The self-driving cars that were recently announced are still far off. The Head of R&D at Google called AI just "augmented intelligence".

Positive consequences

Other advantages of digital technology are that consumers can now buy goods simply by clicking on their home computer or smartphone. Competition is therefore increasing, which is good for their purchasing power[8] (but difficult at times for companies). Poorer countries with lower labour costs[9] are developing faster as jobs are created to produce goods for the whole world. The Digital Revolution also helps people to be better educated and possibly better paid. It thus contributes to decreasing extreme poverty worldwide, and people can protect themselves more efficiently from exploitation. Social networks created by interconnected tools help people communicate, get more information, find or offer jobs and services, create communities, circulate new ideas, etc. Despite growing automation, the new services and equipments conceived by R&D create new jobs and opportunities.

Negative consequences

Existing jobs are destroyed, so that people have to retrain[10] for new skills[11]. Not everyone can rise to this challenge. In addition to job displacement, a lot of expensive appliances or machines quickly become obsolete. The spreading of information, now out of control, can lead to fake news, shady dealings[12], the surveillance state, and even terrorism. Human relations are both dwindling[13] and exploding. The high-tech world and markets tend to be dominated by a few American Internet giants—called Big Tech in the US or GAFA (Google, Amazon, Facebook, Apple) in Europe—and Chinese networks such as Alibaba. Big Data threatens people's privacy. It is difficult to keep up with[14] all innovations, to manage all the information we get and use all these technologies efficiently.

New developments

The Digital "Revolution" is now practically behind us, except for a continuous flow[15] of practical innovations that are just improvements on and for Big Data. But another revolution is looming[16]: quantum computing based on quantum physics[17] where qubits replace bits. Its even more fantastic calculating speed is highly promising and already attracting investments. Today, it is still "a distant dream". But in the long term, who knows?

1. upheaval: *bouleversement.*
2. shift: *changement.*
3. to disrupt: *transformer.*
4. breakthrough: *percée technologique.*
5. data set: *base de données.*
6. device: *appareil, système.*
7. pattern: *schéma, tendance.*
8. purchasing power: *pouvoir d'achat.*
9. labour costs: *coûts de main-d'œuvre.*
10. to retrain: *se recycler.*
11. skill: *métier, compétence.*
12. shady dealings: *trafics suspects/ illégaux.*
13. to dwindle: *diminuer.*
14. to keep up with: *se tenir au courant de.*
15. flow: *flux.*
16. to loom: *s'annoncer.*
17. quantum physics: *physique quantique.*

Repérer les notions essentielles

Answer the following questions.

a. Explain what the Digital Revolution consists of.
b. Why is the Digital Revolution an upheaval and for whom?
c. Name four objects that have been digitalised.
d. What is the Word Wide Web and to what extent has it contributed to digitalising the world?
e. How does Big Data work?
f. Can Artificial Intelligence replace the human brain? Why or why not?
g. Name three positive consequences of the Digital Revolution.
h. Does the Digital Revolution create unemployment?
i. What advice is given at the end about this revolution?

Résumer le texte en français

Résumez ce texte en dégageant les principales caractéristiques économiques et sociales de la révolution numérique. *(150 mots environ, en français.)*

Approfondir

a. **Which "digital" object plays an important role in your life and why? What do you think of it? You can answer in writing *(about 150 words)* or orally.**
b. **Quantum computing: perhaps the next revolution? It is extremely complicated and totally different from today's digital computers and technology: if you are interested, browse the Net to find some information about it.**

Lexical work

to access a site	accéder à un site
analytics	analyse de données
app / application	appli / application
attachment	pièce jointe
B2B / Business-to-Business trade	commerce interentreprises
Big Data	données de masse, mégadonnées
blockchain	stockage et transmission de données
to browse the Net	surfer / naviguer sur Internet
broadband	haut débit
C2C / Consumer-to-Consumer trade	transaction(s) entre particuliers
computer chip	puce électronique
cut and paste	copier-coller
cyberthief	pirate de données
cybertheft	vol/piratage de données
cyber security	cybersecurité
data capture/processing	saisie/traitement de données
data flow	flux de données
digital divide	fracture numérique
disclaimer	décharge de responsabilité
disposable	jetable
to download/upload to/from	télécharger vers/depuis (un ordinateur)
e-bill / e-business	facture/commerce électronique
to email sb	envoyer un email/courriel à qqn
to encrypt	crypter
file/data-sharing	partage de dossiers/ données
hacker	pirate (informatique)
to hack	pirater
to hold a conference call	avoir une conférence téléphonique
Internet / file server	serveur sur Internet
Internet provider	fournisseur d'accès à Internet
junk mail / spam	courrier indésirable, pourriel
to key in / to capture data	saisir des données
keyboard	clavier
to mine data	extraire des données
online auction site	site d'enchères en ligne
to operate / to power	activer, faire fonctionner
to order online	commander en ligne
password	mot de passe
piracy / hacking	piratage

• to p**o**wer	faire marcher
• to pr**o**cess	traiter
• to pr**o**gram (in comp**u**ting)	programmer *(Informatique)*
• search **e**ngine	moteur de recherche
• sec**u**red trans**a**ction	transaction sécurisée
• skill	compétence, métier
• s**o**ftware	logiciel(s)
• to subscr**i**be	s'abonner
• switch off	se déconnecter
• touch screen	écran tactile
• **u**pgrade	nouvelle version
• to **u**pgrade	améliorer
• to **u**pdate	mettre à jour
• up-to-date	le plus récent, moderne
• **u**sername	identifiant
• voice mail, mail box	boîte vocale, messagerie Internet
• w**i**dget	petit gadget, truc
• w**i**red	branché, câblé

Use the list

Fill in the gaps with words from the list, making the necessary changes, then translate the sentences.

data mining – voice mail – to power – wired – to process – cybersecurity – to hold a conference call – chips – to upgrade – chip

a. How much would it cost to … my computer?
b. "Please record your message on my … ."
c. Some … simply store information, others can perform certain elaborate tasks.
d. To … Artificial Intelligence, an American start-up has created a giant computer … .
e. The data we have gathered will be … by their computers.
f. Our whole society is now … .
g. Don't disturb the boss: he is … .
h. … has now become a major issue for companies.
i. Our … methods will help you make good decisions more quickly.

Grammar work

Comparatifs de supériorité, d'infériorité, et d'égalité

› Aide-mémoire grammatical, p. 174

Analysez et traduisez les exemples suivants :

1. The deadline for sending our order is getting <u>closer</u>.
2. There are <u>fewer</u> computing bugs now <u>than</u> there were in the past.
3. Up-to-date printers use <u>less</u> ink <u>than</u> the old ones.
4. Children play <u>more</u> videogames <u>than</u> they should.
5. This new chip is <u>as</u> big <u>as</u> a dinner plate.
6. My mobile is <u>not as</u> up-to-date <u>as</u> yours.
7. This computer is <u>less</u> expensive <u>than</u> that one.

- **Quels éléments faut-il utiliser après un comparatif de supériorité, d'infériorité ou d'égalité ?**
- **Quels sont les trois exemples de comparatif exprimant l'infériorité présentés ici ? Quelles en sont les différences ?**

1 Employez chacun de ces adjectifs au comparatif de supériorité, d'égalité ou d'infériorité dans des phrases de votre choix .

Attention à la différence entre adjectifs longs et courts !

a. difficult
b. cheap
c. expensive
d. intelligent
e. slow
f. profitable
g. useful
h. efficient
i. reliable
j. fast
k. easy
l. convenient
m. high
n. bad
o. good

2 Traduisez les phrases suivantes en anglais.

a. Ce nouveau smartphone est plus cher que mon précédent, mais il peut être connecté à beaucoup plus d'applis et de jeux en ligne.
b. Notre nouveau logiciel est plus rapide mais plus difficile à utiliser que l'ancien.
c. Je ne suis pas d'accord : je l'utilise aussi facilement que l'ancien, qui était effectivement bien plus lent.
d. Les gens ont plus d'ordinateurs et de téléphones que jamais, et consomment moins de papier.
e. Les ordinateurs d'aujourd'hui consomment moins d'énergie que les anciens.
f. Votre fournisseur d'accès à Internet est-il aussi efficace et fiable que le mien ?
g. De nos jours, les gens passent moins de temps devant leur télévision, mais beaucoup plus sur les réseaux sociaux.
h. L'intelligence artificielle peut-elle réagir aussi vite qu'un cerveau humain ?

Expression de la continuité : *still, (yet) again, (not) yet, no / not any longer, no / not any more.*

› Aide-mémoire grammatical

Analysez et traduisez les exemples suivants.

1. Many people still need to talk with someone when they call a public service.
2. I can no longer access the Internet on my computer. What's going on?
3. I cannot access the Internet (yet) again!
4. I still cannot access the Web, this is maddening.
5. I have no more e-mails to answer, at last!
6. This client does not email orders any more / any longer. I wonder why.

3 Complétez les phrases ci-dessous en ajoutant une des expressions de continuité ci-dessus et en effectuant les changements nécessaires ; puis, traduisez-les.

Ex. : I do not have a cell phone because mine has been stolen.
→ *I no longer have a cell phone because mine has been stolen.*

a. Are you using this outdated software?
b. Even though Bill has a mobile phone, he uses his fixed-line telephone.
c. I have not received the order I made online. What's going on?
d. She has not decided to change her Internet provider.
e. We have not subscribed to this service, there is no hurry.
f. We do not receive any bills from your accounting department. Why?
g. Our office computer network does not work and has not been repaired.
h. Our technician has not arrived.
i. Do you use paper in your firm?
j. I cannot find my mobile. Where on earth did I put it?
k. We do not have their phone number. Do you have it?
l. Boris does not use this email address because it gets too many spams.

Exam work

Document 1

Accounting in the fourth industrial revolution

(…) We are currently living in an age referred to as the "fourth industrial revolution." (…) The tax and accounting industry is no longer in the business of preparing more tax returns[1] at a faster rate, since technology does this for us and it will continue to get better at it. In fact, it's likely that how tax and accounting professionals serve their clients isn't really going to change. There will still be compliance[2] work to do, but the paradigm[3] flips[4] in how we think about it. Once you adopt that mindset[5], you can rebuild your business around it. At that point, you're ready to build your skills differently.

The skills you build should be focused on communication and client relationship management, sales, managing different kinds of talent in your firm, and most importantly, translating real-time data into insights[6] while tapping into[7] your vast experience working across many different kinds of businesses. This affords you the opportunity and unique capability of advising clients on their current and future financial health and growth. (...) This lowers prices for consumers, since the suppliers create it faster and cheaper, which then frees the supplier to add more services or focus on a niche in the market. (...) Technology simply allows you to produce these things faster and at greater scale so that you can focus on the next most important thing to serve your customers and clients: advice.

So when new intelligent technology comes along, will I still even be needed or relevant[8]? Of course I will; it's simply what I will focus on that will be different. I'll be able to spend time feeding new technology my ideas, testing creative approaches that AI couldn't know, and focus my energy on building relationships to increase my market penetration.

That's because technology is an augmentation of me, my skills and my ability to advance. Not to mention the time technology saves me will be time back in my pocket for relaxing, spending time with family or investing in my business. And this is what technology really affords us—options and the flexibility to choose how we spend our time and energy.

Jasen Stine, www.accountingtoday, 6 August 2019.

1. tax return: *déclaration fiscale.* **2.** compliance: *conformité aux règles comptables.* **3.** paradigm: *paradigme, modèle.* **4.** to flip: *connaître une révolution.* **5.** mindset: *façon de penser.* **6.** insight(s): *idées claires et en profondeur.* **7.** to tap into: *faire appel à.* **8.** relevant: *à la hauteur, adapté.*

1 ***Compréhension.*** Summarise the text, analysing the positive and negative changes brought about by the fourth industrial revolution in accounting, and the advice given to accountants on how to adapt to them.
(About 100 words, in English.)

Document 2

Silicon Valley siphons our data like oil. But the deepest drilling has just begun.

Silicon Valley is an extractive industry. Its resource isn't oil or copper, but data. Companies harvest[1] this data by observing as much of our online activity as they can. This activity might take the form of a Facebook like, a Google search, or even how long your mouse hovers[2] in a particular part of your screen. Alone, these traces may not be particularly meaningful. By pairing them with those of millions of others, however, companies can discover patterns[3] that help determine what kind of person you are – and what kind of things you might buy. These patterns are highly profitable. Silicon Valley uses them to sell you products or to sell you to advertisers. But feeding the algorithms that produce these patterns requires a steady[4] stream of data. And while that data is certainly abundant, it is not infinite. (...) Together, Facebook and Google receive a staggering 76% of online advertising revenue in the United States.

Putting a listening device in your living room is an excellent way for Amazon to learn more about you. Another is conducting aerial surveillance of your house. In late July, Amazon obtained a patent for drones that spy on people's homes as they make deliveries[5]. An example included in Amazon's patent filing[6] is roof repair: the drone that drops a package on your doorstep might notice your roof is falling apart, and that observation could result in a recommendation for a repair service. Amazon is still testing its delivery drones. But if and when they start flying, it is safe to assume[7] they'll be scraping[8] data from the outside of our homes as diligently as the Echo[9] does from the inside.

Ben Tarnoff, *The Guardian*, 23 August 2017.

1. to harvest: *moissonner*. **2.** to hover: *planer, rester en l'air*. **3.** pattern: *schéma*. **4.** steady: *constant*. **5.** delivery: *livraison*. **6.** to file: *déposer une demande*. **7.** to assume: *supposer*. **8.** to scrape: *récolter laborieusement*. **9.** Echo: *enceinte nomade vendue par Amazon*.

2 ***Compréhension.*** Résumez ce texte en français en expliquant quelles données personnelles sont récoltées, comment, par qui, et à quoi elles servent. *(150 mots environ.)*

Exam work

Document 3

The Domino's 'pizza checker'[1] is just the beginning – workplace surveillance is coming for you

(...) Earlier this year, Domino's, the worldwide purveyor[2] of mediocre pizza, introduced a snazzy[3] tool called the Dom Pizza Checker to its Australia and New Zealand locations. According to its website, in-store cameras "use advanced machine learning, artificial intelligence and sensor technology to identify pizza type, even topping[4] distribution and correct toppings". If your food doesn't match your order, or internal quality standards, workers are ordered to make it again. Basically, Big Brother is watching your pizza. (...)

At first glance[5], this may sound benign. The tech ensures customers receive consistent quality; what could be wrong with that? The answer, dear reader, is that it is 2019: everything is problematic – even pizza. Nick Knight, who runs Domino's in the region, provided more details about the tool at a recent investor day, revealing that it will be incorporated into a "'scorecard'[6] bonus system" for franchises and used to identify underperforming stores. In short, it is a workplace surveillance tool. (...)

But (...) Domino's, after all, is far from the only company tracking[7] workers: workplace surveillance is becoming increasingly pervasive[8] and worryingly sophisticated. (...) According to the research firm Gartner, 50% of businesses monitor employees, a figure it expects to rise to 80% by 2020. This monitoring takes a variety of forms. Your employer may be taking remote screenshots[9] of your computer. It may be logging your keystrokes or recording your Google searches. It may be tracking the time you are spending reading this, so it can plug[10] that data into an algorithm to analyse your behaviour and predict whether you are likely to quit. (...)

(...) We are entering a new world of workplace surveillance in which we are watched 24/7 and every move is scrutinised. And things are only going to get more intrusive[11] as corporations treat us less like human beings and more like machines. (...). But, hey, while the future may look bleak, at least there is consistently prepared pizza to look forward to[12].

Arwa Mahdawi, *The Guardian*, 15 October 2019.

1. checker: *vérificateur*. **2.** purveyor: *fournisseur*. **3.** snazzy: *du dernier cri*. **4.** topping: *garniture*. **5.** at first glance: *à première vue*. **6.** scorecard: *fiche de notes*. **7.** to track, to keep track of, to monitor: *surveiller*. **8.** pervasive: *envahissant*. **9.** screenshot: *capture d'écran*. **10.** to plug: *brancher, introduire*. **11.** intrusive: *envahissant*. **12.** to look forward to: *espérer voir arriver*.

3 *Compréhension.*

Explain what "workplace surveillance" consists in, how it is carried out and by what means, what its good and bad effects are, and for whom. *(About 150 words, in English)*

Document 4

The Revolution Will Be Digitized

New-collar jobs will require digital skills and critical thinking.

In 2012, *New York Times* writer Thomas Friedman visited and wrote about a small Minnesota-based manufacturing company whose forays[1] into the aerospace and military spheres had shifted its work into a higher-tech realm of welding[2]. Noting this shift, Friedman wrote: "Who knew? Welding is now a STEM[3] job..."

Author Sarah Boisvert employs this anecdote in her 2018 book *The New Collar Workforce* to illustrate the transformation of manufacturing jobs into ones that utilize science and technology, as well as the training[4] gaps that must be filled in order to meet the needs of the changing workforce.

These needs also drive Boisvert's work as founder of Fab Lab Hub, which is part of the MIT[5]-based Fab Lab Network. Fab Lab Hub operates labs in Santa Fe at Santa Fe Community College and the Santa Fe Business Incubator. Like the other fab labs[6] around the country, Santa Fe's all have 3D printers, laser cutters, computer numerical control (CNC) machines and vinyl cutters, all of which are tied[7] together with computer-aided design, aka[8] CAD.

This fall[9], she will teach 3D printing courses through SFCC's Continuing Education program, both of which will allow students to earn "digital badges", one tool, Boisvert says, in helping train people to enter a swiftly[10] changing workforce. That training requires learning digital skills, but more importantly, the critical thinking to adapt to new technologies as they emerge. "We have devalued a part of our population," she says, "and it's wrong." The new-collar jobs of the future, she notes, such as CNC machinists and welders, pay well and offer good benefits[11]. If we can find opportunities—for people, for our communities—that (...) end up with engaging, fun, inspiring jobs that pay well (...), then we can bring back the middle class. And I think if we can do that, we'll have more harmony."

By Julia Goldberg, abridged from *The Santa Fe Reporter*, 13 August 2019.

1. foray: *incursion.* **2.** to weld: *souder.* **3.** STEM = Science, Technology, Engineering and Math. **4.** training: *formation.* **5.** MIT (Massachusetts Institute of Technology): *grande université scientifique aux États-Unis.* **6.** fab lab: *atelier de fabrication ouvert au public.* **7.** to tie: *lier.* **8.** aka = also known as. **9.** fall (US): autumn (GB). **10.** swiftly: *rapidement.* **11.** benefit: *avantage (pour un employé).*

4 ***Compréhension.*** Explain how, according to this text, the digital revolution has impacted industry, schools and education, and even society. *(About 200 words in English.)*

Document 5

"No letters to Santa this year. Just tell the tree what you want."

Santa: Santa Claus = Father Christmas

5 ***Compréhension.*** Describe this cartoon, analysing some effects of the Digital Revolution such as the invention of a smart or Internet connected "Christmas tree" on age-old Western traditions, which are satirized here. *(About 100 words, in English.)*

6 ***Synthèse.*** En vous appuyant sur ces cinq documents, vous montrerez les principaux aspects positifs et négatifs de la Révolution numérique. *(Environ 250 mots, en français.)*

7 ***Expression. Letter of application*** Souhaitant vous spécialiser dans le marketing numérique ou dans une autre spécialité du secteur numérique de votre choix, et améliorer votre anglais, vous avez cherché et trouvé un cours *(course)* intéressant au Newcastle Technical College qui a une excellente réputation, situé dans une grande ville en pleine expansion dans le nord-est de l'Angleterre. Dans le cadre de votre dossier d'inscription à renvoyer par mail, vous rédigez une courte note en anglais (maximum 150 mots) résumant votre CV et décrivant vos motivations pour suivre cette formation afin de convaincre cette université de vous sélectionner.

8 ***Expression* (oral or in writing).** Are you optimistic or pessimistic concerning the "Digital Revolution"? Give your reasons. *(About 200 words, in English.)*

CHAPITRE

3

Corporate citizenship

L'entreprise citoyenne

Definition

Corporate citizenship refers to the responsibilities and duties of a company towards society. All companies need to be profitable. However, they have to respect the law and participate in social protection; they also influence standards of living and have an impact on the environment, now a major challenge. They simply cannot ignore these issues. Ethics has become a dimension to be taken into consideration too. Companies are becoming interested in diversity and inclusion, philanthropy, supporting the arts and culture, etc.

Stakeholders

Businesses are accountable to[1] their stakeholders[2]. These include customers, employees, suppliers[3], local communities, government officials, investors, and shareholders[4]. Traditionally, companies mainly focus on profitability to satisfy their shareholders. However, increasing consumer pressure and new regulations have compelled businesses to become interested in the whole business ecosystem to create value for all their stakeholders, who expect them to participate in social progress.

CSR – Corporate Social Responsibility

Companies decide to set up standards of governance for their operations in order to comply with[5] ESG guidelines – environmental, social and governance practices. The idea is to behave[6] ethically, hoping this will boost a company's competitiveness. Incorporating CSR in a company's business plan can bring about a number of benefits. It can lead to better staff loyalty, engagement and productivity. Some companies offer family-friendly benefits or enable workers to do charity work. However, implementing[7] CSR has a cost and small businesses cannot always afford[8] it.

Respecting employees' rights and needs

Employees not only need to be paid decent wages but also expect recognition, rewarding[9] jobs, training opportunities, and engaging career plans. By law, companies have to offer safe working conditions, and discrimination against employees on criteria of gender or race are forbidden. Today companies also need to reconsider work patterns[10] and introduce flexibility, as workers want to achieve a satisfactory balance between work and family life.

Customers have a say

Customers have to be taken very seriously as their loyalty is fundamental to a company's success. Today, consumers care about how products are produced or sourced and they look for products with an ethical dimension, such as the guarantee that workers are paid fairly and work in safe conditions. Consumers are also aware[11] of greenwashing[12] and woke washing[13] However, with the rise in eco-labels, consumers may end up being confused and wary[14] of CSR messages and sustainability[15] claims. It has become more difficult for them to know what brands to trust.

Get woke or go broke

To do sustainable business, companies now have to deliver a social message. This is called "purpose driven marketing". They need to deal with social issues in the production process and in the management of their image. "Woke" means being aware of social stakes and taking action to fix injustice. With social media, consumers are easily informed of companies' misdeeds[16] and they are quick to demand action when a company is found guilty of abuse, discrimination, racism, or misogyny. The young, who now account for 40% of shoppers in the USA, today vote with their money, which means that they express their political views through their purchases[17]. Many of them prefer to buy "woke brands" that stand for strong values.

Climate change

Some companies include the fight against climate change into their strategic planning. They do not wait for governments to regulate carbon emissions, which is a good bet[18] because they often have stronger returns on equity[19] as consumers are increasingly aware of global warming issues. With governments failing to address climate change properly, many private companies take on the burden[20] of climate responsibility. Consumers are becoming more aware of how companies respond to natural disasters.

Green products

Green products are the future of consumerism. Electric cars, zero emission buildings, locally grown vegetables and fruit, vertical farming, soja meat, reusable water bottles, LED bulbs, etc. are making their way into our lives.

Companies today need to produce eco-friendly products that do not harm the environment to attract consumers. Also, recycling and finding alternatives to plastic are a matter of urgency.

Conscious capitalism

Many ethically-minded companies today play a strong role in the fight against unemployment or the protection of the environment. They create shared value by combining their economic competitiveness and the well-being of society. This is sometimes called "conscious capitalism". This approach does not minimize profit-making but includes the pursuit of the common interest in the company's business plan. However, such appealing[21] principles sometimes fail as they may be viewed as utopian.

1. accountable to: *qui a des comptes à rendre à.*
2. stakeholder: *partie prenante.*
3. supplier: *fournisseur.*
4. shareholder: *actionnaire.*
5. to comply with: *respecter.*
6. to behave: *se comporter.*
7. to implement: *mettre en œuvre.*
8. to afford: *se permettre.*
9. rewarding: *gratifiant.*
10. work pattern: *mode de travail.*
11. aware: *conscient.*
12. greenwashing: *écoblanchiment.*
13. woke washing: *engagement de façade.*
14. wary: *méfiant.*
15. sustainability: *durabilité.*
16. misdeed: *méfait.*
17. purchase: *achat.*
18. bet: *pari.*
19. return on equity: *rentabilité financière des capitaux.*
20. burden: *fardeau.*
21. appealing: *séduisant.*

Repérer les notions essentielles

Answer the following questions.

a. Why is corporate citizenship important for companies?
b. Why must companies take all stakeholders into account?
c. What is the aim of CSR?
d. What employees' needs must companies respect?
e. Why do customers matter for companies?
f. How have consumers evolved over the past few years?
g. Why does "woke" matter to young people today?
h. Is climate change a concern for companies today? Why?

Résumer le texte en français

Résumez ce texte en français, en 200 mots environ.

Approfondir

How can companies reduce their ecological footprint?

Lexical work

• accountable	(légalement) responsable / qui doit rendre des comptes
• to adapt to the times	s'adapter à l'époque
• to behave ethically	agir de façon éthique
• brand image	image de marque
• brand loyalty	fidélité à une marque
• to build up customer loyalty	fidéliser la clientèle
• built-in obsolescence	obsolescence programmée
• business ethics	éthique en affaires
• carbon footprint	empreinte carbone
• cause marketing	marketing engagé
• to be committed to	être engagé à
• commitment	engagement
• consumer	consommateur
• to contribute to	contribuer à
• CSR (Corporate Social Responsibility)	RSE (Responsabilité Sociale des Entreprises)
• customer / client	client
• ecolabel	label vert
• employee	employé / salarié
• to ensure	garantir
• environmentally-friendly	écologique / qui respecte l'environnement
• ethical investment	investissement éthique
• ethically-minded	qui comporte une dimension éthique
• ethics	l'éthique
• fair trade	commerce équitable
• goods / wares	marchandises
• green-washing	écoblanchiment
• to implement CSR	mettre en œuvre / en pratique la RSE
• to implement a policy	mettre en place une mesure / une politique
• to improve quality	améliorer la qualité
• industrial dispute	conflit social
• industrial tribunal	conseil de prud'hommes
• investor	investisseur
• to launch a campaign	lancer une campagne
• to look for solutions	rechercher des solutions
• loyalty	loyauté, fidélité
• to file a complaint	faire une réclamation
• to meet expectations	satisfaire des attentes

• to mislead consumers	tromper les consommateurs
• to participate in	participer à
• partner	associé
• principle	principe
• profits	bénéfices financiers
• progressive cause	cause progressiste
• prospective customer	client potentiel
• quality standard	norme de qualité
• to raise awareness	faire prendre conscience
• reliable	fiable
• renewable energy	énergie(s) renouvelable(s)

Use the list

1 Use the following words to fill in the gaps, then translate the sentences.

consumers – customers – shareholders – stakeholders

One must not confuse … who are all the people with an interest in what a company does and … who are people who own at least one share of a company's capital. One must not confuse … who are all the people who buy and use products and services and … who are the clients of a particular company.

2 Fill in the sentences with a preposition. If none is necessary, leave a blank.

a. Consumers need to trust … companies.
b. Managers participate … CSR activities.
c. This company shows commitment … ethics.
d. The new policy will contribute … reducing global warming.
e. Businesses need to adapt … today's global problems.
f. When problems arise, we need to look … solutions.

3 Finish the following words with a suffix (*-ation*, *-ee*, *-er*, *-ing*, *-ness*, *-ty*) to build a noun, then translate these nouns into French.

Ex. : commit ⇨ commitment

a. aware… b. custom… c. employ…
d. expect… e. greenwash… f. loyal…

Grammar work

Les noms dénombrables et indénombrables

› Aide-mémoire grammatical, p. 188

Analysez et traduisez les exemples suivants :

1. Companies do business with dozens of stakeholders.
2. In all countries, small businesses are more numerous than multinationals.
3. Our main supplier is a small catering business.
4. She loves her new job but there is a lot of work to do.

- **Les noms soulignés sont-ils dénombrables ou indénombrables ?**

1 Dites si les noms suivants sont indénombrables, dénombrables, ou les deux. Utilisez un dictionnaire.

loan – trust – commitment – advice – information – progress – time – growth – job – work.

2 Utilisez les mots de l'exercice précédent pour compléter ces phrases en effectuant les changements nécessaires. (Certains mots peuvent être employés deux fois.) Ensuite, traduisez les phrases.

a. The company's relationships have to be based on …, but within reason.
b. It takes … to build a positive brand image.
c. Banks grant … to companies which want to invest in development.
d. We sent our customer the invoice three … but he didn't pay us.
e. Some retailers try to collect as much … about their customers as they can.
f. A lot of … has been achieved targeting customers according to their needs.
g. The … expect rapid return on investment.
h. People who are out of … try to find a new … .
i. Economic … is due to different factors such as demography and monetary policies.
j. Companies now publish their … to respecting Human Rights.
k. Good bankers provide reliable … for their customers to make the right choice.

3 Traduisez les phrases en utilisant les noms indénombrables suivants.

business – evidence – growth – information – oil – petrol – progress – waste

a. Les entreprises doivent recycler leurs **déchets**.
b. On a des **preuves** du réchauffement climatique.
c. Le **pétrole** permet de fabriquer de l'**essence**.
d. Les consommateurs veulent des **renseignements** fiables.
e. Notre entreprise connaît une **croissance** forte.
f. Les ampoules LED sont un **progrès**.
g. Aujourd'hui, pour faire des **affaires**, il faut être vert.

L'expression de la quantité

› Aide-mémoire grammatical, p. 204

Analysez et traduisez les exemples suivants :

1. As they had a little money, they were able to buy presents for the whole family.
2. When consumers have little money, they cannot afford to buy luxury products.
3. Banks tend to lend less money these days.
4. A few days ago, they launched their marketing campaign.
5. A shop that has too few customers cannot make enough profit.
6. They have fewer customers than before because of the crisis.

4 Complétez les phrases suivantes avec *less* ou *fewer*, puis traduisez-les.

a. There were … customers than usual.
b. There should be … advertising on TV.
c. Ten years ago, there were … advertisements in cinemas.
d. They have been exporting … wool from Australia.
e. I was given … advice than I expected.
f. … and … consumers use plastic bags when they shop.
g. There should be … waste in the oceans.
h. Companies with a negative brand image don't always make … profit.

5 Traduisez les phrases suivantes.

a. Il y a aujourd'hui moins d'entreprises dans les petites villes anglaises.
b. Ils auront peu de temps pour améliorer leur image de marque.
c. Le magasin m'a accordé quelques réductions sur mes achats de Noël, avant les soldes.
d. L'entreprise a fait moins de bénéfices l'année dernière.
e. La publicité a probablement moins d'influence sur les consommateurs que l'on ne croit.
f. Un peu de confiance est nécessaire dans les relations avec les fournisseurs.
g. Peu de clients ont fait confiance à cette société de vente par correspondance.
h. Cette banque accorde trop peu de prêts à ses clients.
i. Il y a quelques années, peu de gens faisaient leurs achats sur Internet.

Exam work

Document 1

Unilever boss says brands using 'woke-washing' destroy trust

The chief executive[1] of Unilever has lashed out[2] at companies that engage in woke-washing[3] by using the language and imagery of worthy[4] causes to increase sales, without backing up this rhetoric with action. Alan Jope, who holds the purse strings[5] to a multibillion-dollar advertising budget for brands such as Dove, Persil, PG Tips and Hellmann's mayonnaise, said: "Woke-washing is beginning to infect our industry. It's putting in peril the very thing which offers us the opportunity to help tackle many of the world's issues."

Speaking at a conference in Cannes, the head of the consumer goods company said brands that highlight purpose but do not "walk the talk"[6] could "further[7] destroy trust in our industry, when it's already in short supply."[8] He added: "Purpose-led[9] brand communications is not just a matter of 'make them cry, make them buy.' It's about action in the world."

A host of major companies have come under fire[10] over concerns that they are trying to cash in on[11] causes seen as "woke" – a term that has come to mean worthy, or aware of social injustice. Last month, Marks & Spencer was criticised for launching a sandwich to mark LGBT Pride month. (...) Some fashion companies have been criticised for using plus-size models to cash in on sentiment around body positivity, despite offering very few clothes for people of a similar size. Earlier this year, *The Guardian* revealed Spice Girls T-shirts sold to raise money[12] for Comic Relief's "gender justice" campaign were made at a factory in Bangladesh where women earn the equivalent of 35p an hour.

Mark Borkowski, a branding expert, said: "There's nothing wrong with having a purpose and a drive[13], but it has to run through every element of your brand.

The younger generation are much more aware that they're being marketed to. Every brand wants that immediate idea that's going to lift them above the noise[14], but the messaging and authenticity – really making a change – isn't easily achieved in the blink of an eye[15]. We all end up even more cynical."

By Rob Davies, *The Guardian*, 19 June 2019.

1. chief executive: *directeur général.* **2.** to lash out at: *s'en prendre à.* **3.** woke-washing: *engagement de façade pour une cause.* **4.** worthy: *respectable.* **5.** to hold the purse strings: *tenir les cordons de la bourse.* **6.** to walk the talk: *faire ce que l'on dit.* **7.** further: *davantage.* **8.** in short supply: *rare.* **9.** purpose-led: *engagé.* **10.** to come under fire: *essuyer des critiques.* **11.** to cash in on: *tirer profit de.* **12.** to raise money: *lever des fonds.* **13.** drive: *motivation.* **14.** to lift them above the noise: *les faire connaître.* **15.** in the blink of an eye: *en un clin d'œil.*

1 ***Compréhension.***

a. What is Unilever's CEO angry about and why? (*About 100 words, in English.*)

b. Résumez ce texte en français en 150 mots environ.

Document 2

What Are the Disadvantages of Corporate Social Responsibility?

(…) When you plan a CSR strategy, don't just quietly go about executing it. Part of the goal of CSR is to show that you care about the community you call home, thereby[1] making consumers feel good about giving you their business. Press releases[2] will help you get the word out, but once you've announced your CSR gameplan[3], be ready to back it up[4] with future success. A failed CSR plan can ultimately fare worse[5] for your company than no CSR at all. Use corporate social responsibility to show consumers that you follow through with your promises and put your money where your mouth is[6]. Press releases that prove to be[7] false promises over time lead to greater scrutiny from both the media and consumers. You have a chance to earn their trust[8], so make sure all your ducks are in a row[9] before making any announcements. (…)

From an administrative perspective, CSR strategies can end up being expensive endeavors[10] with difficult-to-track return on investment. After all, you must pay a team of people to devise[11] and execute a corporate social responsibility plan, and their salaries alone can be difficult for some small businesses to stomach[12]. Plus, CSR campaigns often have a financial component[13], whether it's donating money outright[14] or allowing employees to spend a day out of the office doing volunteer work[15]. But small businesses can still find ways to balance[16] CSR efforts with profitability. Often, social responsibility begins with employee-friendly policies, like paid sick days and vacation time. (…)

A final disadvantage of CSR is that it can be easy to misinterpret your community's or consumers' values. For example, you might decide that sending employees on a mission trip to another country is the perfect way to show that you care about people in every corner of the globe. But if most of your consumers and employees live in a totally different country or region, they may be upset[17] because you did not choose to dedicate resources to local issues. Understanding the values that your employees, community and consumers have in common helps lead to a successful and profitable CSR campaign. Without a unifying message, your corporate social responsibility strategy will struggle[18] to succeed.

By Cathy Habas, reviewed by Jayne Thompson, bizfluent.com, 20 October 2018.

1. thereby: *ainsi*. **2.** press release: *communiqué de presse*. **3.** gameplan: *plan d'action*. **4.** to back up: *renforcer*. **5.** to fare worse: *se passer plus mal*. **6.** to put money where your mouth is: *joindre l'acte à la parole*. **7.** to prove to be: *s'avérer*. **8.** to earn trust: *gagner la confiance*. **9.** all your ducks are in a row: *tout est prêt*. **10.** endeavour (UK), endeavor (US): *entreprise, initiative*. **11.** to devise: *concevoir*. **12.** to stomach: *supporter*. **13.** component: *composante*. **14.** outright: *directement*. **15.** volunteer work: *bénévolat*. **16.** to balance: équilibrer. **17.** upset: *contrarié*. **18.** to struggle: *avoir du mal*.

2 ***Compréhension.*** According to the blog writer, what matters most when establishing a good CSR strategy? Write your answer in English. (*About 150 words.*)

Exam work

Document 3

Boots faces backlash[1] over 'hypocrisy' for making switch from plastic to paper bags

(...) On Monday 24 June, Boots announced plans to ditch plastic bags in all its stores by next year and replace them with paper alternatives. The high street retail[2] giant said 53 stores will lose[3] plastic bags at checkouts[4] from Monday, with all 2,485 shops only offering customers paper versions from early next year.

However, several customers have pointed out that the retail store recently introduced medical prescription bags made of plastic. In a message posted on Twitter following Boots' announcement regarding paper bags, one user tweeted: "Trust this means your prescription bags are going to be all paper ones as well!" Another wrote: "They have changed to using plastic bags for dispensing[5] now though instead of paper ones! Total hypocrisy!" (...) Another customer, named Roisin Moriarty, told the *BBC* that the company's continued use of plastic bags for prescriptions was "a classic case of paying lip service[6] while not really caring." "They've ignored the pleas from environmental agencies and customers to reverse their plastic packaging for prescriptions policy," she told the news outlet.

Last month, Boots came under fire[7] from customers after it began handing out repeat drug prescriptions in plastic bags instead of its traditional paper alternatives. Charities including Friends of the Earth and Greenpeace were "baffled"[8] by the decision and called on the Government to improve its legislation on single-use plastics. (...)

At the time, Boots explained the decision for using plastic bags was due to some prescriptions[9] being assembled at a DPS (Dispensing Support Pharmacy) based in Preston before being sent out to individual stores. The company said the bags needed to be "heat-sealed shut"[10] to reduce the risk of products falling out during transportation.

In light of the new backlash, Boots said on Twitter that it was "actively" looking into alternatives to plastic prescription bags "including cellulose (compostable), potato starch[11] and a paper solution". (...)

By Kathy OMalley, *The Independent*, 25 June 2019.

1. backlash: *réaction violente contre qqch.* **2.** retail: *vente au détail.* **3.** lose (inf.): get rid of. **4.** checkout: *caisse.* **5.** dispensing: *distribution, vente.* **6.** to pay lip service: *faire quelque chose pour la forme.* **7.** to come under fire: *être critiqué.* **8.** baffled: *stupéfait.* **9.** prescription: *ordonnance.* **10.** heat-sealed shut: *scellé thermiquement, thermocollé.* **11.** starch : *amidon.*

3 ***Compréhension.*** Sum up this text in English. *(About 150 words.)*

Document 4

Removing mini-shampoos from hotel rooms won't save the environment

InterContinental Hotels Group will replace mini-shampoos and conditioners with possibly more efficient bulk products[1] by the year 2021. Marriott Hotels recently followed suit[2], vowing[3] to ban miniature toiletries by next year.

But environmental activists shouldn't rejoice just yet.

These announcements are yet another example – such as banning plastic straws, false sustainability claims[4] and corporate commitments that are far in the future – that seem to be more of a PR exercise than real attempts to move the needle[5]. (…)

InterContinental Hotels Group CEO Keith Barr says that replacing miniature bathroom products "will allow us to significantly reduce our waste footprint and environmental impact" at the conglomerate's hotel chains, which include InterContinental, Crowne Plaza and Holiday Inn.

It's true that the British foundation Clear Conscience estimates that 200 million travel-size toiletries end up in UK landfills[6] every year, but there's another motivation: With 5,600 hotels, the savings for IHG can mount to over US$11 million annually.

Additionally, studies we have carried out at MIT and elsewhere show that evaluations of a product's environmental impact can mislead[7] if economists don't consider the entire supply chain management process[8].

For example, most of the carbon footprint of companies like Apple, Microsoft and Cisco comes from the suppliers who actually make the iPhones, routers and Xboxes, not directly from the company itself.

Additionally, the net reduction in discarded[9] plastic could be minimal at best if the larger containers are filled from single-use plastic pouches[10]. Also, we do not yet know if the larger containers are recyclable, nor the cost and environmental impacts of making, transporting, installing and maintaining them.

Even if replacing miniature toiletries does reduce waste somewhat – as other hotel chains join the movement and California moves to ban them – a transition to bulk products will barely[11] put a dent[12] in the plastic waste that now clogs the planet's rivers and oceans. It is another "feel good" initiative which help avoid the move to more serious actions that can actually make a difference.

Banning plastic straws is another such example. While outlawing plastic straws makes for excellent public relations copy[13], it has virtually no impact on the global accumulation of plastic garbage.

By Yossi Sheffi, *The Conversation*, 23 August 2019.

1. bulk product: *produit en gros.* **2.** to follow suit: *faire de même.* **3.** to vow: *promettre.* **4.** claim: *allégation.* **5.** to move the needle: *prendre un nouveau virage.* **6.** landfill: *dépotoir.* **7.** to mislead: *induire en erreur.* **8.** supply chain management process: *processus de gestion de la chaîne logistique.* **9.** to discard: *jeter à la poubelle.* **10.** pouch: *sac.* **11.** barely: *à peine.* **12.** to put a dent: *réduire.* **13.** copy: *documents.*

4 ***Compréhension.*** D'après le journaliste, pourquoi des mesures en apparence vertueuses et écologiques inscrites dans les pratiques d'entreprises ne font pas de ces dernières des entreprises citoyennes ? *(Environ 150 mots, en français.)*

Document 5

"Make sure everything is done ethically. Within reason*, of course."

* within reason: *dans les limites du raisonnable.*

5 ***Expression.*** Comment on the cartoon. To what extent does it apply to the other documents? Write your answer in English. (*About 150 words.*)

6 ***Compréhension.*** En vous appuyant sur les documents 1 à 5, vous ferez une synthèse qui dégagera les enjeux de la responsabilité sociale des entreprises. (*250 mots environ, en français.*)

7 ***Expression. Write an email.***

Vous êtes responsable des fournitures de bureau et des fournitures pour la cafétéria de votre entreprise. Vous rédigez un courriel destiné au responsable environnement de votre entreprise pour lui proposer que votre service se fournisse désormais en produits écologiques, plus chers, mais plus éco-responsables. Expliquez-lui l'intérêt de la démarche.
Présentation et formules d'usage. (*150 mots environ, en anglais.*)

CHAPITRE

4

Strategy and competitiveness

Stratégie et compétitivité

General definition

The word "strategy" comes from the Greek word meaning "generalship" or "commanding an army". Just as a general wants to lead his army to victory, so[1] a manager wants to make his company win by being competitive and, whenever possible, even more competitive than its competitors to make profits grow.

The strategy of a large or medium-sized[2] company is the responsibility of the strategic committee who sets its objectives, of the top management who implements[3] it and of the Board of Directors[4] who, having no operational functions, controls these structures.

The objectives of strategy

The first objective of a firm is of course to make money in order to survive and face competition. There are other objectives that depend on its size, type (manufacturing or services), structure and the area where it operates; the objectives have to be legitimate and ethical, respect laws, rules and regulations, and benefit the firm and its stakeholders, who work for and with it: clients, employees, subcontractors, suppliers and investors. The essential requirement[5] is to attract clients, develop their loyalty, and diversify the production according to the markets: a good strategy is market-oriented. As a result, strategy must answer the questions: "How big are we and how big can we become? How can we offer lower prices or better value for money[6]? What can we do differently from, and better than our competitors? What innovations can we launch to prepare the future?" The objectives are usually discussed at various levels of the company: how far down and to what extent is part of the strategy and of the management style. These objectives may also have to adapt to political and economic changes.

Leadership

As a result, it is important to have a good leader (usually the CEO) who must bring in ideas, imagination, a vision and a perspective that should be both long term and fairly realistic.

He/She needs a clear and wide understanding of what his/her company is and can do by carrying out a SWOT analysis (Strengths, Weaknesses, Opportunities and Threats), and studying its environment.

How to attain the objectives: strategy and tactics

Strategy is long-term thinking defined by those who govern, whereas tactics is short-term acting carried out by the various managers and their subordinates. They are jointly[7] responsible for utilising the company's human and financial resources. The best advice for a successful strategy was perhaps given by Steve Jobs, the founder of Apple: "Think different." That is why innovation, as much as, or perhaps more than, prices, is essential today to outdo[8] one's competitors. With a good strategy, this can also be achieved by small companies.

Growth in a globalised environment

The need to grow and make economies of scale (essential goals in strategy) is often due to global competition, a long-term trend in a free-trading[9] world. So, decisions must be made either to hire and expand (internal growth), or to launch mergers and acquisitions (external growth). The latter are sometimes difficult to achieve successfully, especially in the case of international ones. A good strategy is then essential to merge harmoniously not only production and financial elements, but also employees' mindsets[10], cultures and values. However, if the merger or acquisition is successful, the new company will probably enjoy long-lasting competitiveness.

Management policy

Management tries to achieve these goals by implementing a specific strategy. It should therefore communicate well and listen to the employees to establish trust, make the right decision at the right moment and inform people clearly about it. Hiring and motivating employees (and sometimes streamlining[11], which may mean lay-offs) are also key ingredients. They will be motivated by a strategy meeting their demands and promising rosy perspectives. Success is 5% strategy and 95% execution. There are different management styles, depending on management's philosophy, the current fashions, the type and size of the firm, with their advantages and drawbacks. They shape[12] the company's culture, *i.e.*[13] its values and traditions.

New trends

In our changing world, other strategic obligations have recently surged:

– First transparency in finance, production, governance, etc. has become a must: hence[14] the importance of communication. Accountability[15], which is linked, is a growing requirement.

– Then, environmental issues now make sustainability[16] and decarbonisation[17] policies necessary. A company accused of polluting or producing greenhouse gases risks losing environmentally-minded clients, employees and even investors, and not just in most Western countries, but also in China now.

– CSR (or corporate social responsibility) has become a necessity for a company, especially if it wants to attract and retain talented people. Millennials[18] usually prefer motivating, well-balanced jobs enabling them to combine family and work, to well-paid ones – unlike previous generations.

1. just as ... so: *de même que … de même.*
2. medium-sized company: *société de taille moyenne.*
3. to implement: *mettre en œuvre.*
4. Board of Directors: *conseil d'administration.*
5. requirement: *obligation.*
6. value for money: *rapport qualité-prix.*
7. jointly: *conjointement.*
8. to outdo/outperform: *faire mieux que.*
9. free-trading: *de libre-échange.*
10. mindset: *mentalité.*
11. to streamline: *rationnaliser, dégraisser.*
12. to shape: *structurer.*
13. i.e (id est): *c'est-à-dire.*
14. hence: *d'où.*
15. accountability: *responsabilité de ses actions.*
16. sustainablity: *durabilité.*
17. decarbonisation: *fait de ne plus produire de CO_2.*
18. millennials: *jeunes nés de 1980 à 2000.*

Repérer les notions essentielles

A. Les propositions suivantes sont-elles conformes au texte ? Dans le cas contraire, donnez la bonne réponse en français.

a. Le mot « stratégie » est un terme d'origine militaire.
b. Il veut dire à peu près la même chose que « tactique ».
c. Le conseil d'administration décide de la stratégie conjointement avec les dirigeants.
d. Le premier objectif de toute stratégie est de créer des emplois.
e. Le client est au cœur de la stratégie d'une entreprise.
f. L'utilisation de technologies ultramodernes est le pilier de la stratégie.
g. Toute stratégie doit savoir s'adapter au changement.
h. Il n'y a qu'une façon de bien diriger une entreprise.
i. La compétitivité d'une entreprise dépend fortement de la stratégie qui l'oriente.

B. Trouvez dans le texte les mots ou expressions correspondant aux expressions suivantes:

a. fixer des objectifs
b. effectuer une analyse
c. conseil(s)
d. mettre en œuvre une politique
e. des perspectives à long terme prometteuses
f. la mode actuelle
g. permettre à un employé de concilier famille et travail

Résumé

Résumez ce texte en français (*150 mots environ*), en faisant bien ressortir les objectifs, la méthode et les conditions d'une bonne stratégie.

Approfondir

What is "a market-oriented strategy" in your opinion? Why is it so important? Do you agree?

Lexical work

• to **a**llocate res**ou**rces	affecter des ressources
• to app**oi**nt	nommer (à un poste)
• app**oi**ntment	nomination ; rendez-vous
• to b**a**lance	compenser, contrebalancer, équilibrer
• b**a**lance sheet	bilan
• b**o**ttom line	résultat financier
• branch	filiale, succursale
• to chart a str**a**tegy	planifier une stratégie
• to close down	fermer (ses portes)
• comp**e**titive adv**a**ntage / edge	avantage compétitif / concurrentiel
• c**o**rporate / c**o**mpany m**a**nager	chef d'entreprise
• cost-eff**e**ctiveness	rentabilité
• c**o**sting	estimation du prix de revient
• cre**a**tive destr**u**ction	destruction créatrice
• to cut / c**u**t back	supprimer ; réduire
• cut / cutback	compression ; réduction ; suppression
• decision m**a**king	prise de décision
• to dev**i**se	concevoir
• to differ**e**ntiate	(se) différencier, faire une différence
• to displ**ay** manag**e**rial skills	montrer des qualités de manager
• to d**o**wnsize	réduire les effectifs
• drive	dynamisme, énergie
• effic**i**ent	efficace, performant
• emp**o**werment	responsabilisation ; dynamisation
• fac**i**lities	installations, infrastructures
• fl**ou**rishing / thr**i**ving	florissant, prospère
• to f**o**cus	(se) concentrer
• to fores**ee**	prévoir ; anticiper
• f**o**resight	vision (de l'avenir)
• to hire / recr**ui**t / take on sb	embaucher qqn
• in ch**a**rge of / resp**o**nsible for	responsable de, en charge de
• inc**e**ntive	stimulation, encouragement
• job cut	suppression d'emploi
• joint m**a**nagement	cogestion
• to launch	lancer
• to lay off / dism**i**ss / make red**u**ndant	licencier
• m**a**nagement by obj**e**ctives	management par objectifs
• market s**e**gment / dyn**a**mics	segment / dynamique de marché
• to **o**rient	orienter
• **ou**tput	rendement ; productivité

• to **ou**tsource / subcontr**a**ct	externaliser / sous-traiter
• perf**o**rmance	résultats
• to plan	prévoir, organiser, planifier
• to prom**o**te	promouvoir
• to prov**i**de for / fores**ee**	prévoir
• to reloc**a**te	délocaliser
• to rel**y** on	compter sur
• ret**u**rn on inv**e**stment	retour sur investissement
• to run / **o**perate a b**u**siness	diriger / faire marcher une affaire
• scope	envergure, portée, objectifs, périmètre d'action
• sch**e**dule / plan / ag**e**nda	plan, programme d'action
• str**u**ggling	en difficulté
• to turn ar**ou**nd	redresser
• turn**o**ver / r**e**venue	chiffre d'affaires
• uncomp**e**titive	non compétitif
• to underc**u**t compet**i**tion	offrir des prix inférieurs à ceux des concurrents

Use the list

1 Fill in the gaps with words from the list, making the necessary changes, then translate.

a. Let us hope that this new plan will raise our company's r… .
b. Yes, but don't forget that the t… is not the same as the profit.
c. If you want to r… your own business, you will have to work very hard.
d. In order to c… the production costs, the CEO has decided to o… the manufacturing of this line of products in China.
e. Why doesn't he at least s… this task to a factory in Eastern Europe?
f. The boss is both very humane and incredibly e… .
g. This CEO is very good at p… ahead and f… all the possible difficulties.
h. I wonder if m… by o… can really make the workers more e… .
i. L… this new product very early on will give us a tremendous c… a… .
j. Assessing the c… e… of all its products is an essential aspect of a company's strategy.
k. E… consists in giving more power and responsibility to employees to motivate them.
l. If we don't adapt our strategy, we will rapidly become u… .

2 Choose five words from the list above which you think are important and make sentences with them, with the help of a dictionary or of the Internet if necessary.

Grammar work

Prétérit et *present perfect* (simple ou en *-ing*)

› Aide-mémoire grammatical, p. 199

Analysez, puis traduisez les exemples suivants :

1. Unfortunately, our financial results showed an operating loss in 2019.
2. When did we last make a profit?
3. We made some bad decisions two years ago in India.
4. Their sales have been dropping for several months now, since last January in fact.
5. This company struggled for years before the arrival of a new manager.

1 Mettez les verbes entre parenthèses au temps du passé approprié selon le contexte, puis traduisez les phrases ci-dessous :

a. We just *(receive)* some bad news from our subsidiary in India.
b. You ever *(visit)* their factory in Mumbai?
c. Our plan of action so far not *(be)* ambitious enough to increase our turnover.
d. Five years ago, this pharmaceutical company *(start)* selling a new medicine. But it *(not cure)* anyone. So they *(withdraw)* it from the market.
e. Then they *(launch)* a really innovative treatment in 2017.
f. Since then it *(be)* successful.

Futur et expression de l'avenir

› Aide-mémoire grammatical, p. 183

Analysez les exemples suivants, puis traduisez-les.

1. We are going to buy new equipment soon.
2. We will become more competitive when we modernize.
3. The new CEO will reorient the business as soon as this is feasible.
4. What will we produce once we relocate?

2 Mettez les verbes entre parenthèses dans les phrases ci-dessous à la forme appropriée pour exprimer une action future, puis traduisez le tout.

a. I wonder if the department's performance *(increase)* when the new manager *(be appointed)*.
b. When we *(change)* our strategy, I am sure we *(improve)* our performance.
c. Empowerment *(be)* probably an excellent incentive for our staff.
d. As long as the right resources *(be)* allocated to the R&D department, the researchers *(be able to)* find innovations fairly rapidly.

Les différentes traductions de « faire + verbe »

› Aide-mémoire grammatical, p. 182

Analysez, puis traduisez les exemples suivants en utilisant la construction « faire + verbe ».

1. The CEO wants to get this department to increase its output.
2. He had the factory renovated last year.
3. We must have them improve their bottom line.
4. The boss's jokes don't make me laugh at all.
5. Our new manager makes us work much harder.

3 Complétez les phrases avec *make, have* ou *get* au temps approprié, puis traduisez-les.

a. I do not know what … her do it, but she did it!
b. The boss … me believe I would get a pay rise, but I did not get one, in the end.
c. I will … him call you back as soon as possible.
d. The CEO … the investors put more money in his project.
e. The idea … them smile.
f. The traffic was so bad it … me arrive late at the office.
g. They want to … the buildings refurbished next year.
h. Before launching this product, they should have … more market research carried out.

4 Traduisez en anglais.

a. Nous avons sous-traité ce travail à un fabricant en Inde, c'est-à-dire que nous faisons maintenant exécuter le travail par un autre fabricant moins cher.
b. Ce patron fait venir ses subordonnés très tôt au bureau le matin.
c. Elle a fait rénover son bureau complètement l'an dernier.
d. Je me suis fait acheter un nouvel ordinateur par l'entreprise.
e. Cette nouvelle stratégie nous a fait améliorer nos résultats.
f. Nous avons fait changer l'implantation de notre siège social il y a six mois.
g. Mme Patel a-t-elle jamais fait vérifier ses rapports par le directeur ?
h. Nous avons fait faire une analyse de la rentabilité de ce produit par notre service financier il y a quelque temps déjà.
i. Que va décider la direction pour faire connaître ce produit révolutionnaire ?
j. Qu'est-ce qui fait qu'une entreprise gagne plus ou moins d'argent ?

Exam work

Document 1

Sparking[1] breakthrough[2] ideas

Creativity shouldn't be confined to just the "creative types" in your organization. As technologies and strategies change and customers' demands evolve, companies increasingly expect everyone at every level to contribute ideas. So how can you spark new thinking about products, processes, and problems?

Simple logistical changes in the way you schedule[3] your day or where you sit can be a good place to start. Research by Carnegie Mellon's Sunkee Lee shows that sitting next to unfamiliar colleagues can make you more likely to come up with an innovative solution to a problem: Your new neighbors expose you to new knowledge, which allows you to connect ideas in novel ways.

Perhaps for this reason, groups, especially diverse groups, can often generate more creative ideas than individuals – thus, the ubiquitous[4] group brainstorming session. But if you're running one of these sessions, you also need to guard against an opposite problem: the stultifying[5] effects of groupthink. The key, (...) is to move back and forth between individual and group idea generation to get the most out of everyone's voices.

Creativity may seem by definition inherently unmanageable, but you can manage for it, write Harvard Business School professors Teresa Amabile and Mukti. By choosing the right people and perspectives, putting in place a lighter process, and motivating people to participate, a manager can become a "producer of creativity."

But there are some pitfalls[6] to popular approaches to soliciting creativity. When it comes to creating new products, for example, experimenting with early prototypes and brainstorming ideas with customers can cause more problems than they solve, warn Paul Leonardi and Peter C. Verhoef. Creativity may seem like an innate power: Either you have it or you don't. But adopting proven approaches and logistical tweaks[7] can help even the most "stuck in the mud[8]" among us come up with better ideas.

The Editors, abridged from *Harvard Business Review*, Spring 2019.

1. to spark: *déclencher*. **2.** breakthrough: *percée technologique*. **3.** to schedule: *planifier*. **4.** ubiquitous: *omniprésent*. **5.** stultifying: *abêtissant*. **6.** pitfall: *piège*. **7.** tweak: *ajustement*. **8.** stuck in the mud: *encroûté*.

1 ***Compréhension.*** Summarize this text in 100 words in English, pointing out the various ways of stimulating innovative ideas that are mentioned in this editorial.

2 ***Expression.*** In your opinion, why are the strategies described here important to increase competitiveness? *(About 100 words in English.)*

Document 2

How Wells Fargo is Ponying up[1] for its Digital Transformation

Henry Wells and William G. Fargo started Wells Fargo & Company (...) in 1852 to provide express banking services to the people of California. Wells and Fargo had previously founded the express mail company, which would eventually[2] become credit card heavyweight[3], American Express in 1950. Over the next century, Wells Fargo expanded rapidly to the point where it stands today as the world's second largest bank by market capital (...). Wells Fargo didn't get where it is today by shying away[4] innovation, and has long been demonstrating its commitment to remaining an industry leader during the global digital transformation. (...)

The Wells Fargo Innovation Labs

Like many modern businesses, Wells Fargo has its own department dedicated to coming up with innovative technologies and/or initiatives with which to better serve their account holders. (...) All this is designed to create an idea of community between the innovation team at Wells Fargo, and the users who will ultimately benefit from the initiatives if and when they are implemented[5]. Working out of a brand new[6] and high-tech location in San Francisco, the Well Fargo Innovation Lab is supplied with all the tools it needs to perform its role. (...)

IoT Pony

Another innovation (...) is a new take[7] on the iconic Wells Fargo plush[8] pony. The Wells Fargo ponies are a range of plush toys, each based on and named after a real workhorse from the company's history. To honor these animals – without which the company wouldn't have been able to function in those early years – Wells Fargo commissions and sells a range of adorable cuddly[9] toys. Inspired by these iconic plush toys, and Internet of Things (IoT) technology, Wells Fargo has created a lovable soft companion which also serves as a tool to teach children about finance. When a child's parents deposit money in their progeny's savings account, a small screen on the toy lights up and displays the account balance, providing children with a handy[10] and adorable reminder regarding how their savings are progressing.

Riding into the Future

(...) With the innovations already being put out by its brand-new Innovation Lab – and those still in development – Wells Fargo certainly isn't ready to ride off[11] into the sunset. The last word goes to the Director of Wells Fargo Innovation Group, Miranda Hill. "I hope to provide more team members with a front-row seat[12] to innovation," she says. "It is critical for the lab to continually push the boundaries on the future of personal finance and money management. The more we motivate team members to reimagine experiences, the more[13] successful we'll be as an organization in redefining the future of banking."

Worldwide Business Research
and Future Digital Finance, January 2020.

1. to pony up (fam.): *miser du fric.* **2.** eventually: *finalement.* **3.** heavyweight: *poids lourd.* **4.** to shy away from: *craindre de.* **5.** to implement: *mettre en œuvre.* **6.** brand new: *tout neuf.* **7.** take: *clip vidéo.* **8.** plush: *peluche.* **9.** cuddly: *à câliner.* **10.** handy: *pratique.* **11.** to ride off: *partir à cheval.* **12.** to provide with a front-row seat to: *pousser au maximum pour.* **13.** the more... the more: *plus ... plus.*

3 *Compréhension.* Summarize the basic strategy of Wells Fargo to remain a successful leader in banking. What is at its core: people (what people), money, horse-riding, or what else, and how? To what extent is this strategy both new and linked to the bank's glorious past? *(About 150 words, in English.)*

4 *Expression.* **(oral or in writing)**

Browse the Internet to find other facts about Wells Fargo, or about the strategies of the other American banks mentioned here, or about other banks that you know of. Then write a report *(about 150 words)* or make an oral presentation about it.

Document 3

General Motors Company 2019 Annual General Meeting[1]

Questions and answers about GM's business strategy and operations

Will further[2] brand consolidation save money and time to market with respect to[3] product innovation?

We constantly analyze the business to see where we can be more efficient. And you have seen us take action in areas of the business where we didn't have a line of sight[4] to generating appropriate returns. We take a holistic view[5] when it comes to cost savings, speed to market, and innovation. Each brand in our current portfolio[6] serves a different customer with unique needs. Last fall[7] we announced a global transformation that aligns our product portfolio with changed customer preferences for trucks, SUVs, and crossovers. We also integrated our vehicle and propulsion engineering teams; we are doubling resources allocated to electric and autonomous vehicle programs; and we are investing in newer, highly efficient vehicle architectures so that 75% of our global sales volume will come from just five architectures by early next decade.

Will GM make a small car for 2020, excluding the Cruze?

In North America, Chevrolet continues to offer the Spark, Sonic, Malibu, Camaro, and Corvette. This gives us strong offerings for first-time and price-sensitive buyers, families, enthusiasts, and fleet[8] customers. The midsize segment where the Malibu competes[9] accounts for about 10 percent of retail sales alone, and it's also a very popular choice for commercial fleets, which are very important customers for GM. We are also investing to build the next generation of Cadillac luxury cars at our Lansing Grand River assembly plant.

•••

...

General Motors is changing to zero emissions with electric vehicles (EV). How do you plan to sell vehicles that people do not want?

Every year, cars and trucks account for nearly one-fifth of US carbon emissions. With vehicles that are more fuel efficient than ever—and EVs becoming more affordable—we can help customers save money and reduce their carbon footprint[10]. GM is committed to[11] developing a next-generation battery-electric vehicle architecture that makes EVs desirable and obtainable for the customer—and profitable for the company and its shareholders. Additionally, GM will ramp up[12] marketing efforts around EVs over time to increase awareness; these efforts will educate consumers on the benefits of EVs and help drive consumer adoption.

General Motors Company 2019
Annual General Meeting.

1. annual general meeting (AGM) (of shareholders): *assemblée générale annuelle des actionnaires*. **2.** further: *supplémentaire, nouvelle*. **3.** with respect to: *en ce qui concerne*. **4.** line of sight: *vue claire*. **5.** holistic view: *vision d'ensemble*. **6.** product portfolio: *gamme, portefeuille de produits*. **7.** fall (US): *automne*. **8.** fleet: *flotte d'entreprises*. **9.** to compete: *être en concurrence*. **10.** carbon footprint: *empreinte carbone*. **11.** to be committed to: *être engagé dans/à*. **12.** to ramp up: *augmenter*.

5 ***Compréhension.*** Summarize this document: first present it in its context, then describe General Motors' strategy for the near future concerning its car production:
– Which types of cars will it make, how and why did it make these choices?
– What final difficult decision has it made for the future and what are its plans for coping with it? *(About 150 words, in English.)*

6 ***Expression.*** **(oral or in writing)**

What would you say about the final strategic choice announced here, from an investor's, from an employee's, and from your own viewpoint?
Write your analysis *(about 150 words)* or make an oral report about the subject.

Exam work

Document 4

7 ***Expression.***

What is paradoxical about this picture? You can refer to document 1.
(About 100 words, in English.)

8 ***Synthèse.***

Rédigez une note de synthèse en français rendant compte de tous les documents étudiés, en dégageant les caractéristiques d'une bonne (ou d'une mauvaise) stratégie entrepreneuriale pour la compétitivité d'une entreprise.
(Environ 250 mots, en français.)

9 ***Expression.***

Write a cover letter to one of the CEOs of the companies appearing in documents 2 or 3, choosing the one that appeals to you most because of its strategy. Explain that you would like to work as an intern or trainee in his/her firm for three months. Give your motivations and say why you think you are suited for the company. Date, usual greetings and salutations. *(About 150 words, in English.)*

CHAPITRE

5

The social and solidarity economy

L'économie sociale et solidaire

Definition and objectives

The social and solidarity economy (SSE) has existed for a long time in different forms, like cooperatives or workers' unions[1], etc. but today a global SSE movement is emerging and has gained popularity since the 1990s. Since the crisis in 2008, it has gained greater visibility. The social and solidarity economy as a whole provides 6.53% of total paid employment in the European Union, or 14.5 million jobs. Its aim is to make the economy socially inclusive. The fundamental values of SSE are solidarity, equity, responsible consumption, human rights and dignity, self-determination, self-help and cooperation. Its goals are to favour the well-being of society, promote inclusion, preserve the environment, support education, encourage participatory democracy, favour sustainability, empower women, protect health and so on. It is viewed as an alternative to capitalism and state-dominated economies. It is also an ethical approach to economic development where the welfare[2] of people and of the environment prevails over[3] profits and blind[4] growth. For instance, citizens feel concerned by social inequalities, or wish to encourage the circular economy, which is an economic system aimed at eliminating waste and reusing resources.

In France, the SSE has been enshrined in law since 2014. In the UK, this concept is less recognised, being sometimes called "the third sector", and includes charities and social business. In the USA, it is relatively small in scale.

The people involved

Volunteers, and even some users of services, who are mainly ordinary people, play an active role, create and run unions, cooperatives, mutual benefit societies, community organisations or fair-trade[5] networks. SSE is most of the time grounded[6] in local activities. Sometimes, individuals set up a venture to address social issues. This is called "social entrepreneurship". The aim is not to make a profit but to improve society.

Technology

New communication tools contribute to making the SSE more widespread and popular. They are an opportunity for this type of economy to develop. The Internet and smartphones are effective tools to help to set up digital platforms where economic exchanges are organised by individuals, without intermediaries. Online platforms also enable people to share tools, goods or even time. The idea is to share and use rather than buy, in order to reduce waste. Paradoxically, new tech has brought barter[7] back into fashion, especially in contexts of economic crises where it is easier to exchange goods for food without needing to use money.

Microcredit

The aim of microcredit is to compensate for the inadequacies of regular banks through a flexible system of loans and to reduce poverty. Microcredit and small loans[8] are granted to small, impoverished entrepreneurs who cannot get a loan from a bank. These sums enable them to set up a small business more easily and so reduce poverty. Interest rates are extremely low. In 1983, economist Muhammad Yunus established the Grameen Bank in Bangladesh to assist the poor, for which he was awarded the Nobel Prize for Peace.

Alternative currencies

The SSE is based on peer-to-peer exchanges, hence the creation of local currencies used as an alternative means[9] to exchange time, services and good. The idea is to recreate traditional community bonds and to encourage local networks. These currencies take different forms like printed vouchers[10] or digital credit. Their aim is to keep the money out of the hands of big corporations. They are a financial force to be reckoned with[11] today.

Crowdfunding

Originally launched to support artistic activities, it is now a way of raising money online by asking the public for donations in order to fund a business venture[12]. The idea is that a large number of participants can give small sums of money, which in the end will make up huge sums. It is now viewed as an alternative to traditional investment. This is how the film *Demain*, dealing with a possible green future for the planet, was able to complement its budget.

Fair trade

Fair trade promotes environmental sustainability[13] and fairness in trading conditions for small producers in developing countries. It is seen as an alternative to conventional international trade. Various fair-trade labelling organisations work together to develop this approach and organise supply chains which respect their values all along the process from production to selling. Consumers in developed nations often back[14] this approach.

Worker cooperatives

The number of cooperatives has grown steadily[15] over the past decades. They are companies owned and managed by the workers themselves and not by outside shareholders[16]. Representation is democratic to the extent that one member equals one vote, and workers benefit from the profits made by the cooperative.

CSA – Community supported agriculture

Born in Japan in the late 1960s, it includes two essential pillars: food sovereignty and solidarity economy. It implies the involvement of eaters (consumers) with the producers, shared risks and benefits, based on a local and ecological farming model. Western consumers today want to know where their food comes from but also to benefit from locally-grown, pesticide-free produce[17] and a chance to taste new vegetables and fruit.

1. union: *syndicat.*
2. welfare: *bien-être.*
3. to prevail over: *l'emporter sur.*
4. blind: *aveugle.*
5. fair trade: *commerce équitable.*
6. grounded: *implanté.*
7. barter: *troc.*
8. loan: *prêt.*
9. means: *moyen.*
10. voucher: *bon.*
11. to be reckoned with: *avec laquelle il faut compter.*
12. venture: *projet qui comporte des risques.*
13. sustainability: *durabilité.*
14. to back: *soutenir.*
15. steadily: *régulièrement.*
16. shareholder : *actionnaire.*
17. produce: *produits agricoles.*

Repérer les notions essentielles.

Answer the following questions.

a. What is the aim of the Social Solidarity Economy?
b. What has given rise to this type of economy?
c. Who is involved in the SSE?
d. Why are new communication technologies useful for such an economy?
e. What funding systems have been invented to support small economic projects?
f. What is the objective of fair trade?
g. What characterises workers' cooperatives?
h. What benefits does CSA provide?

Résumer le texte en français.

Faites un résumé de ce texte en *200 mots environ*.

Approfondir

Do some research on one of these topics by answering the questions.

a. Present an NGO of your choice. When was it created? Where was it created? What does it do? What is its aim? Etc. Make a presentation to your class.
b. What are the drawbacks and benefits of fair trade?
c. Fast food is often criticised. Today, the Slow Food movement is gaining popularity. What does it consist in ?

Lexical work

• activist	militant
• alternative currency	devise alternative
• access to health care	accès aux soins de santé
• barter system	système de troc
• to benefit society	profiter à la société
• to benefit from	profiter de
• boycott campaign	campagne de boycott
• to bridge a gap	combler un fossé
• to call into question	remettre en question
• cause marketing	marketing de cause sociale ou humanitaire
• charity	organisme caritatif
• consumer pressure	pression des consommateurs
• commitment	engagement
• crowdfunding	financement participatif
• CSR (Corporate Social Responsibility)	RSE (responsabilité sociale de l'entreprise)
• to donate money	faire un don d'argent
• economic problem	problème économique
• the economy	l'économie
• egalitarian	égalitaire
• to empower	autonomiser, émanciper
• empowerment	autonomisation
• environmental awareness / challenge	conscience / défi écologique
• environmental footprint	empreinte écologique
• equal in rights	égaux en droits
• ethical investment	investissement éthique
• to foster solidarity	favoriser la solidarité
• fundraising	levée de fonds
• to involve local actors	impliquer des acteurs locaux
• to lend money	prêter de l'argent
• moneyless trading	commerce sans argent
• NGO (Non-Governmental Organisation)	ONG
• to overcome inequalities	surmonter les inégalités
• to pool skills	mutualiser des compétences
• peer lending	prêt(s) entre pairs
• to reduce inequalities	réduire les inégalités
• to raise awareness	faire prendre conscience
• to raise funds	lever des fonds
• self-help group	groupe d'entre-aide
• to set up a cooperative	monter une coopérative
• to share	partager

Lexical work

• social entrepreneurship	entrepreneuriat social
• social benefit / businesses	prestation sociale / entreprises sociales
• sustainability	durabilité
• sustainable economy	économie durable
• stakeholder	partie prenante
• value	valeur
• to volunteer	faire du bénévolat
• volunteering	bénévolat
• to widen a gap	creuser un fossé

Use the list

1 Fill in the sentences with these verbs from the list. Make the necessary spelling changes.

bridge – call – donate – lend – overcome – pool – share – volunteer – widen

a. For a decade, the gap between the poor and the rich has …ed.
b. The SSE economy attempts to … the gap between social classes.
c. You can participate by …ing money.
d. Many people … after work in order to build up a fairer society.
e. …ing skills is a way not to waste human resources.
f. The relation between labour and capital is sometimes …ed into question.
g. In cooperatives, people agree to … risks collectively.
h. The SSE is aimed at …ing social disparities.
i. Microcredit consists in …ing money to help people set up a small business venture.

2 Translate into English.

a. L'économie peut bénéficier de projets communautaires.
b. Réduire les inégalités entre les femmes et les hommes est nécessaire.
c. Les agriculteurs ont monté une coopérative pour être plus forts.

3 Translate into French.

a. Better education fosters the empowerment of poor communities.
b. Lending small sums of money can help people to set up small ventures.
c. Barter makes it possible not to use money.
d. Consumers want to participate in a more sustainable economy.
e. Unknown artists sometimes use crowdfunding to fund projects.
f. CSR is a business practice that takes ethical values into account.
g. Volunteering implies commitment on the part of participants.

Grammar work

Le superlatif

› Aide-mémoire grammatical, p. 174

Analysez les éléments soulignés et traduisez les exemples suivants.

1. SSE takes into account the most vulnerable individuals in society.
2. The least advantaged members of society need assistance.
3. The precariat are people with the lowest incomes.
4. This NGO has the strongest foothold in Africa.
5. The best diet is based on local, organic food.
6. They believe the easiest thing to do is to share services.
7. The worst cases of poverty are sometimes found in developed countries.
8. Cooperatives are the most commonly known legal structures of SSE.

1 Traduisez en anglais les phrases suivantes.

a. Les personnes âgées qui travaillent encore n'ont pas toujours les plus hauts revenus.
b. Les handicapés sont les moins susceptibles de trouver un emploi.
c. Les pires inégalités concernent les enfants.
d. La solution la plus facile consiste à prêter de petites sommes d'argent.
e. L'économie solidaire utilise les meilleures pratiques pour aider la communauté.
f. Les plus petites organisations caritatives peuvent faire beaucoup de choses.

Comment traduire le pronom relatif français « dont »

› Aide-mémoire grammatical, p. 179

Observez les exemples suivants et leur traduction en français.

1. Volunteers whose work is useful must be thanked.
   → *Les bénévoles dont le travail est utile doivent être remerciés.*
2. This cooperative produces 80 tons of coffee, half of which are exported to Europe.
   → *Cette coopérative produit 80 tonnes de café, dont la moitié est exportée vers* l'Europe.
3. Where is the accommodation (which) we need for poor students?
   → *Où sont les logements dont nous avons besoin pour les étudiants pauvres ?*

- **Dans quel exemple le pronom relatif français « dont » permet-il :**
  – de préciser une sous-partie d'un ensemble ?
  – d'exprimer la possession ?
  – de reprendre le complément d'un verbe introduit par « de » ?
- **Observez les trois équivalents anglais de « dont » dans chacun de ces cas.**

2 Complétez les phrases en traduisant l'élément donné entre parenthèses.

a. We are going to meet the farmers … yesterday. *(dont je t'ai parlé)*

b. The SSE is an economy … is to reduce inequalities. *(dont l'objectif)*

c. They have set up different shelters for the homeless, … will be open for the winter. *(dont beaucoup)*

d. Children … do not earn enough need financial help to go on holiday. *(dont les parents)*

e. Unemployment and poverty, … , have been increasing since last year. *(dont les gens ont peur)*

f. Our community enterprise is run by volunteers … is an essential asset. *(dont l'engagement)*

3 Traduisez en anglais.

a. Les bénévoles dont nous avons parlé ce matin partiront au Chili demain.

b. L'argent dont ils ont besoin sera envoyé le plus tôt possible.

c. Les femmes dont les opportunités étaient réduites peuvent désormais produire et vendre leurs légumes.

d. Nos bénévoles, dont beaucoup sont retraités, aident des jeunes à réussir leurs études.

e. Les travailleurs sociaux dont on a besoin ne sont pas assez nombreux.

f. Les difficultés, dont les origines sont nombreuses, affaiblissent l'organisation de ce projet risqué.

g. C'est une association dont les membres sont solidaires.

h. Les dons, dont la moitié provient d'entreprises, seront très utiles.

i. C'est une coopérative dont le but est d'améliorer la vie des petits producteurs.

j. Nous ne savons pas ce dont ils ont besoin.

k. J'ai visité plusieurs ONG, dont deux m'ont semblé sérieuses.

Exam work

Document 1

Can co-ops solve the housing[1] crisis?

(...) Housing co-ops are not a new phenomenon. In the UK, they emerged out of the squatting scene of the 70s and 80s. Squatters were given licences to live in short-life houses – typically, low-quality housing stock – in exchange for maintaining the properties. Some of those co-ops still exist, having been given permanent licences by local councils[2]; others were subsumed[3] into housing associations. Although they take different forms, most housing co-ops consist of buildings lived in by an association of members. These members pay a below-market rent[4], which goes towards upkeep[5], and properties are managed by members on an unpaid basis. If a window needs to be fixed or a boiler serviced[6], residents will arrange for a tradesperson[7] to visit the property, and pay for it out of the communal repair fund.

Members of housing co-ops do not usually own equity[8] in their homes; the properties are owned by the legal entity that is the co-operative itself, rather than individual members. However, in some co-ops, members have pooled[9] finances. (...)

Within co-ops, rules vary: some don't take couples; some welcome families. Members of a housing co-op often hear about it through word of mouth[10]; few advertise, as they don't have the space and already have long waiting lists. As a result, many members end up there through happy accident and connections, rather than through responding to an advert. Although co-ops offer secure housing to their members for as long as they choose to live there, when members leave, the property reverts to[11] the co-operative, which will then allocate[12] the property to someone on its waiting list.

Becoming a member of a housing co-op can be life-changing. Private rents have risen faster than wages in England since 2011, according to data from the housing charity Shelter. London is at the heart of the housing crisis: in some boroughs[13], average rents have jumped 42%, while wages have increased by 2% in the same period. One in seven UK tenants[14] spends more than half their monthly income in rent. (...)

Housing co-ops offer affordability and safety. "It's an oasis," says 50-year-old Helima Zindiani. She has lived in "20/20", a housing co-operative in Balsall Heath, Birmingham, since 1997. When she moved in, she was a single mother of three children, struggling to make ends meet[15]. For her three-bedroom house, she pays £89 a week.

Sirin Kale, *The Guardian*, 27 March 2019.

1. housing: *logement*. **2.** local council: *municipalité*. **3.** to subsume: *intégrer*. **4.** rent: *loyer*. **5.** upkeep: *entretien*. **6.** to service a boiler: *faire réviser une chaudière*. **7.** tradesperson: *artisan*. **8.** equity: *(ici) part de propriété*. **9.** to pool: *mettre en commun*. **10.** word of mouth: *bouche à oreille*. **11.** to revert to: *retomber dans*. **12.** to allocate: *allouer*. **13.** borough: *quartier londonien*. **14.** tenant: locataire. **15.** affordability: *caractère abordable*. **16.** to make ends meet: *joindre les deux bouts*.

1 ***Compréhension.***

Expliquez comment fonctionne le logement coopératif au Royaume-Uni. Quels sont ses avantages ? *(Environ150 mots, en français.)*

Document 2

Worker cooperatives offer real alternatives to Trump's retrograde economic vision

In dozens of cities, worker-owner cooperatives are establishing new enterprises based on joint[1] decision-making, dignified work conditions and fair pay. (...). And in this rising movement, people of color, immigrants and women are leading the way.

There are many reasons why cooperatives are well-suited to these demographics, says Esteban Kelly, executive director of the U.S. Federation of Worker Cooperatives, or USFWC, a nationwide coalition representing over 160 co-ops. "Cooperatives are very appealing[2] for people who have been locked out of the traditional job market, or who tend to get locked in to jobs which have low wages and poor working conditions," he said. "We are seeing a lot of momentum[3] in the service sectors, like child care and elderly care, early education, hospice, and other labor-intensive, low-wage jobs — and these tend to be comprised of many people of color, indigenous people, immigrants and women." (...)

According to USFWC data, the average hourly wage in a worker co-op is $16.54, with an average of 31 hours per week. And while competing in the mainstream[4] economy means these companies aren't able to raise wages significantly above the market rate, Kelly says the cooperative model offers many other benefits to members. Joint decision-making lends more dignity to the workplace, "and many cooperatives have better benefits or offer more in the way of training and career development." (...)

The worker-owner movement is still relatively small — estimates range between 200 and 300 such cooperatives operate nationwide — but a growing number of cities, counties and states are beginning to look at cooperatives more seriously. (...)

A primary barrier to this expansion is difficulty in accessing capital. Many mainstream banks are wary[5] of lending to cooperatives (...) and co-op members often lack[6] the capital to finance themselves. However, there are alternatives to traditional banks, including Community Development Financial Institutions, such as the Local Enterprise Assistance Fund, which focus on supporting cooperatives. In fact, some of these creditors report being underutilized, indicating a disconnect between the needs and know-how[7] of cooperatives. Small co-ops that need outside funding may be able to find it if they have sound[8] business plans (...).

Sarah Aziza, wagingnonviolence.org,
23 January 2018.

1. joint: *en commun.* **2.** appealing: *attrayant.* **3.** momentum: *dynamisme.* **4.** mainstream: *dominant.* **5.** wary: *méfiant.* **6.** to lack: *manquer de.* **7.** know-how: *savoir-faire.* **8.** sound: *(ici) sain.*

2 ***Compréhension.***

What are the objectives, benefits and challenges of workers' cooperatives in the USA? Answer in English. *(About 150 words.)*

Exam work

Document 3

Increasing investment in people's capabilities[1]

The profound changes in the world of work are placing unprecedented pressures on the social contract. (...) The fears generated by the changing nature of work have led to a growing consensus around the need to reinvigorate the social contract which greatly relies on the individual participation of citizens in decisions affecting their lives. As highlighted[2] by the ILO[3] Global Commission on the Future of Work: "The absence or failure of the social contract is to the detriment of all."

Gender Equality – Globally[4], great strides[5] have been made towards gender equality over the last two decades. Nevertheless, deep gender disparities persist across the globe, surfacing in labour markets, as well as other realms[6]. Compared to men, women continue to earn less, are more likely to partake in[7] unpaid labour, and are more apt to be excluded from decent work and opportunities for advancement.

As gender equity is increasingly seen as a pillar for sustainable economic development and broad social well-being, alternative models to development which incorporate women's equality in work are needed. Cooperatives and other SSEEOs[8] are well-suited[9] to advancing women's economic participation in three key ways: increasing access to employment and work, enabling economic democracy and agency and boosting leadership and management experience.

Nine of the biggest 100 cooperative and mutual insurers[10] in the world have women CEOs, compared to only one of the top 100 stock company insurers. Women have opted to work in cooperatives and other SSEEOs for paid work opportunities that can be managed alongside[11] responsibilities associated with unpaid care work. Women workers in the informal economy often choose to come together through cooperatives and other SSEEOs to improve their livelihoods[12], enhance[13] their access to goods, markets and services (like insurance) and improve their collective voice and negotiation power.

In the US, immigrant women homecare workers have been setting up cooperatives, with the support of unions and community organizations, to secure better wages, improved quality of jobs and healthier working environments. Women-only cooperatives exist in countries like Mexico, India, Nepal, and Nigeria to Morocco, Iran, Lebanon and Turkey often in sectors where women are the main producers and service providers. In sectors such as agriculture, women's participation in cooperatives and other producer organizations as members and leaders still lags behind[14].

ILO, May 2019.

1. capability: *potentiel.* **2.** to highlight: *souligner.* **3.** ILO (International Labour Organisation): *Organisation Internationale du Travail.* **4.** globally: *au niveau mondial.* **5.** stride: *avancée.* **6.** realm: *domaine.* **7.** to partake in: *participer à.* **8.** SSEEOs = Social and Solidarity Economy Enterprises and Organizations. **9.** well-suited: *bien adapté.* **10.** insurer: *assureur.* **11.** alongside: *avec.* **12.** livelihood: *moyen de subsistance.* **13.** to enhance: *améliorer.* **14.** to lag behind: *être à la traîne.*

3 *Compréhension.*

What problems do women face in the world of work today? How can these issues be addressed? What roles do women occupy and where? *(About 150 words, in English.)*

Document 4

As garbage[1] piles up in Tunisian cities,waste pickers[2] demand recognition.

(...) The system of plastic recycling in Tunisian cities is largely reliant on[3] an informal workforce of waste pickers, known as *barbechas*, meaning someone who searches, digs[4] or investigates.

And like thousands of other Tunisians who work in the informal sector, *barbechas* lack an official status and lead a precarious life, carrying out their jobs without workers' rights or health insurance, say human rights activists.

Many waste pickers live in poverty, selling the waste they find to middlemen[5] recyclers who then sell it on for a markedv-up price to the national waste collection system or, more often, a private recycling factory.

"There is no legal framework[6] that regulates (this type of) recycling," said Mehdi Barhoumi, Tunis-based project manager for the British non-profit International Alert.

This could change with a proposed law to establish a "social and solidarity economy" which would support collectives and self-governed businesses that both make a profit and have a social objective.

The idea is to create a halfway house[7] between the informal sector and regular employment by giving workers the opportunity to self-organize and register their activity without setting up a company, Barhoumi explained.

He hopes the law will give Tunisia's waste pickers better protection from health risks and exploitation by middlemen. (...)

In an attempt to build a support system for Tunisia's waste pickers, the non-profit Environmental Protection and Recycling Association (EPRA), based in Ettadhamen, provides vaccines as well as protective clothing for its 70 members, and operates its own waste disposal unit.

International Alert help the collective with funds and equipment so that members can sell their collected plastic to the association, which grinds[8] it down and then sells it straight to recycling companies at a fair price.

Layla Foroudi, Reuters, 10 August 2019.

1. garbage: *ordures.* **2.** waste picker: *chiffonnier, collecteur de déchets.* **3.** reliant on: *dépendant de.* **4.** to dig: *creuser.* **5.** middleman: *intermédiaire.* **6.** framework: *cadre.* **7.** halfway house: *transition.* **8.** to grind: *moudre.*

4 *Compréhension.*

Answer the following questions in English: Who are barbechas? What problems do they face? What is being done about it, and how? *(About 150 words, in English.)*

Document 4

www.caritas.org

5 ***Expression.***

Describe and explain the meaning of these illustrations taken from Caritas's site. Caritas is a non-profit relief (*aide humanitaire*) and development agency. *(About 150 words, in English.)*

6 ***Compréhension.***

En vous appuyant sur les documents 1 à 5, présentez les divers aspects de l'économie sociale et solidaire aujourd'hui.

7 ***Expression*. Write an email.**

Vous êtes le responsable marketing d'une coopérative d'agriculteurs producteurs et tisserands de coton bio située en Inde (GreenCotton.in) qui cherche des débouchés commerciaux.

Vous rédigez un courriel en anglais à une société de confection de vêtements (EcoGarment.co.uk) qui est connue pour ses valeurs d'engagement social et éthique. Vous voulez les convaincre de l'utilité de développer une ligne de vêtements en coton bio *(organic cotton)* qui pourrait intéresser leurs acheteurs, de jeunes urbains désireux de préserver l'environnement. Dans votre argumentaire, vous insistez entre autres sur vos engagements : ne pas recourir au travail des enfants, supprimer les pesticides, accorder de meilleurs salaires aux ouvriers, baisser le taux d'endettement des agriculteurs, préserver les sols et les ressources en eau, etc. Présentation et formules d'usage. *(Environ 150 mots dans le corps du courriel.)*

CHAPITRE

6

Working conditions and social dialogue

Les conditions de travail et le dialogue social

Working conditions

Working conditions are the environment in which workers operate[1]. They include various elements such as wages, health and safety, commuting, benefits, working hours, employment terms, autonomy or work-life balance.

Social dialogue

Social dialogue includes all types of negotiations and exchanges between partners, which are the government, workers and employers. The aim of negotiations is to find solutions to conflicts through consensus and to achieve[2] economic and social goals. Bipartite dialogue means that only two of the above three partners discuss and tripartite ones include all three partners, the government often playing the role of a neutral facilitator. Most countries in the world are members of the International Labour Organization (ILO). As such, they should follow the ILO guidelines[3] concerning social dialogue. This includes strong trade unions, the political will to establish social dialogue and respect of fundamental workers' rights, etc.

Trade unions

Unions defend the interests of workers. Their role is to make sure fair wages are guaranteed, working conditions are acceptable and that workers engage in meaningful and productive work. France has a low union membership density (about 11% in the public sector, and 8% in the private sector) but it is higher in the UK (around 23%). Tripartite social dialogue does not exist in the USA, where only bipartite dialogue between management and unions exists. The clout[4] of unions has been declining since the end of the 20th century in the USA, with now a 10% density.

Negotiating

Labour market regulations and labour laws protect workers' rights in every country but conditions differ from country to country. Companies also have collective agreements in which wages, hours, benefits, etc. are agreed on. Works councils[5], which comprise employers, workers and union representatives, discuss improvements and changes. Thanks to collective bargaining, management and unions can negotiate working conditions. Industrial relation laws[6] define the powers on each side. Labour disputes[7] occur when they disagree. Sometimes, when disagreements last too long, strikes are organized by workers to put pressure on public authorities or companies themselves.

Flexibility

Workers all over the world are nowadays concerned with achieving a better work-life balance[8]. Moreover, with the "24-hour society", businesses operate outside the standard hours to increase productivity and meet consumer demand. Companies implement[9] policies, which help to set up flexible working patterns, with practices such as job-sharing[10], flexi-time, teleworking and so on.

Stress – the new occupational disease

Long hours end up reducing productivity because workers lose energy and motivation. The Japanese have invented a term which refers to death by overworking – *karoshi*. Without going to such extremes, "burn out" syndromes have become an issue in many countries. Some workers end up completely exhausted, physically and emotionally. This is now reaching near epidemic proportions in various countries.

Workplace bullying and discrimination

Workplace bullying[11] consists in physical or psychological threats, unfair criticism, exclusion, etc. It is the second most reported professional health problem after stress. The underlying cause is often a management culture of bullying. Victims may have panic attacks, sleep disorders, anxiety and higher blood pressure. Being bullied makes people less able to perform and they end up losing self-esteem.

Gender, race or age discrimination at work are illegal in most countries. However, applying for a job is often harder for minorities. Sometimes, unionists are discriminated against for their activities and often have lower wages as a result.

The gig economy

In the gig economy, many workers are self-employed (other workers have short-term or zero-hour contracts). The gig economy is based on self-employment. With the rise of Internet platforms, self-employment is increasing, with the result that some workers are no longer protected by the traditional framework[12] of employer-employee relationship. Even if the new "non-standard" jobs enable job-seekers to find a job more easily, workers are often excluded from social protection or face more discrimination because they cannot participate in collective bargaining.

The fear of robots

Robot use is growing rapidly and this raises widespread fear[13] that robots and AI (Artificial Intelligence) will destroy millions of jobs. Sometimes, we hear that new jobs will be created in order to monitor[14] and collaborate with robots. The purpose of automation is to get rid of dull[15] or dangerous tasks and so robots are good news for workers. Robots cannot completely replace humans because many tasks require dexterity, judgement[16] or appreciation. However, low-skilled workers are more likely to face disruption[17] and so it is important that unions safeguard their interests and maintain a good balance of power in the world of work.

1. to operate: *fonctionner.*
2. to achieve: *réaliser.*
3. guideline: *directive.*
4. clout: *influence.*
5. works council: *comité d'entreprise.*
6. industrial relation laws: *législation relative au travail.*
7. labour disputes: *conflits sociaux.*
8. work life balance: *équilibre entre vie professionnelle et privée.*
9. to implement policies: *mettre en œuvre des mesures.*
10. job sharing: *partage de poste.*
11. to bully: *harceler.*
12. framework: *cadre.*
13. to raise widespread fears: *soulever des craintes généralisées.*
14. to monitor: *surveiller.*
15. dull: *rébarbatif.*
16. judgement: *discernement.*
17. disruption: *bouleversement.*

Repérer les notions essentielles

Answer the following questions.

a. Why are good working conditions essential?
b. What is the purpose of social dialogue? Who is involved?
c. How important are unions?
d. What is the purpose of negotiating?
e. What are the new patterns of work?
f. Why is workplace stress a serious issue?
g. What is the gig economy? What are its consequences on workers' rights?
h. Are robots a real threat on jobs or not? What needs to be done?

Résumer le texte en français

Résumez ce texte en 200 mots environ.

Approfondir

a. **Should we fear the presence of artificial intelligence in the world of work? *(About 250 words, in English.)***
b. **Do some research to find out about working hours in various countries in the world. Make comparisons.**

Lexical work

• to address problems / an issue	s'occuper de problèmes / d'une question
• to agree on wages	se mettre d'accord sur les salaires
• automation	automatisation
• to axe jobs	supprimer des emplois
• to be out of work / unemployed	être au chômage
• bargaining	négociations
• boreout	épuisement professionnel par ennui
• burnout	épuisement
• collective bargaining	négociations collectives
• to commute	faire les trajets pour aller à son travail
• danger money	prime de risque
• day off	jour de congé
• employees' rights	droit des employés
• employment contract	contrat d'embauche
• empowerment	émancipation, autonomisation
• to fear layoffs	craindre des licenciements
• fixed-term work	contrat à durée déterminée
• flexitime	horaire à la carte / variable
• full-time / part-time work	travail à temps plein / partiel
• gender pay gap	le fossé salarial homme-femme
• to go on strike	faire grève
• holidays with pay	congés payés
• hourly rates	taux horaires
• inclusiveness	inclusion, non exclusion
• industrial umpire	arbitre du dialogue social
• health hazards	risques liés au travail
• job losses / cuts	suppressions d'emplois
• job security	sécurité de l'emploi
• job sharing	partage du travail
• labour dispute	conflit social
• labour laws / talks	droit du travail / négociations de travail
• to lay off / make redundant	licencier
• living income	revenu minimum vital
• minimum wage	salaire minimum
• occupation	métier
• overtime	heures supplémentaires
• parental leave	congé parental
• pay cut / rise	réduction / hausse de salaire
• pay dispute	conflit salarial
• permanent contract	contrat à durée indéterminée

• representative	représentant (un)
• safety	sécurité
• schedule	horaire, programme
• seasonal work	travail saisonnier
• to be self-employed	travailler à son compte
• sick leave	congé maladie
• social partner	partenaire social
• to take legal action	intenter une action en justice
• telecommuting / teleworking	télétravail
• time off	congés
• union	syndicat
• wage growth / rise	croissance / augmentation des salaires
• wage rise	augmentation de salaires
• to walk out	claquer la porte
• to work long hours	faire de longues journées
• to work overtime	faire des heures supplémentaires
• work patterns	modes de travail
• workload	charge de travail
• working time regulations	réglementation du temps de travail
• zero-hour contract	contrat à la tâche / zéro heures

Use the list

1 Match the following words and add an article if necessary, then translate the phrases. Ex.: *to take a day off.*

a. to take (x2) b. to fear c. go on
d. to axe e. to address f. to agree on

1. jobs 2. wages 3. legal action
4. day off 5. issue 6. layoffs 7. strike

2 Complete the following sentences.

self-employed – working time regulations – overtime – holiday – unions – burnout – representatives

a. If workers are overworked, they sometimes do .... . Their stress is called occupational stress and if they don't stop, they will suffer from … and be very sick. What they need is a … .

b. During negotiations, … and management discuss topics like … or wages rises.

c. In the gig economy, … workers don't have many … and have to demonstrate in order to be heard.

Grammar work

Les auxiliaires modaux : obligation, interdiction, absence d'obligation, forte probabilité

› Aide-mémoire grammatical, p. 167

Analysez et traduisez les exemples.

1. The court ruled that companies must pay employees' cell phone expenses.
2. But they don't have to pay for employees' clothing expenses.
3. Night workers must not work more than an average of 8 hours in a 24-hour period.
4. British businesses had to follow the EU working time directive.
5. Some American employees work 50 hours a week. They must be exhausted.
6. He looks exhausted: he must have worked all night long.
7. I saw my colleagues in a bar at 6 pm. They can't have worked as late as they say.
8. In the 19th century, people had to work much longer hours.

1 Complétez et traduisez les phrases avec une des formes ci-dessus.

a. The British government has ruled that NHS workers … speak English fluently.
b. Company workers … belong to a union. Nobody can force them to do so.
c. He arrived late at the office: he … have been held up by traffic jams.
d. Employees sometimes feel they … answer all the emails they get.
e. But he is only 15! He … have been hired by a company. It's illegal.
f. In the 19th century, workers … take their work home when it was badly done.
g. Regulations stipulate that workers … work more than 4 hours in succession.
h. Stress at work … be tackled by companies to improve productivity.
i. It … be hard to leave the office earlier than everyone else when there is so much pressure to succeed.
j. Working hours … comply with national law.

2 Traduisez en anglais.

a. La semaine dernière, ils ont dû demander un congé pour raisons familiales.
b. Il a l'air mécontent. Il a dû être contrarié par les critiques du directeur.
c. On ne doit pas faire travailler les enfants.
d. Le train est en retard. Ils doivent être énervés.
e. Il faut que les entreprises respectent les taux horaires.
f. Ce n'est pas la peine de travailler autant. Il faut rester performant.
g. Ils ne sont pas encore partis à la retraite. Ils doivent attendre d'avoir 65 ans.
h. Il n'est là que depuis deux semaines. Impossible qu'il ait pris des vacances.
i. Il ne faut pas arriver en retard. J'ai toujours suivi ce principe.
j. Ils n'ont pas fait de pause-café, mais ils ne sont pas obligés d'en faire une.

3 **Traduisez en français.**

a. Women must not be discriminated against.
b. Do workers have to belong to a union?
c. He must have lost his job.
d. They can't have reduced our wages.
e. Must we go on strike?
f. They don't have to participate in the negotiations.

Les quantificateurs : expression de la quantité

› Aide-mémoire grammatical, p. 204

Analysez et traduisez les exemples.

1. Too few workers belong to a union today.
2. Only a few workers went on strike last week.
3. Workers who take public transport realise they have little time for themselves.
4. If you finish early, you will have a little time to rest.
5. Many parents want longer parental leaves.
6. Some workers are tired because they have too much work.
7. They sometimes don't take any breaks.

4 **Complétez les phrases suivantes par des quantificateurs : *little / a little / few / a few / much / many / some / any*, puis traduisez les phrases.**

a. Last year, only … employees were promoted. a few
b. If there are too … strikes, companies can be in financial trouble. many
c. Too … men take care of their children. few
d. Too … anxiety raises stress levels. much
e. Even when there is … pressure, workers may feel stressed. a little
f. He had some personal problems which prevented him from concentrating.
g. Workers who are criticized all the time don't have … self-esteem in the end. much
h. There was very … inclusiveness in this company's policies. much
i. There is ... fear about robots replacing employees. Some

5 **Traduisez les phrases suivantes.**

a. Ils ont très peu de robots dans cette usine. they have very few robots
b. Il avait peu de temps pour effectuer cette tâche. he had little time
c. Il n'y a pas de dialogue social sans lois. Theres isn't any Social dialogue
d. Quand on a trop d'heures de travail, on devient malade. When we have too many hours
e. Trop peu de dialogue social donne lieu à des conflits. Too little social dialogue
f. Certains syndicats défendent mal les employés. Some Unions defend badly
g. Il y a eu une grève pendant quelques jours. There was a strike for a few days

Exam work

Document 1

Union stages[1] final protest over "horrific" Amazon work practices

Union workers have staged the final in a series of protests outside an Amazon warehouse[2] in Doncaster over "unsafe" and "appalling[3]" working conditions. According to the GMB union, workers urinate in plastic bottles rather than go to the toilet during their shifts[4], and pregnant women are forced to stand for hours on end. The protest follows international campaigns last week to coincide with the retail giant's[5] Prime Day promotion, with demonstrations being held outside seven British warehouses – what the company calls "fulfilment[6] centres" – and in seven US cities.

Mick Rix, the GMB's national officer, said Amazon workers wanted to send a message to Jeff Bezos, the company's founder and CEO, that they were people, not robots. "The conditions our members work under at Amazon sites are appalling. The reports we get from GMB members are horrific and suggest the practices Amazon employed at Doncaster create unsafe work, in comparison to some other warehouse distribution centres," he said. (…)

Amazon workers were joined by Jack Dromey MP[7], the Shadow Pensions Minister[8], outside the Milton Keynes warehouse on Friday. He pledged[9] to call for a joint health and safety audit of Amazon with the HSE[10] and the GMB union "so no more Amazon workers are injured[11] at work." "It's unacceptable that Amazon workers are subjected to working practices that would shame[12] a 19th-century mill owner[13] while the company makes ever increasing profits and Jeff Bezos gets even richer," he said.

Amazon said workers can use the toilet whenever they want to and that nobody urinates in plastic bottles. It said figures from the HSE show that the company has more than 40% fewer injuries on average than other transportation and warehousing companies in the UK.

An Amazon spokesperson[14] said: "Events like Prime Day have become an opportunity for our critics, including unions, to raise awareness for their cause, in this case, increased membership dues[15]. These groups are conjuring[16] misinformation to work in their favour when, in fact, we already offer the things they purport[17] to be their cause – industry-leading pay, benefits and a safe workplace for our employees."

By Maya Wolfe-Robinson, *The Guardian*, 22 July 2019.

1. to stage: *organiser*. **2.** warehouse: *entrepôt*. **3.** appalling: *lamentable*. **4.** shift: *période de travail*. **5.** retail giant: *géant de la distribution*. **6.** fulfilment: *accomplissement*. **7.** MP = Member of Parliament: *député*. **8.** Shadow Pensions Minister: *parlementaire de l'opposition spécialisé dans les retraites*. **9.** to pledge: *promettre*. **10.** HSE (Health and Safety Executive): *Direction de la Santé et de la Sécurité*. **11.** injured: *blessé*. **12.** to shame: *couvrir de honte*. **13.** mill owner: *patron d'usine*. **14.** spokesperson: *porte parole*. **15.** dues: *cotisations*. **16.** to conjure: *inventer*. **17.** to purport: *prétendre*.

1 ***Compréhension.***
Why are Amazon workers on strike? How have politicians and Amazon managers reacted? Answer the questions in English. *(About 200 words.)*

Document 2

Revealed: catastrophic effects of working as a Facebook moderator

The task of moderating Facebook continues to leave psychological scars[1] on the company's employees, months after efforts to improve conditions for the company's thousands of contractors, the *Guardian* has learned. A group of current and former[2] contractors who worked for years at the social network's Berlin-based moderation centres has reported witnessing colleagues become "addicted" to graphic content[3] and hoarding[4] ever more extreme examples for a personal collection. They also said others were pushed towards the far right by the amount of hate speech and fake news they read every day.

They describe being ground down[5] by the volume of the work, numbed[6] by the graphic violence, nudity and bullying[7] they have to view for eight hours a day, working nights and weekends, for "practically minimum pay". A little-discussed aspect of Facebook's moderation was particularly distressing to the contractors: vetting[8] private conversations between adults and minors that have been flagged[9] by algorithms as likely sexual exploitation. (…)

In February, the technology site The Verge produced one of the first behind-the-scenes reports from a US Facebook contractor. Similar to their Berlin colleagues, the Americans reported that "the conspiracy videos and memes that they see each day gradually led them to embrace fringe views[10]", and that a former moderator "now sleeps with a gun at his side" after he was traumatised by a video of a stabbing[11].

Others were dealing with trauma by self-medicating. Just as the Arizona moderators were reportedly turning to drugs and alcohol, so were those in Germany. "I saw a lot of big consumer drugs in the company," Daniel said. "We don't have any way to destress. The company, technically, is against drugs."

When trying to go down a more legitimate route of self-help, the American moderators complained about the psychological help that was provided. "The on-site counsellors were largely passive," the Verge reporter Casey Newton wrote, "relying on workers to recognise the signs of anxiety and depression and seek help."

Berlin moderators were also critical of the counselling services[12] provided and suggested they leaned too heavily on the state's universal healthcare. Daniel said: "In the end, we didn't have proper psychological support. We had some colleagues who went to the [counsellor], and when they showed that they had real problems, they were invited to go outside the company and find a proper psychologist."

By Alex Hern, *The Guardian*, 17 September 2019.

1. scar: *cicatrice.* **2.** former: *ancient.* **3.** graphic content: *contenu choquant.* **4.** to hoard: *stocker.* **5.** to grind down: *broyer.* **6.** to numb: *rendre insensible.* **7.** bullying: *harcèlement.* **8.** to vet: *examiner.* **9.** to flag: *signaler.* **10.** fringe views: *idées extrémistes.* **11.** stabbing: *attaque à l'arme blanche.* **12.** counselling services: *soutien psychologique.*

2 ***Compréhension.***
Why do content moderators suffer from and why? What is done about it?
(About 120 words, in English.)

Exam work

Document 3

EU introduces new minimum rights for "gig economy"[1] workers

The European Parliament has approved new minimum rights for workers in so-called "gig economy" jobs such as Uber drivers and Deliveroo riders.

Under the EU regulations, casualised[2] employees across Europe will have a right to compensation from their bosses for last-minute cancellation[3] of work.

Any mandatory[4] training will have to be provided free of charge to workers, and counted as paid working time.

"Exclusivity clauses" that ban[5] workers from taking other jobs will also be banned, and probation[6] periods will be restricted to one, with a maximum of six months.

Employers will also have to give workers a description of their duties "from day one", a formal starting date and pay information, and an indication of what the standard working day will be.

The rules, which will apply to everyone who works at least three hours a week, are intended as a baseline[7], with member states able to raise standards to higher levels.

The new regulations are not intended to apply to "genuinely[8] self-employed" people, EU officials say.

Enrique Calvet Chambon, a Spanish liberal MEP[9] overseeing the rules, said: "All workers who have been in limbo[10] will now be granted minimum rights thanks to this directive, and the European Court of Justice rulings. From now on no employer will be able to abuse the flexibility in the labour market."

Member states, which have already approved the plan at the European Council, will have to enforce the rules in their own domestic laws within three years. (...)

The issue of employment rights for casualised workers has come into focus in recent years with the growth of a new generation of service companies styling themselves as[11] tech firms.

In June last year, a group of 50 couriers working for the food takeaway service Deliveroo won a six-figure payout after they successfully argued they had been unlawfully denied the minimum wage and paid holiday. (...)

By Jon Stone, *The Independent*,
17 April 2019.

1. gig economy: *économie basée sur le travail indépendant payé à la tâche.* **2.** casualised: *précaire.* **3.** cancellation: *annulation.* **4.** mandatory: *obligatoire.* **5.** to ban: *interdire.* **6.** probation: *essai.* **7.** baseline: *base de référence.* **8.** genuinely: *réellement, véritablement.* **9.** MEP (Member of the European Parliament). **10.** limbo: *incertitude.* **11.** to style oneself as: *se faire passer pour.*

3 ***Compréhension.*** De quelles avancées bénéficient désormais les livreurs des plateformes de services de livraison en ligne ? Répondez en français en 150 mots environ.

4 ***Expression.*** In what ways have new information technologies transformed jobs? Do some research and find specific examples.

Key words: CVs, hacking, working hours, telecommuting, applications, car-pooling, facial recognition, flexibility, communication.

Document 4

Making use of global agreements in the garment industry

3 October, 2019 – Over 80 trade union leaders from Turkey, Bangladesh, Cambodia, India, Indonesia, Mauritius and Morocco met in Cesme, Turkey, to see how global framework agreements (GFA) can be better used to boost union organizing, collective bargaining agreements and social dialogue. Global fashion brands, Asos, Esprit, H&M, Inditex and Tchibo, which have signed GFAs with IndustriALL Global Union, also joined the meeting on 23 and 24 September. GFAs are becoming a stronger tool for improving labour relations in the supply chain[2] and there was a call for IndustriALL to negotiate such agreements with more global brands.

Participants discussed how GFAs and social dialogue could be used to promote the new ILO Convention 190 and Recommendation 206 on Violence and Harassment in the garment sector[3]. Gender-based violence, and particularly sexual harassment, is prevalent in the industry. Most garment workers are women and many are young and migrant workers, who are not aware of their rights. They have little access to safe housing and transportation, while the fashion industry generates excessive overtime, low pay, and long working hours.

The meeting concluded that it was urgent for trade unions and brands to promote the ratification of the new Convention. Trade unions should also push to review existing collective agreements and GFAs, to ensure[4] they are in line with the Convention 190.

Unions exchanged experiences on the best ways to monitor[5] global framework agreements and there was strong support for trade unions in production country to play a greater role. National unions are essential in ensuring that the GFAs are implemented in the global brands' supplier factories.

Christina Hajagos-Clausen, IndustriALL director for the textile and garment industry, said: "The increase of unionization rate in GFA supplier factories is key to enable trade unions to monitor the agreements and to ensure that workers' rights are respected in the global garment supply chain."

(...) Global framework agreements are negotiated at a global level between trade unions and a multinational company. They put in place the very best standards of trade union rights, health, safety and environmental practices, and quality of work principles across a company's global operations, regardless of[6] whether those standards exist in an individual country.

From Industriall-union.org, October 2019.

1. IndustriALL Global Union: *nom d'une fédération de syndicats.* **2.** supply chain: *chaîne logistique.* **3.** garment sector: *confection.* **4.** to ensure: *garantir.* **5.** to monitor: *surveiller.* **6.** regardless of: *indépendamment de.*

5 ***Expression.*** Rédigez en français une note résumant les informations de ce document émanant d'un syndicat. *(Environ 150 mots.)*

Document 5

6 ***Expression.*** What does this cartoon imply about working conditions today? To what extent do you agree with it? *(About 250 words, in English.)*

7 ***Synthèse.*** En vous référant aux documents 1 à 5, rédigez en français une note de synthèse qui rendra compte de la problématique générale du dossier. *(Environ 250 mots.)*

8 ***Expression.*** Vous êtes chauffeur contractuel d'une entreprise en ligne de VTC « Call a Ride ». Vous écrivez un mail **en anglais** à votre représentant syndical (Adresse : 721 Broadway, New York, NY 10003) pour vous plaindre des conditions imposées par la société qui vous fournit vos clients. Vous citez notamment la faible rémunération, le taux trop élevé des commissions, les longues heures de travail nécessaires pour rentrer dans vos frais, la fatigue, etc.
Vous indiquez que vous souhaiteriez que des négociations soient entamées pour obtenir un statut de salarié. Vous lui demandez d'intervenir et d'organiser une consultation avec la plateforme « Call a Ride ».

CHAPITRE

7

Communication and corporate culture

Communication et culture d'entreprise

Internal communication

The aim of internal communication is to transmit information within a company. It is essential to make employees and managers better informed. If workers feel involved[1] in the life of their company, they will contribute to its success even more. Their motivation will also enable them to deal with any change that might occur. To be successful, companies have to help the workforce to understand the goals, values and procedures of the organisation. Otherwise, employees might not be confident or efficient enough.

A clear, shared organisational culture can reduce day-to-day conflict, which is good for the employees' morale and for the running of the company. Most importantly, management behaviour and decisions must be consistent[2] with the messages sent out to the workforce. An inconsistent approach to communication may cause resentment[3] and cynicism.

Methods

Companies use various methods to create a common culture, first in their written communication: memos, brochures, newsletters, billboards[4], slogans, e-mails, performance appraisal[5] documents; they also develop oral communication through meetings, periodic speeches by the CEO, open house sessions, etc. When possible, some form of informal communication is also very effective because it can encourage two-way communication which gives management a good idea about how the company is perceived among employees.

External communication

The objective of external communication is to maintain relationships with outside parties. Companies communicate with the public by means of public relations and advertising. They also use catalogues, marketing communication, trade shows[6], etc. External communication also comprises crisis communication when a problem occurs.

Public relations (PR)

Public relations are a strategic communication process. They consist in making sure that a company has a strong, positive public image and in helping the public and the stakeholders[7] to understand the company and its products. Public relations are often carried out through the media. Publicity is essential in public relations rest: journalists discuss the company and/or its products in the media. It is they and not the company that will decide what is said. Companies don't have total control of what is said about them in the media.

Advertising

Advertising is meant to persuade customers to buy products or use services. Companies pay to have ads placed in newspapers or online and have control over the message. Advertisements have less credibility than the coverage a company may obtain through PR. Advertising is usually done by means of billboards, leaflets, brochures, ads in newspapers and magazines, television and radio commercials, direct mailings or e-mail messages, personal contact, buzzing, and above all, social media platforms.

Brand image

Brand image is essential when you want to build loyalty[8] to your firm or brand. Basically, it is a company's reputation. It is not just a matter of logos or slogans, business cards or clean premises, though they do count. Consumers are very sensitive to what may happen to a company, especially when problems occur. Building a company's brand image takes a long time but when it is achieved, the company can benefit from a distinctive image, or personality.

The rise of social media

Companies increasingly rely on[9] social media such as Facebook, Twitter or Instagram to launch campaigns, target[10] consumers, improve PR and promote brand awareness[11]. Social media communication is now an inescapable element of marketing strategies. Today, influencer marketing is all the rage[12], for fashion brands in particular. Influencers can strongly affect the purchasing[13] decisions of consumers.

Corporate culture

The corporate culture of a company determines the way things work within each department and between departments themselves. The way employees work, think and act has direct repercussions on the company's success. Company culture is made of the values and norms which define what is appropriate behaviour in the company. Visible elements such as free meals, dress codes, schedules[14] or job titles shape this culture, but also less visible issues like promotion, innovation and values. From top to bottom, that is to say from the CEO to the most junior trainee, this culture needs to be the same and this set of values has to be understood by everyone. Corporate culture is an essential dimension for employees today – it shapes a company's identity. Workers value culture and career opportunities nearly twice as much as they value perks[15] and benefits[16] when choosing an employer.

The danger of corporate cults

Companies sometimes build a cult-like following among their customers and also encourage cultish behaviour in their employees. They become a replacement for family by encouraging them to centre their lives around their jobs, at the expense of leisure or holidays. Some companies require devotions from their employees. This often happens in startups.

1. involved: *impliqué.*
2. consistent: *en adéquation.*
3. resentment: *rancune.*
4. billboard: *panneau d'affichage.*
5. appraisal: *évaluation.*
6. trade show: *salon commercial.*
7. stakeholder: *partie prenante.*
8. loyalty: *fidélité.*
9. to rely on: *s'appuyer sur.*
10. to target: *cibler.*
11. brand awareness: *(re)connaissance de la marque.*
12. to be all the rage: *faire fureur.*
13. purchasing: *achats.*
14. schedules: *horaires.*
15. perks: *avantages en nature.*
16. benefit: *avantage social.*

Repérer les notions essentielles

Answer the following questions.

a. Why is good internal communication very important?
b. What negative feelings may be produced among employees when communication is bad, and why?
c. Why is informal communication recommended?
d. Why is external communication absolutely essential?
e. What are the various methods used?

Résumer le texte en français

Résumez le texte en français en *150 mots environ*.

Approfondir

a. What techniques are used by advertisers to catch the attention of the public?
b. Are you for or against banning advertisements during children's TV programmes?
c. Do you trust online influencers? Why or why not?
d. Which brands do you think have an excellent brand image? Choose one brand and explain why to your partner.

Lexical work

• to achi**e**ve	accomplir
• ad pl**a**cement	placement publicitaire
• **a**dvertiser ; ad(v**e**rtisement)	un publicitaire ; une pub(licité)
• after-sales s**e**rvice	service après-vente
• b**a**shtag	dénigrement sur les réseaux
• brand b**ui**lding	campagne de notoriété
• brand **i**mage / name	image / nom de marque
• br**a**nding	positionnement d'une marque
• to boost mor**a**le	renforcer le moral
• to build a rel**a**tionship	construire une relation
• cl**i**ckbait	piège à clic
• cons**u**mer	consommateur
• to conv**ey**	faire comprendre, transmettre
• c**o**rporate beh**a**viour (GB) / beh**a**vior (US)	comportement de l'entreprise
• cr**i**sis m**a**nagement	gestion de crise
• to d**a**mage	nuire à, endommager
• d**a**mage contr**o**l	limitation des dégâts
• to dec**ei**ve ; dec**e**ption	tromper ; tromperie
• to **e**mphasize, h**i**ghlight, **u**nderline	souligner
• to ens**u**re	garantir
• f**ee**dback	retour
• to get in touch with	contacter
• gr**ee**nwashing	blanchiment écologique
• g**ui**deline	directive, principe
• to h**a**ndle a cr**i**sis	gérer une crise
• to h**a**rm	faire du mal à
• to impr**o**ve	améliorer
• **i**nfluencer m**a**rketing	marketing des influenceurs
• to l**o**bby	faire du lobbying
• to lose contr**o**l **o**ver	perdre le contrôle sur
• l**o**yalty	fidélité
• the m**e**dia	les médias
• misl**ea**ding	mensonger
• to m**o**nitor c**o**ntent	contrôler un contenu
• op**i**nion s**u**rvey	sondage
• to pr**o**sper	être florissant
• publ**i**city	publicité, renommée
• to reinf**o**rce / to enh**a**nce	renforcer
• rel**i**able	fiable
• responsib**i**lity	responsabilité

• to share	partager
• to smear	salir, calomnier
• social media outlet	plateforme de réseau social
• to solve a problem	résoudre un problème
• spin doctor	expert en relations publiques
• spokesperson	porte-parole
• to spread word of mouth	faire du bouche à oreille
• talent management	gestion des talents
• to target	cibler
• to tarnish	ternir
• tracking	pistage des internautes
• to trust ; (un)trustworthy	faire confiance à ; (non) fiable
• update	mise à jour
• value	valeur
• to walk the talk	faire ce qu'on a annoncé

Use the list

1) Make noun combinations by matching words from the following lists, then translate them.

a. blog **b.** web **c.** market **d.** brand
e. corporate **f.** brand **g.** to gain **h.** to open up

1. a market **2.** image **3.** behaviour **4.** post
5. building **6.** a foothold **7.** banner **8.** survey

2) Use the following words to fill in the gaps in the texts (make the necessary changes), then translate the sentences.

A) *team – prosper – improve – achieve – ensure*

In order to … that a company survives and … , it is necessary to have a public relations … which adds value to the company by helping it to … the employees' understanding of what has to be … .

B) *after sales – customers – loyalty – responsibility – trust – reliable*

To create customer …, companies acknowledge … for mistakes. This is why efficient … services are popular among … . They … companies that not only provide … services but also find solutions when problems occur.

C) *advertise – advertisement – advertisers – advertising – target*

… are people who promote new products by placing an … which may be seen on television. … is an interesting activity because you have to find good ideas in order to … such and such a product and to … different categories of consumers.

Grammar work

Le *present perfect* simple

› Aide-mémoire grammatical, p. 199

Analysez et traduisez les exemples suivants :

1. We are very sorry. We have never received your email.
2. They called us because they haven't received our invitations yet.
3. Have they ever organised a press conference?
4. The journalists have already written two articles about our company.
5. Look! I have just found the brochures you need.
6. They have always placed ads in newspapers.
7. Our company is famous because we have had a distinctive image for many years.
8. Since last year, our employees have benefited from new career opportunities.

- **Comment utilise-t-on *since* et *for* ?**

1 Complétez les énoncés suivants par *since* ou *for*.

a. We have had a green logo … a long time.
b. They have had an opportunity to discuss the problem … 5th January.
c. … the beginning, the crisis has been addressed with new methods.
d. … many years now, we have encouraged good communication methods.

2 Complétez les phrases par *ever*, *never*, *yet*, *always* ou *already*.

a. There has … been any problem with this department.
b. Has such an incident … happened?
c. They haven't found a stylish logo … .
d. I have … met my new manager but not all my colleagues…
e. We have … had any control over what is said about the company.
f. To be efficient, we have … had sets of values understood by everyone.

Les modaux : *should, would, could*

› Aide-mémoire grammatical, p. 167

Analysez les nuances de sens dans les exemples suivants. Traduisez.

1. Here is some good advice: you should send invitations to all the journalists.
2. If we lied too much, we could lose customers.
3. If they had a poor communication strategy, they would lose customers.

Faites la même analyse pour les trois phrases suivantes, puis traduisez-les.

4. We should have sent an apology to our customers, but now it's too late.
5. They could have published fake news but didn't because it was unethical.
6. If they had lied, they would have damaged their reputation.

3 **Completez les phrases avec *would*, *should*, ou *could* puis traduisez-les.**

a. Here is a suggestion: you … organise an emergency meeting.
b. If they had updated the files in time, we … not have had to write the names by hand.
c. If our communication strategy were more consistent, we … gain trust from our customers.
d. If we had not recalled the faulty goods, there … have been complaints.
e. We are running late! We … have prepared this campaign earlier.
f. When talking to customers, you … remain polite.
g. Our logo is black and white but I think it … have been nicer with some red in it.
h. Our boss wrote an article entitled: "Why good communication … be a goal in companies."

Les pronoms relatifs : *who / whom / which / ∅*

› Aide-mémoire grammatical, p. 201

Observez les exemples suivants et traduisez-les :

1. A manager is a person <u>who</u> runs a company.
2. They want to invest in markets <u>which</u> will be profitable.
3. The sales manager Ø / <u>whom</u> I work with is called Mr Jones.
4. This is a problem Ø / <u>which</u> we must solve every day.

- **Qu'est-ce qui détermine le choix entre *who*, *whom* et *which* ?**
- **Dans quel cas peut-on omettre le pronom relatif (Ø) ?**

4 **Complétez avec *which* ou *who(m)*. Indiquez dans quelles phrases il est possible d'omettre le pronom relatif.**

a. Businesses … lose money may go bankrupt.
b. The new employees … the recruiting manager hired will have to be trained.
c. Our production site was visited by investors … would like to buy company shares.
d. The new premises … were inaugurated last week are quite pleasant to work in.
e. The financial statement … the young trainee mislaid has finally been found.
f. The report shows that workers … commute for more than two hours a day are highly stressed.

5 **Traduisez les phrases suivantes.**

a. Si nous organisions une campagne publicitaire qui concerne les jeunes, nous gagnerions de nouveaux clients.
b. Vous devriez rédiger un bulletin d'information qui dise la vérité.
c. Vous auriez dû traiter la question que je vous ai envoyée plus tôt.
d. Si notre image d'entreprise, qui est bonne, était atteinte, nous ferions une campagne pour l'améliorer.
e. Ils pourraient contrôler le contenu des messages qui sont postés sur les réseaux.

Exam work

Document 1

1.
Fluffy language
Words or terms with no clear meaning e.g. 'eco-friendly'

2.
Green products v dirty company
Such as efficient light bulbs made in a factory which pollutes rivers

3.
Suggestive pictures
Green images that indicate a (un-justified) green impact e.g. flowers blooming from exhaust pipes

4.
Irrelevant claims
Emphasising one tiny green attribute when everything else is un-green

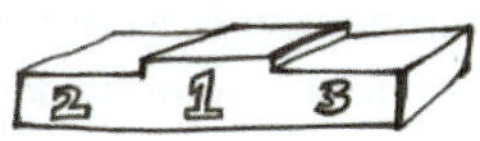

5.
Best in class?
Declaring you are slightly greener than the rest, even if the rest are pretty terrible

6.
Just not credible
Eco friendly' cigarettes anyone? 'Greening' a dangerous product doesn't make it safe

7.
Gobbledygook
Jargon and information that only a scientist could check or understand

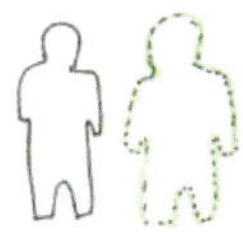

8.
Imaginary friends
A 'label' that looks like third party endorsement … except it's made up

9.
No proof
It could be right, but where's the evidence?

10.
Out-right lying
Totally fabricated claims or data

"The Greenwash guide", www.futerra.co.uk

1. fluffy: *séduisant et creux*. **2.** light bulb: *ampoule électrique*. **3.** to bloom: fleurir. **4.** exhaust: *pot d'échappement*. **5.** to emphasize: *insister sur*. **6.** pretty terrible: *plutôt affreux*. **7.** gobbledygook: *charabia*. **8.** endorsement: *soutien*. **9.** made up: *inventé*. **10.** evidence: *preuves*. **11.** claim: *déclaration*.

1 ***Expression***. D'après ce document, à quoi reconnaît-on qu'une entreprise se livre à un éco-blanchiment de sa marque ou de ses activités ? *(Environ 200 mots, en français.)*

Document 2

The Pros and Cons[1] of Influencer Marketing Campaigns

Many brands invest a lot of time and a vast amount of money into influencer marketing campaigns. The results show that influencer marketing is worth[2] the effort. Most of the research proves that influencer marketing is one of the most sustainable[3] methods to build brand awareness, increase conversions, or establish brand authority. There is, however, the dark side of influencer marketing campaigns. As with every business decision, influencer marketing is not a solution for everyone. (...)

Not only does influencer marketing convert more customers (according to many studies influencers convert people twice as much as paid ads), those customers stay with the brand much longer. Influencers attract customers with much longer lifetime value than customers you appeal to via other marketing channels[4]. No matter which social media platform you choose for your influencer marketing campaign, you will be able to reach brand new audiences you would have missed otherwise[5]. (...)

Influencers are, by many followers, considered friends. Lots of people value their opinion and trust their recommendation. That trust can transfer to your product or service. You won't be just another brand that posts paid banners[6] on social media, on the contrary, your company will be associated with positive feelings and experiences. (...)

Unfortunately, (...) there are some drawbacks[7], and you need to be aware of them. That will help you prepare for many obstacles on the way to a successful influencer marketing campaign. An influencer marketing campaign that serves its purpose[8] takes time and effort to set up. You have to do your research and find an influencer that suits[9] your brand, prepare terms and conditions of your cooperation, approve the content your influencer prepared, and measure the results of your campaigns. But there are some rare cases when influencer marketing campaigns backfired[10]. Either[11] the influencer profile didn't suit the brand, the content was ill-prepared, or there was some other type of social media crisis.

By Marta, brands24, 25 February 2019.

1. pros and cons: *avantages et inconvénients.* **2.** to be worth: *valoir.* **3.** sustainable: *durable.* **4.** channel: *canal.* **5.** otherwise: *sinon.* **6.** banner: *bannière.* **7.** drawback: *inconvénient.* **8.** purpose: *objectif.* **9.** to suit: *convenir.* **10.** to backfire: *être contreproductif.* **11.** either: *soit.*

2 ***Compréhension***. Expliquez dans quelle mesure le marketing d'influence est bénéfique pour une marque. *(Environ 150 mots, en français.)*

Document 3

Inside Facebook's 'cult[1]-like' workplace, where dissent[2] is discouraged and employees pretend to be happy all the time

At a company-wide town hall[3] in early October, numerous Facebook employees got in line to speak about their experiences with sexual harassment. (...)

A young female employee was among those who got up to speak, addressing her comments directly to COO[4] Sheryl Sandberg. "I was reticent to speak, Sheryl, because the pressure for us to act as though everything is fine and that we love working here is so great that it hurts," she said, according to multiple former Facebook employees who witnessed[5] the event. "There shouldn't be this pressure to pretend to love something when I don't feel this way," said the employee, setting off[6] a wave of applause from her colleagues at the emotional town hall in Menlo Park, California.

The episode speaks to an atmosphere at Facebook in which employees feel pressure to place the company above all else in their lives, fall in line with their manager's orders and force cordiality with their colleagues so they can advance. Several former employees likened[7] the culture to a "cult."

This culture has contributed to the company's well-publicized wave of scandals over the last two years, such as governments spreading misinformation to try to influence elections and the misuse of private user data, according to many people who worked there during this period. They say Facebook might have caught some of these problems sooner if employees were encouraged to deliver honest feedback. Amid[8] these scandals, Facebook's share[9] price fell nearly 30 percent in 2018 and nearly 40 percent since a peak in July, resulting in a loss of more than $252 billion in market capitalization.

Meanwhile, Facebook's reputation as being one of the best places in Silicon Valley to work is starting to show some cracks[10]. (...)

Facebook declined to comment on former employees' characterization of the work place as "cult-like." Former employees describe a top-down approach where major decisions are made by the company's leadership, and employees are discouraged from voicing[11] dissent (...)."

Salvador Rodriguez, CNBC, 8 January 2019.

1. cult: *secte.* **2.** dissent: *désaccord.* **3.** company-wide town hall: *réunion qui rassemble tous les employés.* **4.** COO (chief operating officer): *directeur exécutif.* **5.** to witness: *être le témoin de.* **6.** to set off: *déclencher.* **7.** to liken: *comparer.* **8.** amid: *parmi.* **9.** share: *action (boursière).* **10.** crack: *fêlure.* **11.** to voice: *exprimer.*

3 ***Compréhension.*** What problem do Facebook workers face and how do they feel about it? What are the consequences of this situation?

4 ***Expression.*** Do you think employees should be barred from saying what they think about their company? *(About 150 words, in English.)*

Document 4

The Starbucks incident: a crisis management case study

[In 2018, in a Starbucks restaurant, two African-American men asked to use the restrooms, but the manager refused since they didn't order anything. The manager called the police to arrest them because they stayed in the restaurant, waiting for a friend to show up.]

(...) By nearly any measure, Starbucks has been ultra-successful, with now about 28,000 stores worldwide and unmatched[1] influence in the supplier markets[2]. Up until the Philadelphia incident, it's hard to imagine anyone being mad at Starbucks. Clearly it has walked the social responsibility talk[3]. But when a request to use a restroom[4] in the Philadelphia store escalated into the arrests of the two men who had come there to meet a friend, the public reaction was loud and furious.

A cell phone video of the arrests went viral, and it instantly attracted worldwide attention and accusations of racism. The video showed that the arrestees[5] had done nothing to merit such a fate[6]. What's a crisis manager to do[7]?

The first consideration in managing any crisis is to avoid making the situation worse. Starbucks accomplished that by immediately recognizing the threat to its reputation, responding quickly, issuing an unequivocal apology[8] (as opposed to "We're sorry *if* we offended anyone") and by flying across the country to deliver apologies in person to the men who were arrested.

The company also succeeded in positioning the incident as a "teachable moment." Starbucks CEO Kevin Johnson, in an ABC interview on the Monday following the incident, repeated the apology, took responsibility and said he wanted to apologize in person to the men and "invite them to join me in finding a way to solve this issue." (...)

In the face of an organized protest at the site of the arrests and calls for a national boycott of the company, Johnson announced plans to close 8,000 U.S. stores on May 29 to provide employees with bias sensitivity training[9]. (...)

Johnson was right to accept responsibility for the incident. The company's policies, procedures, training and culture fell short of[10] preventing an outcome that should not have occurred and ran counter to[11] one of the organization's stated values of "creating a culture of warmth and belonging, where everyone is welcome."

(...) Depending on the nature of the crisis, some stakeholders may turn away for good. At the same time, handling a crisis well can strengthen an organization's relationships and strength.

By Rick Kelly, extracted from bernsteincrisismanagement.com

1. unmatched: *inégalé.* **2.** suppliers market: *marché des fournisseurs.* **3.** to walk the talk: *agir comme annoncé.* **4.** restroom: *les toilettes.* **5.** arrestee: *personne arrêtée.* **6.** fate: *sort.* **7.** is to do: *doit faire.* **8.** apology: *excuse.* **9.** bias sensitivity training: *formation contre les discriminations.* **10.** to fall short of: *ne pas réussir à.* **11.** to run counter to: *aller à l'encontre de.*

5 ***Compréhension.*** What incident happened at an American Starbucks outlet? What may be said about the way the company handled the crisis? *(About 150 words, in English.)*

Document 5

"Fred, I want you to sanitize[1] this, punch it up[2], dumb it down[3], leak[4] it to the media and then be fully prepared to deny it!"

© Bradford Veley / www.CartoonStock.com

1. to sanitize: *édulcorer*. **2**. to punch up : *rendre plus attractif.* **3**. to dumb down: *simplifier en nivelant par le bas*. **4**. to leak : *faire fuiter*.

6 ***Compréhension.*** What does this carton denounce concerning corporate communication and press releases? *(About 100 words, in English.)*

7 ***Compréhension***. Rédigez une note de synthèse en vous basant sur les documents 1 à 5, sur les enjeux de la communication dans le monde de l'entreprise. *(Environ 200 mots, en français.)*

8 ***Expression.*** Le Directeur des Ressources humaines de votre entreprise veut améliorer la communication entre les employés et la direction. Il vous demande de préparer une note de service à transmettre par mail à tous les employés. *(Environ 150 mots, en anglais.)*

Vous proposerez diverses mesures : réunions internes régulières, animations, amélioration des possibilités de rendez-vous, nouvelle offre de stages de formation, etc.

Vous présenterez également de nouveaux outils de collaboration : documents concernant la communication interne en ligne, ouverture d'une plateforme d'échanges, tableaux de clarification des responsabilités de chacun, etc.

Terminez en expliquant que la direction reste ouverte aux échanges sur ce sujet.

CHAPITRE

8

Energies

Les énergies

The production of energy has always entailed[1] lots of problems, and now more than ever, to feed economic expansion and improve living standards in both developed and emerging countries. All energy sources, fossil and renewable fuels, and nuclear plants, have pros and cons: there is no ideal one.

Fossil fuels

Coal

This primary fossil fuel is the world's most abundant and cheapest source of energy and accounts for 40% of world electricity production today. But it has many harmful effects: it is responsible for large scale air pollution and for emitting large quantities of CO_2 (carbon dioxide[2]), which is a greenhouse gas[3] that causes climate change. Its extraction has killed hundreds of thousands of people. It is nowadays mostly produced in and exported from the USA, China, India, Ukraine, Russia, South Africa, China, Australia, and other countries. Coal reserves are enormous, vastly superior to petroleum or gas.

Petroleum or crude oil

In 2019, total world production averaged over 80 million barrels (bbl) per day. Today's main producers are the USA, Saudi Arabia (OPEC[4] member), Russia, Iraq (OPEC), Iran (OPEC), China, Canada, Venezuela, etc. Oil is found on all continents and under water, sometimes at huge depths. Far from dwindling[5] (as was feared a few decades ago) more oil reserves keep being found, but exploitation costs are rising. The prices of oil vary a lot according to its quality and country of origin, world demand, the political and economic situation, and speculation. These fluctuations cause frequent and at times serious crises. It is a source of pollution (but there is progress in refining and using it) and of CO_2. That is why it is increasingly criticised.

It is also a cause of the dependence of non-producing countries on exporting ones, especially OPEC.

Shale oil[6]

It is mostly produced and consumed in the USA, and extracted by fracking[7], a method that is harmful to the environment. It has helped to make the USA almost independent energetically, which has big political and strategic consequences.

Natural gas

It is widely used especially in Europe. The main producers are the USA, Russia (now Europe's biggest supplier), and far behind, Iran, Qatar, Canada, China, Algeria, and some EU countries whose reserves are declining. It is considered relatively clean, but like petroleum and coal, it produces CO_2 and makes non-producing countries dependent on producing ones.

Renewable fuels

For some years now, the sustainability[8] factor and climate change have made the transition to clean, renewable, job-creating energies necessary, and many countries are therefore embarking on it.

Hydro energy

It is the oldest and largest contributor of all renewable sources (6.7% of world electricity production). It is flexible, reliable[9], and can be stored. But damming[10] a river is extremely expensive, highly polluting, and has a huge disruptive impact on populations and local environment. Its expansion is therefore limited.

Wind power

Wind is free and endless: a big advantage. Wind turbines which are getting bigger and bigger can be installed on land and offshore[11]. But wind power is limited, intermittent, and above all cannot be stored. Even if wind turbines can be spread out[12] over large areas to make their output more constant, transport over long distances means a big energy loss. Its costs have dropped, but are still high. Also many people object to wind farms that are noisy and can spoil landscapes[13].

Solar energy

It is captured in solar panels installed on roofs to heat water or buildings, or turned into electricity by photovoltaic panels on roofs and in solar farms that cover huge areas. To be really efficient, they must be installed in sunny regions: Africa, South East Asia, southern Europe. However, it is expensive, and manufacturing the panels, essentially in China, is very polluting.

A key issue is **storing energy**: a lot of research is still necessary to invent long-lasting batteries. Thermal power plants are therefore needed to take over[14] when there is no wind or sun.

Biomass

It recycles organic materials: certain crops, manure[15], some types of waste residue, forest and other wood debris, etc. It generates biogas (methane, etc.) which is turned into both electricity and heat, and fuels vehicles. Not only is it renewable but a biomass power plant can work non-stop, unlike wind and solar. But like fossil gas it emits CO_2.

Hydrogen

It can be produced by renewable sources and is itself a promising way of generating and storing energy through fuel cells[16] (a kind of battery). But it is still much too difficult or expensive to produce and insufficient to meet all the needs of industry, transport and heating.

Nuclear power

Nuclear power is a decarbonised energy. Thanks to it and thanks to hydro-electricity, France and Finland have the lowest carbon imprint[17] in the world. However, nuclear power produces very long-lasting radioactive waste, and, even if they are rare, accidents in nuclear plants have disastrous consequences on people's health and the environment. That is why this energy arouses widespread concern and controversy.

Energy conservation

Energy conservation offers an excellent solution to energy problems. Walk or bike if you can. Put on warm clothes when it is cold. Insulate your home. The best waste is the waste we do not produce. That is why more and more people try to reduce their consumption of energy.

1. to entail: *entraîner.*
2. carbon dioxide: *gaz carbonique.*
3. greenhouse gas: *gaz à effet de serre.*
4. OPEC (Organisation of Petroleum Exporting Countries): *OPEP (Organisation des Pays Exportateurs de Pétrole).*
5. to dwindle: *diminuer.*
6. shale oil: *huile de schiste.*
7. fracking: *fracturation.*
8. sustainability: *durabilité.*
9. reliable: *fiable.*
10. to dam: *construire un barrage sur.*
11. offshore: *en mer.*
12. to spread out: *étaler.*
13. spoil a landscape: *défigurer un paysage.*
14. to take over: *prendre le relais.*
15. manure: *fumier.*
16. fuel cell: *pile à combustible.*
17. carbon imprint: *empreinte carbone.*

Repérer les notions essentielles

Answer the following questions about the text.

a. Why is energy an essential issue?
b. Which is the most plentiful source of energy on earth?
c. What are the advantages and drawbacks of natural gas?
d. Name three renewable sources of energy.
e. Why is nuclear energy a controversial source of energy?
f. Which countries currently produce the cleanest energy?

Résumer le texte en français

Résumez ce texte en 150 mots environ.

Approfondir

Carry out further research online about one of these sources of energy worldwide or in one country. Then present your findings orally or in writing.

Lexical work

• air conditioning	air conditionné
• barrel (of crude oil)	baril (de brut) (≈ 160 litres)
• boiler	chaudière
• coal / nuclear (power) plant	centrale à charbon / nucléaire
• to conserve energy	faire des économies d'énergie
• to cool	refroidir
• to curb / cut	réduire
• dam	barrage
• decade	décennie
• to deplete	réduire, épuiser
• to diversify	(se) diversifier
• downswing, drop	baisse
• to drill	forer, effectuer un forage
• to drop	chuter, baisser
• energy provider/supplier	fournisseur d'énergie
• fuel efficient / economical vehicle	véhicule sobre
• gas	gaz / essence *(Am.)*
• geothermal energy	énergie géothermique
• glut	surplus, excès
• to heat / heating	(se) chauffer / chauffage
• heavy/light oil	pétrole lourd/léger
• to hold reserves	détenir des réserves
• insulation	isolation
• to light / lighting	éclairer / éclairage
• off shore	en mer
• oil crisis (crises)	choc(s) pétrolier
• oil tanker	navire pétrolier
• output	rendement
• overconsumption	surconsommation
• petrol	essence *(Brit.)*
• to push prices up	faire grimper les prix
• proven reserves	réserves confirmées/prouvées
• reliable	fiable
• (re)processing	(re)traitement
• research and development / R&D	recherche et developpement
• to rise / surge / go up	augmenter, monter
• to save	économiser, épargner
• shortage	pénurie
• sluggish/upward/downward demand	demande au ralenti/en hausse/en baisse

• to soar	monter en flèche
• to stave off	retarder, éviter, stopper
• stiff price	prix élevé
• to store	stocker
• stove	poêle, cuisinière
• to s**u**bsidise / s**u**bsidy	subventionner / subvention
• sust**ai**nable dev**e**lopment	développement durable
• to switch on/off	allumer / éteindre
• to t**a**rget / t**a**rget	cibler / cible, objectif
• tr**a**nsport / a means of tr**a**nsport	transports / un moyen de transport
• **u**pswing	redressement, amélioration
• v**o**latile price ≠ stable/st**ea**dy price	prix instable ≠ prix stable
• waste	gaspillage, déchets

Use the list

1 Fill in the blanks with words from above, making the necessary changes and translate the sentences.

a. A drop in energy prices usually brings about an u… in the economy.
b. Oil prices have suddenly s… in the Middle East: could it result in an oil c…?
c. After r… , high-level nuclear w… makes 3% of the total volume of the spent fuel.
d. Nuclear waste can be s… for 50 years in a water pool or dense material like concrete or steel, then deep underground.
e. It is a sensible t… for any country to have d… energy sources.
f. Many countries today are trying to reduce the emission of carbon dioxide in order to s… o… climate change.
g. The coal-fired Ratcliffe-on-Soar power station in the UK has an o… of 2 gigawatts.
h. Energy transition requires a lot of R… and D…to turn away from dirty energies to clean ones.
i. To h… this huge building better, you will need an extra b… .

2 Choose five words which you think are important in this list and write sentences with them with the help of a dictionary.

Grammar work

Présent simple et présent en *be* + V*ing*

› Aide-mémoire grammatical, p. 197

Analysez et traduisez les exemples suivants :

1. France <u>produces</u> a lot of nuclear energy.
2. Many European countries <u>import</u> energy from France.
3. Will these wind turbines produce electricity when the wind <u>drops</u>?
4. Analysts <u>reckon</u> that this situation can't go on for ever.
5. World energy needs <u>are growing</u> steadily.
6. The sun <u>is shining</u>: our solar panels <u>are heating</u> our water. Good!

1 Mettez les verbes ci-dessous entre parenthèses au présent simple ou avec *be* + V*ing* selon le cas, puis traduisez les phrases :

a. Demand for renewable energies *(soar)* today in southern California.
b. SIT is an American company which *(produce)* solar equipment.
c. It *(manufacture)* both solar and photo-voltaic panels.
d. But its managing director now *(complain)* that the demand for solar energy often *(depend)* on irrational decisions.
e. Some Californian politicians now *(try)* to change that.
f. They *(want)* to subsidise renewable energies more efficiently.
g. The problem *(be)* that solar energy producers now *(hire)* lobbyists to get even more subsidies.
h. As this industry *(grow)*, this policy *(cost)* tax payers more and more money.
i. Nowadays many scientists *(work)* on ways to store energy for the long term.
j. At home we usually *(try)* to conserve energy so we *(set)* a fairly low temperature.
k. I will turn on our boiler when it *(get)* much colder tomorrow as is forecast.
l. However, I will switch it off as soon as the weather *(improve)*.

Used to et to be/get used to

› Aide-mémoire grammatical, p. 208

Used to **+ V (infinitif) et t*o be/get used to* + V*ing***

Il ne faut pas confondre ces deux constructions, qui n'ont pas le même sens.

Analysez et traduisez les exemples suivants :

1. Coal used to be the main energy for powering the Industrial Revolution in Europe.
2. During that period, people got used to breathing the noxious fumes emitted by coal-powered machines.
3. Chinese coal miners are used to working in very hard conditions.

2 Traduisez ces phrases en utilisant *used to* ou *get/be used to* selon le cas.

a. Dans les pays occidentaux, beaucoup de gens ont maintenant l'habitude de bien chauffer leur maison.
b. Dans le passé, en hiver, ils avaient souvent froid chez eux. Mais ils y étaient habitués.
c. Je ne parviens pas à m'habituer à vivre dans l'air conditionné de ce bureau.
d. Et pourtant, en général, je suis habituée à porter des vêtements chauds, même en été, à cause de cela.
e. Autrefois dans certains états américains du Middle West et du sud, lorsqu'il n'y avait pas d'air conditionné, les gens avaient terriblement chaud l'été. Mais ils étaient habitués à ce climat.
f. Jusque dans les année 50, les locomotives à vapeur consommaient beaucoup de charbon et produisaient beaucoup de fumée.
g. Dans les années 1950, les grosses voitures américaines n'étaient pas du tout économiques.
h. Actuellement, les Français sont habitués à avoir une électricité peu chère.
i. Nous devons maintenant nous habituer à faire des économies d'énergie.

3 Name an activity or an action that you or somebody else:

(1) are used to doing,
(2) are not used to doing,
(3) are (not) getting used to doing.

Ex.: (1) Now I am used to commuting by train every day to work.
(2) I am not used to taking the bus.
(3) I can't get used to spending a lot of time commuting.

Exam work

Document 1

Renewable energy to expand by 50% in next five years

Global supplies of renewable electricity are growing faster than expected and could expand by 50% in the next five years, powered by a resurgence in solar energy.

The International Energy Agency (IEA) found that solar, wind and hydropower projects are rolling out[1] at their fastest rate in four years. Its latest report predicts that by 2024 a new dawn[2] for cheap solar power could see the world's solar capacity grow by 600GW[3], almost double the installed total electricity capacity of Japan. Overall, renewable electricity is expected to grow by 1,200GW in the next five years, the equivalent of the total electricity capacity of the US. "This is a pivotal time for renewable energy," said the IEA's executive director, Fatih Birol. "Technologies such as solar photovoltaics (PV) and wind are at the heart of transformations taking place across the global energy system. Their increasing deployment is crucial for efforts to tackle[4] greenhouse gas emissions, reduce air pollution, and expand energy access." (...)

Renewable energy sources make up 26% of the world's electricity today, but according to the IEA, its share is expected to reach 30% by 2024. The resurgence follows a global slowdown[6] last year, due to falling technology costs and rising environmental concerns.

However, Birol warned that the role of renewables in the global energy system would need to grow even faster if the world hopes to meet its climate targets. (...) Growing climate ambitions in the European Union and the US played the biggest role in driving the IEA's forecasts higher, but it will be China which leads the way in rolling out wind and solar energy projects.

Billian Ambrose, *The Guardian*,
21 October 2019.

1. to roll out: *se déployer*. **2.** dawn: *aube*. **3.** GW: *gigawatt*. **4.** to tackle: *s'attaquer à*. **5.** ahead of : *avant, en avance sur*. **6.** slowdown: *ralentissement*.

1 ***Compréhension.***

Summarise this article which predicts the future of renewable energies by 2024. Is this future perfectly predictable according to the text? *(About 100 words, in English.)*

Document 2

Renewables push fails to dent[1] reliance[2] on fossil fuels

Unprecedented efforts to install renewable power capacity have met only 2 per cent of global energy demand, meaning the overwhelming[3] reliance on fossil fuels shows no sign of abating[4]. Coal, oil and gas are forecast to contribute about 85 per cent of primary energy supply by 2040, compared with 90 per cent today, a report shows, jeopardising[5] efforts to contain the worst impacts of climate change.

Wood Mackenzie, the energy consultancy, said 1 terawatt of installed solar and wind capacity makes up about 8 per cent of total power generation as of 2019, a fraction of total consumption.

"The world risks relying on fossil fuels for decades to come," the report says. It forecasts that carbon emissions will continue to rise, their growth slowing only in the 2030s. This will leave the world far short in its efforts to meet the Paris climate goals of limiting global warming to well below 2°C, despite growing political momentum[6] to prevent climate change.

Energy demand, led by swelling[7] populations in emerging economies in Asia and Africa, will increase at least 25 per cent by[8] 2040. Yet carbon emissions would need to halve over the same period to comply with[9] the Paris accord, a huge challenge for energy systems.

"This is a wake-up call[10] for governments and the energy industry," said David Brown, an author of the report. Policymakers needed to work more closely together even though some countries, such as the US, were moving away from multilateral diplomacy. If the world wants to decarbonise, they need to take a leap and come up with targeted policies," he said.

While there is much focus on renewable electricity, Mr Brown said greater attention needs to be paid to cleaning up sectors such as aviation and shipping.

Anjli RAVAL and Leslie HOOK,
The Financial Times Europe Edition, 2 August 2019.

1. to dent: *entamer, réduire*. 2. reliance: *dépendance*. 3. overwhelming: *écrasant*. 4. to abate: *baisser*. 5. to jeopardise: *menacer*. 6. momentum: *mouvement*. 7. swelling: *croissant*. 8. by: *d'ici*. 9. to comply with: *respecter*. 10. wake-up call: *avertissement*.

2 *Compréhension.*

Résumez ce texte en français en précisant les chiffres de l'accord de Paris sur le climat et leurs conséquences théoriques et réelles sur la consommation mondiale d'énergie, ainsi que les causes et conséquences de la différence entre les deux. *(Environ 150 mots).*

Document 3

Energy: Hopes Clash With Reality Of Curbing Its Use

Spencer Dale, group chief economist at oil group BP, says there is a "mismatch between hopes and reality" when it comes to controlling energy demand. Global energy consumption grew last year at its fastest rate since 2010, as countries including the US suffered a colder than average winter while the use of air conditioning in developed and developing countries continued to rise to cope with hot weather.

Much of this increased demand was met by fossil fuels, particularly gas, according to the Paris-based International Energy Agency. That pushed global carbon dioxide emissions to a record high of 33bn tonnes.

When economists, campaigners and academics look back on the current period, they will probably observe a world in which there was growing societal awareness[1] and demands for urgent action on climate change, but where the actual energy data continued to move stubbornly[2] in the wrong direction," Mr Dale said in a speech last month.

Others point to a mismatch between political pledges[3] and accelerated policies. "We have seen this rhetoric around climate change making its way into the political agenda – the words are there, the policies are not there," says Ms Kennerley a campaigner at environmental group Friends of the Earth. Even some countries that have set ambitious climate change targets — including the UK, which last month became the first G20 economy to legislate for net zero-carbon emissions by 2050 — are struggling to[4] meet near-term targets for cuts in emissions.

Certain governments also stand accused of pushing through[5] policies that campaigners see as counter to climate change ambitions. The UK, for example, plans to expand its biggest airport, London's Heathrow. The country is not yet on course to meet its nearer-term emissions targets for 2023-27, according to the Committee on Climate Change, an advisory group.

"We have to tackle[6] lifestyles," says Prof Sovacool, although he admits this is tricky[7] territory for any politician as consumers take it as "an insult" if they are told to stop using so much electricity or curb their air travel…"

By Nathalie Thomas,
The Financial Times, 8 July 2019.

1. awareness: *prise de conscience.* **2.** stubbornly: *obstinément.* **3.** pledge: *engagement.* **4.** to struggle to: *avoir du mal à.* **5.** to push through: *faire passer.* **6.** to tackle: *s'attaquer à.* **7.** tricky: *délicat, épineux.*

3 ***Compréhension.***

Summarise the text explaining what hopes clash with what reality, how and why? *(About 150 words, in English.)*

Document 4

World Energy Consumption 2018

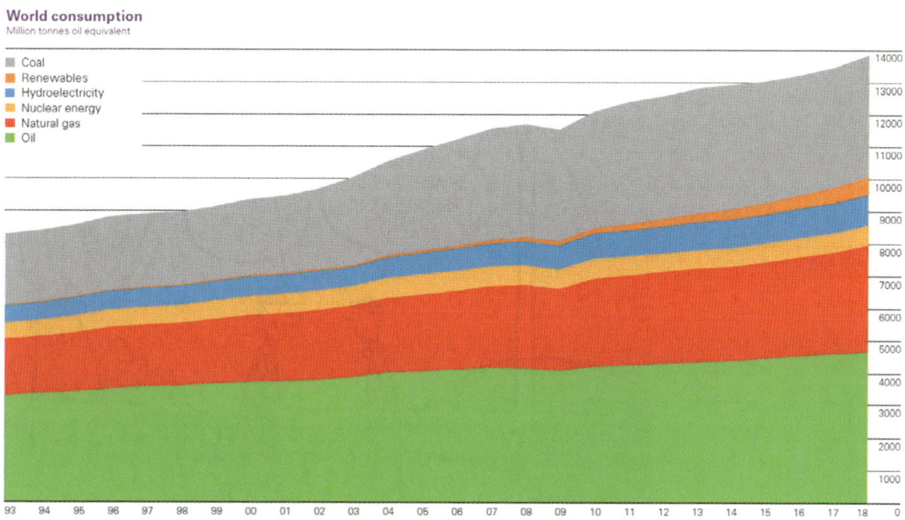

Global energy consumption increased by 2.9% in 2018. Growth was the strongest since 2010 and almost double the 10-year average. The demand for all fuels increased but growth was particularly strong in the case of gas (168 mtoe[1], accounting for 43% of the global increase) and renewables (71 mtoe, 18% of the global increase). In the OECD, energy demand increased by 82 mtoe on the back of strong gas demand growth (70 mtoe). In the non-OECD, energy demand growth (308 mtoe) was more evenly distributed with gas (98 mtoe), coal (85 mtoe) and oil (47 mtoe) accounting for most of the growth.

From *BP Statistical Review of World Energy 2019*, BP p.l.c.

1. mtoe (= Million Tons of Oil Equivalent): *tep (tonne d'équivalent pétrole).*

4 ***Compréhension.***

Describe this chart. What does it show about world energy consumption as a whole from 1993 to 2018? In what year was there a drop? Do you know why? Compare the different sources of energy, from the largest to the smallest, and their growth rates. Which ones did not exist in the 1990s? To what extent does the chart confirm documents 1, 2, 3? What do you think of this evolution? *(About 150 words, in English.)*

Document 5

5 ***Compréhension.***

Describe this cartoon: in what way does it satirize the main disadvantage of wind power? What does it reveal about the two men on the picture? *(About 100 words, in English.)*

6 ***Synthèse.***

Rédigez une note de synthèse des cinq documents en analysant les tendances concernant l'évolution passée, actuelle et espérée de la production et de la consommation des principales sources d'énergie au plan mondial. *(Environ 200 mots, en français.)*

7 ***Expression.***

Write an email.

Vous êtes Ms Pamela Gifford et dirigez une société internationale. Vous envoyez un mail rédigé en anglais à tous vos services présentant votre nouvelle politique d'économies d'énergie. Vous demandez une réduction de 5 % au moins d'ici un an de la consommation totale d'énergie de votre entreprise, surtout celle des transports et des bureaux (éclairage, chauffage et air conditionné). Vous demandez un rapport précis et chiffrés des moyens employés et résultats en particulier financiers, de ces efforts dans un an.

Présentation et formules d'usage.
(Environ 150 mots, en anglais.)

CHAPITRE

9

Competition and the law

La concurrence et le droit

Market economies are based on free trade, free enterprise, and above all fair competition, which is seen as the best way to guarantee better goods and lower prices for consumers. Fair competition, however, is not natural and has to be protected by strict laws. Any business, whatever[1] its legal status, size and sector, must therefore respect these laws, so that it can meet its obligations, assert[2] its rights and defend its own position against unfair competition. That is why collusions, cartels and monopolies are illegal, and mergers and acquisitions are strictly controlled by the law and the antitrust authorities.

Competition law and antitrust authorities in the European Union

As in most other countries, EU competition or antitrust laws (Articles 101 and 102 of the Treaty on the Functioning of the European Union) prohibit two main types of anti-competitive activity:

– **anti-competitive agreements**, which prevent, restrict or distort[3] competition and might affect trade in the EU. Usually secret, they are between major competitors who fix purchase or selling prices, or any other trading conditions (for example discounts or rebates[4]); or who limit or control production, markets, technical development or investment with production quotas; or who share markets or sources of supply; or apply dissimilar conditions to similar transactions.

– **abuse of dominant position**: if a business has a large market share (40 or 50%), it can be in a dominant position. What is illegal is abuse of this dominance by imposing unfair trading prices or excessive pricing exclusivity, refusal to supply or provide access to essential facilities[5], supply agreements, tying sales[6], etc.

Being anti-competitive, social dumping is prohibited throughout the EU.

In the EU, antitrust laws are enforced[7] by the Commission in Brussels through a specialised Commissioner. In addition, all states have their own antitrust laws and authorities.

Antitrust authorities in the UK

In the UK, in 2013, the Department for Business, Innovations and Skills (BIS) which enforces the same legal principles as in the EU, reinforced the consumer protection and competition regimes with the Enterprise and Regulatory Reform Act[8], and set up a Competition and Markets Authority (CMA) to ensure fair competition between businesses and protect consumers.

Antitrust laws in the United States

Contrary to what many people say, the US market economy is very strictly controlled and regulated. In addition to state[9] antitrust laws, there are three major federal ones:

– **the Sherman Antitrust Act** (dating back to 1890) guarantees a free market economy, and outlaws[10] trusts, cartels, monopolies and other combinations and conspiracies that restrain interstate trade. This includes agreements among competitors to fix prices, rig[11] bids[12] and allocate[13] consumers;

– **the Clayton Act** is a civil statute[14] passed in 1914 and amended in 1950. It prohibits mergers or acquisitions that are likely[15] to lessen[16] competition;

– **the Federal Trade Commission Act** (1914) prohibits unfair methods of competition, and created the powerful Federal Trade Commission (FTC), an independent antitrust agency.

Antitrust authorities in the US (or "trustbusters")

They are very active. FTC lawyers protect consumers from violations of antitrust acts and unfair business practices. The Federal Department of Justice (DOJ) and its Antitrust Division investigate possible antitrust activities, prosecute[17] and punish their authors severely. These authorities can interact: the DOJ's sanctions can be appealed[18] before the FTC. But they disagree at times.

Contravention of these laws

Whether[19] in the EU, UK, or USA, firms which breach[20] these laws can face hefty fines[21] from the authorities, or expensive actions for damages[22] from customers and competitors who can show that they have been harmed by anti-competitive behaviour. In some cases, companies accused of being monopolies have had to split[23]. For example, in 2015, Google was split into several smaller companies (Nest, Calico, and even Google) which all became part of a big holding: Alphabet. Individuals, even CEOs, may receive criminal sanctions.

A major issue today is the anti-competitive attitude of the Big Tech corporations, called the GAFA in Europe (Google, Amazon, Facebook and Apple): they have too much power and influence thanks to their huge budgets and the worldwide masses of data they capture, and are practically uncontrollable. The EU Commission and the Americans have tried to reduce their power, in vain so far.

Some actions are considered anti-competitive in one country but not in another: for example, comparative advertising is unlawful in some EU countries (France, in particular), but authorised in others such as the USA.

Most countries, including China, now have comparable laws. The World Trade Organisation (WTO) enforces antitrust laws around the world to avoid unfair competition from countries using child labour, sweatshops, etc.

1. whatever: *quel que soit.*
2. assert: *affirmer.*
3. distort: *dénaturer, fausser.*
4. discount / rebate: *remise / rabais.*
5. facilities: *équipements, installations.*
6. tie sales: *imposer des ventes liées.*
7. enforce: *mettre en application.*
8. act (of Parliament or Congress): *loi votée par le parlement anglais/le congrès américain.*
9. state: *État (l'État fédéral est divisé en 50 États).*
10. outlaw: *déclarer illégal.*
11. rig: *truquer.*
12. bid: *enchère, réponse à un appel d'offres.*
13. allocate: *(se) répartir, (se) partager.*
14. statute: *loi.*
15. likely: *susceptible.*
16. lessen: *diminuer.*
17. prosecute: *poursuivre en justice.*
18. appeal: *faire appel de.*
19. whether: *que ce soit.*
20. breach: *enfreindre.*
21. hefty / huge fine: *lourde amende.*
22. damages: *dommages et intérêts.*
23. split: *se scinder.*

Repérer les notions essentielles

Answer the following questions.

a. What is this text about?

b. Why is competition guaranteed by strict laws, and in which countries?

c. What must firms do regarding competition?

d. What is competition protected by in the EU, the UK and the USA?

e. What is prohibited, in particular?

f. Point out some similarities and differences between competition laws in the UK, the EU, and the USA.

Résumer le texte en français

Résumez ce texte en français (*100 mots environ*) à l'aide de vos réponses aux questions.

Approfondir

a. Browse the Net to find more information about antitrust laws and recent changes that have affected them in the EU, the UK, the US or another country.

b. Do you know of a company which has recently been penalised for breaking competition laws in one of these countries?

Lexical work

• agreement / cartel	entente / cartel
• to be guilty of	être coupable de
• to be liable (in/under law) (for)	être civilement responsable (de)
• to be responsible for	être responsable de
• to bring / file a lawsuit against sb	poursuivre qqn en justice
• case/common law	jurisprudence
• to charge (with)	accuser (de), mettre en examen pour
• to claim (for) damages	réclamer des dommages et intérêts
• to claim one's innocence	clamer son innocence
• class-action suit (US)	recours collectif en justice
• to compensate (sb for sth)	indemniser (qqn pour qqch)
• compensation	dédommagement, indemnisation
• to complain (to a court of justice)	se plaindre, déposer une plainte, saisir la justice
• conviction	condamnation
• corporate lawyer	juriste / avocat d'entreprise
• counterfeit	faux *(nom ou adjectif)*
• to counterfeit	contrefaire
• counterfeiting	contrefaçon, falsification
• criminal offence	délit
• criterion *(pl.* criteria)	critère(s)
• defendant	défendeur
• to defraud sb of sth	escroquer qqch à qqn
• to file a complaint	déposer une plainte
• to impinge on sb's rights	porter atteinte aux droits de qqn
• to infringe a regulation / sb's rights	enfreindre un règlement / les droits de qqn
• infringement, impingement	violation, infraction, transgression
• to investigate sth	enquêter sur qqch
• legal department	service juridique
• to levy a fine on sb	infliger une amende à qqn
• loss of earnings	manque à gagner
• to make charges against sb	porter des accusations à l'encontre de qqn
• to make up for (a loss)	compenser (une perte)
• patent	brevet
• to patent	breveter
• penal / civil law	code pénal / civil
• penalty	peine, pénalité, amende, sanction
• plaintiff	plaignant
• prohibition	interdiction
• proof	preuve
• registered trademark	marque déposée

• to rule	décider, ordonner
• sentence, conviction / to sentence	condamnation / condamner
• to set a precedent	faire jurisprudence
• to settle a legal dispute	régler un contentieux
• sharp / stiff / tough / fierce competition	concurrence vive / dure / rude / féroce
• to sue sb (for damages)	poursuivre qqn (en dommages-intérêts)
• suit, lawsuit, litigation, trial, case	procès, action en justice
• to take over a company	racheter une société
• tender	soumission (à un appel d'offres)
• tribunal, court (of justice)	tribunal, cour

Use the list

1 Fill in the gaps with words from the list above, making the necessary changes. Then translate the sentences.

a. Amazingly, selling c… luxury articles in some EU countries openly is tolerated, which creates unfair competition.
b. And yet, c… is considered a c… o… by EU law.
c. The sellers of c… goods are l… to be c… with a crime.
d. Our company has been harmed by unfair competition and will have to c… to a c… of j… .
e. We will have to ask our l… d… to f… a c… .
f. Hopefully, we will be able to c… for d… because of a serious loss of earnings.
g. By t… o… their only serious competitor, this multinational risks being c… with trying to monopolise the market.
h. He was disqualified from being a company director following his c… for breach of Chapter I of competition law.
i. In the USA, many people s… businesses for sometimes huge d… .
j. The d… tried to settle the case out of court by paying $5 million in c… .

2 Fill in the gaps using a dictionary if necessary.

	Noun	Verb		Noun	Verb
a.	…	to prohibit	g.	…	to restrain
b.	agreement	…	h.	bid	…
c.	competition	…	i.	…	to prosecute
d.	breach	…	j.	…	to sue
e.	monopoly	…	k.	patent	…
f.	…	to investigate	l.	…	to defend

3 Choose five words from these lists which you think are important and write sentences with them.

Grammar work

Subordonnées de but

› Aide-mémoire grammatical, p. 207

Observez et traduisez les exemples suivants :

1. This law was voted to protect competition.
2. In order to safeguard our interests, we will have to investigate the case.
3. In order not to undergo a long trial, he pleaded guilty.
4. A company must know the law so that all its employees can respect it.

- **Quelles différences remarquez-vous ? Attention au modal obligatoire après *so that*.**

1 Reliez les deux propositions de chaque phrase en utilisant une expression de but. (Attention aux temps.) Puis traduisez les phrases.

Ex.: Bestdrugs took over a competitor because it wants to make economies of scale.
→ *Bestdrugs took over a competitor to make economies of scale.*
Bestdrugs a racheté un concurrent pour faire des économies d'échelle.

a. They sued the company because they wanted to get better value for money.
b. You must fill in a form if you want to claim damages.
c. If you wish to get a refund, you will have to apply for it.
d. The FTC has set an example since it does not want this to happen again.
e. We must stop trading with them if we do not want to lose any more money.
f. They will do it as they want companies not to repeat those mistakes.

Propositions infinitives en anglais

› Aide-mémoire grammatical, p. 202

Observez et traduisez les exemples suivants :

1. The judge ordered the culprit to pay a huge fine.
2. Thanks to antitrust laws it is illegal for competitors to agree on prices.

2 Traduisez les phrases suivantes :

a. Nous ne voulons pas que les entreprises imposent des prix trop élevés.
b. Le patron voudrait que notre avocat enquête sur cette accusation de contrefaçon.
c. La loi interdit que les fusions-acquisitions éliminent les concurrents.
d. Le plaignant a demandé au tribunal qu'il inflige une lourde amende à ses concurrents pour entente illégale.
e. Serait-il possible que nous brevetions cette invention rapidement afin qu'elle ne soit pas copiée ?

Expression de quantités chiffrées

› Aide-mémoire grammatical, p. 204

Observez et traduisez les exemples suivants :

1. They spent millions / thousands / hundreds of dollars on that operation.
2. The operation cost them €3bn. (= three billion euros)
3. This will require a lot of capital / efforts.
4. How much (money) will they need?
5. How many patent medicines do they produce?
6. One never has too much money / too many guarantees.

3 Complétez les phrases suivantes avec une expression de quantité, en effectuant les changements nécessaires (ajout de *-s*, *of*, ou article).

million – much – many – a lot – hundred – thousand

a. "How … jobs have been eliminated because of this takeover?"
"Unfortunately, three … at least."
b. "How … work went into preparing this report?"
"…, I am sure."
c. Too … people came to attend the trial, so they could not all get in.
d. The drugmaker spent over four … dollars to develop this new drug.
e. This online bookshop has already sold two … copies of that novel.
f. Unfortunately, he did not get … royalties out of his book.
g. Too … competition may drive … companies out of business, and therefore destroy … jobs.
h. "This company will need … of dollars to take over its main competitor."
"I would say as much as eight … dollars."

4 Traduisez en anglais.

a. Pour gagner beaucoup d'argent, il faut beaucoup travailler.
b. – Il y a des centaines de millions de citoyens dans l'Union européenne. Savez-vous combien ?
– Environ 500 millions.
c. La Commission de Bruxelles fait beaucoup pour protéger les intérêts des 500 millions de consommateurs européens.
d. Il a gagné dix-huit millions d'euros en revendant sa société à un concurrent. Cela fait vraiment beaucoup d'argent pour un seul homme.
e. Le PDG a tout de suite annoncé la nouvelle afin que les autorités anti-trust ne poursuivent pas la société en justice.
f. Beaucoup d'entreprises se plaignent qu'il y a trop de concurrence dans le monde entier et font du lobbying pour qu'il y en ait moins.

Exam work

Document 1

How Qualcomm shook down[1] the cell phone industry for almost 20 years and was finally sued about it

In 2005, Apple contacted Qualcomm as a potential supplier for modem chips in the first iPhone. Qualcomm's response was unusual: a letter demanding that Apple sign a patent licensing agreement[2] before Qualcomm would even consider supplying chips. (...)

Most suppliers are eager[3] to talk to new customers—especially customers as big and prestigious as Apple. But Qualcomm wasn't like other suppliers; it enjoyed a dominant position in the market for cellular chips. That gave Qualcomm a lot of leverage[4], and the company wasn't afraid to use it.

(...) The FTC (Federal Trade Commission) filed this lawsuit in 2017 partly at the urging of Apple, which had chafed[5] under Qualcomm's wireless[6] chip dominance for a decade.

Last week, a California federal judge provided the FTC and Apple with sweet vindication[7]. (…) Judge Lucy Koh ruled[8] that Qualcomm's aggressive licensing tactics had violated American antitrust law.

(…) The legal document outlines[9] a nearly 20-year history of overcharging smartphone makers for cellular chips. Qualcomm structured its contracts with smartphone makers in ways that made it almost impossible for other chipmakers to challenge Qualcomm's dominance. Customers who didn't go along with[10] Qualcomm's one-sided terms[11] were threatened with an abrupt and crippling[12] loss of access to modem chips.

"Qualcomm has monopoly power over certain cell phone chips, and they use that monopoly power to charge people too much money," says Charles Duan, a patent expert at the free-market R Street Institute. "Instead of just charging for the chips themselves, they required people to buy a patent license and over-charged for the patent license."

Now, all of that dominance might be coming to an end. In her ruling, Koh ordered Qualcomm to stop threatening customers with chip cutoffs[13]. Qualcomm must now re-negotiate all of its agreements with customers and license its patents to competitors on reasonable terms. And if Koh's ruling survives the appeals process[14], it could produce a truly competitive market for wireless chips for the first time in this century.

Timothy B. Lee, arstechnica.com, 30th May 2019.

1. to shake down: *extorquer de l'argent à.* **2.** patent licensing agreement : *accord de licence (d'exploitation de brevets).* **3.** to be eager to: *s'empresser de.* **4.** leverage: *poids, influence.* **5.** to chafe: *renâcler.* **6.** wireless: *(téléphone) sans fil/mobile.* **7.** sweet vindication: *douce revanche.* **8.** to rule: *décider, déclarer, émettre un verdict.* **9.** to outline: *exposer.* **10.** to go along with: *être d'accord avec.* **11.** one-sided terms: *conditions unilatérales.* **12.** crippling: *dévastateur.* **13.** cutoff: *rupture (d'approvisionnement).* **14.** appeals process: *procédure d'appel.*

1 ***Compréhension.***

Résumez l'affaire judiciaire Qualcomm. *(Environ 150 mots, en français.)*

Document 2

Construction firms fined £36 million for breaking competition law

Following an investigation by the Competition and Markets Authority (CMA), the Northern Ireland-based firm FP McCann Ltd is facing a fine of more than £25 million for its part in the scheme[1]. Derbyshire-based Stanton Bonna Concrete Ltd and Somerset-based CPM Group Ltd are due to pay more than £7 million and £4 million respectively.

The fines have been imposed after the CMA found that the companies broke competition law by taking part in an illegal cartel covering Great Britain. From July 2006 to March 2013, they agreed to fix or coordinate their prices, shared the market by allocating customers and regularly exchanged competitively sensitive information. These arrangements continued for nearly seven years and involved meetings attended by senior executives from each of the firms. The CMA recorded a number of these meetings and used them as evidence[2] when arriving at its final decision.

Last year, two of the three firms, Stanton Bonna Concrete Ltd and CPM Group Ltd, both accepted that they broke competition law by engaging in these arrangements. Accordingly, under the CMA's provisions for leniency[3] and settlement processes[4], they have received reductions to their fines.

Pre-cast concrete[5] products, such as drainage pipes[6], are of crucial importance to large infrastructure projects (...) in roads and railways or water management projects. (...) At the time of the infringement the firms were the leading players in the market.

Andrea Coscelli, the CMA's Chief Executive, said: "These companies entered into illegal arrangements where they secretly shared out the market for important building products and agreed to keep prices artificially high. This is totally unacceptable as it cheats customers out of[7] getting a good deal. The CMA will not hesitate to issue appropriately large fines in these cases, and we will continue to crack down[8] on cartels in the construction sector and in other industries."

Press release published by The Competition and Markets Authority, 23 October 2019.

1. scheme: *arrangement, combine*. **2.** evidence: *preuves* **3.** leniency: *clémence*. **4.** settlement process: *procédure de règlement*. **5.** pre-cast concrete: *béton précontraint*. **6.** drainage pipe: *tuyau de drainage*. **7.** to cheat sb out of: *priver frauduleusement qqn de*. **8.** to crack down on: *sévir contre*.

2 ***Compréhension.***

Explain what companies were fined, by whom, and for what reasons.
(About 120 words in English.)

Document 3

Tech giants face no contest[1] when it comes to competition law

Amazon has announced that it is acquiring Whole Foods, a chain of American grocery stores.

(...) According to *New York Times* figures for the US, Amazon now accounts for[2] 43% of all online retail sales; half of all online shopping searches start on Amazon (...); in 2016, the company had revenues of $63bn from online sales – which is more than the next top 10 online retailers combined; it controls 74% of ebook sales, and is soon set to become the biggest *clothing* retailer in the US. (...)

By any common-sense yardstick[3], therefore, Amazon wields[4] monopoly power and its activities should trigger action by regulators. The problem is that US antitrust (competition) law has long parted company[5] with common sense. The rot[6] set in when Robert Bork published *The Antitrust Paradox* in 1978, in which he argued that competition law had become too focused on preventing cartels, price-fixing and mergers that create monopolies, and should return instead to what he claimed was its original concern with protecting consumers. This view was then energetically promulgated by the influential Chicago Law School and seems to have become the conventional wisdom of competition authorities across the world.

Crudely put[7], the implication of the Bork view is that no matter how big[8] or dominant a company becomes, if there's no evidence[9] that its dominance is harming[10] consumers, then there's no antitrust concern. (...)

Although Amazon does not provide free services, it can – and does – argue that it provides excellent customer service and very competitive prices. (...)

Amazon's Whole Foods acquisition will have to be approved by the Federal Trade Commission, but my guess is that it will get through[11]. The company will argue that even after buying Whole Foods Market its share of the American grocery market will be less than 5%. *Monopolist, moi?* will be Mr Bezos's plea[12]. But if the FTC does indeed accept this argument, then we will have a really good measure of how irrelevant antitrust law has become in curbing corporate power in a digital world. "The law does not concern itself with trifles[13]," used to be the proud boast[14] of legal theorists. Now it doesn't seem to concern itself with giants either.

By John Naughton, *The Guardian*, 25 June 2017

1. contest: *contestation*. **2.** to account for: *représenter*. **3.** by any common sense yardstick: *selon n'importe quel critère de bon sens*. **4.** to wield: *détenir*. **5.** to part company with: *abandonner, oublier*. **6.** rot. *pourriture*, (ici) *problèmes*. **7.** crudely put: en gros. **8.** no matter how big: *quelle que soit la taille*. **9.** evidence: *preuves*. **10.** to harm: *nuire à*. **11.** to get through: *passer, être accepté*. **12.** plea: *défense, plaidoyer*. **13.** trifle: *bagatelle*. **14.** boast: *affirmation vantarde*.

3 *Compréhension.*

Explain in what subtle and paradoxical way Amazon is breaking American competition law, the various reasons why it is even helped by it, and some consequences. *(About 150 words, in English.)*

4 *Expression* (oral or written work).

In your opinion, are the efforts to "bust" the big tech companies justified? Why is competition not limited to low prices? Will the efforts of the "trust-busters" be successful or not? Give your reasons. *(About 200 words in English.)*

Document 4

www.rudebarbs.com

1. grim: *sombre*. **2.** to bust up: *démanteler*. **3.** Ma & Pa business: *petite entreprise familiale*. **4.** textbook example: *cas d'école*.

5 *Compréhension.*

Décrivez cette caricature. Qui est caricaturé, et pourquoi ?
(Environ 100 mots en français.)

6 Note de synthèse.

Rédigez une note de synthèse des documents fournis. Présentez les différents aspects des lois sur la concurrence selon diverses législations : avantages, inconvénients, efficacité, conséquences pour les consommateurs et les entreprises.
(Environ 250 mots en français.)

7 *Expression.*

Rédaction d'une lettre d'accompagnement de dossier ***(cover letter)*****.**
(About 150 words.)

Vous êtes Mme Clémentine Lafarge et vous travaillez pour la Papeterie d'Eymoutiers (route de Nedde, 87 120 Eymoutiers, France) qui fabrique du carton ondulé et exporte beaucoup vers le Royaume-Uni, où elle détient l0 % du marché. Votre entreprise projette d'y racheter une usine de carton ondulé, la société UDM, 40 Framewood Road, Slough, SL36PJ, UK. Vous êtes chargée de rédiger la lettre d'accompagnement du dossier, contenant tous les documents et précisions nécessaires, qui va être envoyé à The Competition and Markets Authority (Ms Jessica Muhammad, The Cabot, 25 Cabot Square, London E 144 QZ, UK).

Vous demandez si ce rachat respecte bien la loi britannique sur la concurrence, car après l'opération, votre part du marché au Royaume-Uni représentera probablement 15 % (au maximum) : vous espérez que vous ne serez pas en contravention avec les règles de la concurrence applicables dans ce pays, mais vous préférez vous en assurer. Vous souhaitez une réponse de confirmation la plus rapide possible.

Date et salutations d'usage.

CHAPITRE

10

Globalisation

La mondialisation

A flat world

Globalisation has shaped the world over the past 30 years and made it more complex. Today, the world has become more interconnected and countries work together to produce goods and services. Markets become integrated. People share more knowledge, ideas and technology. They travel and migrate more thanks to cheaper transport. Globalisation has seen the rise of multinational corporations (MNCs) with subsidiaries[1] in many countries. The journalist T. L. Friedman popularised the expression "flat world", to explain that globalised trade, outsourcing[2], supply-chaining[3], and political forces had permanently changed the world, for better and worse.

Advantages

The breaking down of borders[4] was initially meant to increase prosperity thanks to free trade and the idea that countries would each specialise in what they do best, in a win-win situation. This is called "competitive advantage." It was also hoped that the more countries traded, the less they would fight. Globalisation has helped to reduce extreme poverty and to reduce prices of consumer goods, thanks to economies of scale. It has enabled countries to participate in a race to the top and to fuel[5] economic growth. Moreover, cultural exchanges have become enriching and inspiring. This has led to greater tolerance.

Drawbacks

Although globalisation has helped to create more wealth in developing countries, it has not closed the gap between the world's poorest countries and the world's richest. Outsourcing has destroyed blue-collar jobs in the industrial world, and this has resulted in a political backlash[6] in most developed nations, with a rise in populism. Sweatshops[7] where the labour force is exploited have also raised much controversy. As globalisation is synonymous with a shrinking[8] of nation states, it is being now put into question, leading to a return to protectionism and economic nationalism. Globalisation is said to have compounded[9] climate change as well and even widened[10] the rich-poor gap and the urban-rural gap in some countries like China. People are now more aware of these issues, thanks to globalisation.

Outsourcing

Relocating factories and outsourcing services to places where the labour force was cheaper was all the rage in the world during the 1990s and the 2000s. Industrial jobs, but also skilled jobs such as computer programming, bookkeeping[11] or jobs in call centres were outsourced abroad, leading to lay-offs[12] in developed countries. Today, however, only 18% of the trade of global goods is driven by considerations about the cost of labour. There is less need for a low-skilled labour force. One reason is that many emerging countries like China now consume more of what they produce. Also, global value chains are becoming more knowledge-intensive. It means workers need a lot of skills to be efficient.

Insourcing

This happens when offshore production moves back or closer to countries. In the context of the third industrial revolution, with smart technologies and the digitalisation of manufacturing, companies want to be closer to their customers to respond more quickly to changes in demand. Moreover, since the 2008 crisis, multinational economic activity has become more regional with deeper regional block trade agreements.

Deglobalisation

It is an anti-globalisation trend supported by those who view globalisation as a threat for job security and wages and who support protectionism as a result. They wonder whether globalisation means more opportunity or more risk. It aims at reducing interdependence between states and favouring the nation state. The Brexit vote, US President Trump's election and the French Yellow Vest movement highlight this frustration.

Alterglobalisation

This movement, which is not against globalisation, opposes the negative consequences of globalisation because it threatens[13] the environment, economic justice and human rights. Its members meet at the World Social Forum at the same time as the World Economic Forum in Davos, Switzerland, so that they may obtain good media coverage. The Slow Food movement which started to protest against McDonald's and fast food in general is typical of this trend. It has influenced other areas like medicine or travel. Some people believe that slow food is what the planet needs right now in order to reduce CO_2 emissions and economic inequality.

Slowbalisation

"Slowbalisation" is a new term that describes the reactions against globalisation and the fact that the share of trade as part of global GDP[14] has fallen since 2008. Globalisation has become slower. Capital flows have also fallen sharply. Many assumptions[15] about globalisation are undermined today but it does not mean globalisation is collapsing. It has always gone through cycles. The rules of international trade are regularly revised, and new deals are negotiated.

'Belt and road'

It is a Chinese plan for the future, consisting in building a huge network of infrastructure – roads, pipelines, sea routes – in order to boost trade and economic development in Asia. It involves a sea route linking China's southern coast to east Africa and the Mediterranean. It has been nicknamed "globalisation with Chinese characteristics" but also described as neo-colonialism.

1. subsidiary: *filiale.*
2. outsourcing: *sous-traitance.*
3. supply-chain: *chaîne d'approvisionnement.*
4. border: *frontière.*
5. to fuel: *alimenter.*
6. backlash: *réaction de rejet.*
7. sweatshop: *atelier où la main-d'œuvre est exploitée.*
8. to shrink: *rétrécir.*
9. to compound: *aggraver.*
10. to widen: *élargir.*
11. bookkeeping: *comptabilité.*
12. lay-off: *licenciement.*
13. to threaten: *menacer.*
14. GDP (Gross Domestic Product): *PIB.*
15. assumption: *idée reçue.*

Repérer les notions essentielles

Answer the following questions with help from the text.

a. Explain how globalisation has transformed the world.
b. What does the expression "a flat world" mean?
c. What are the main benefits of globalisation?
d. What are the main drawbacks of globalisation?
e. Explain the differences between outsourcing and insourcing.
f. What is the advantage of outsourcing abroad?
g. How has globalised outsourcing evolved from the 1990s to today?
h. What is the difference between deglobalisation and alterglobalisation?
i. What does the term "slowbalisation" imply?
j. How do the Chinese envisage the future of global trade?

Résumer le texte en français

Résumez ce texte en faisant ressortir les points positifs et négatifs de la mondialisation. *(Environ 200 mots.)*

Approfondir

a. Choose a global brand and do some research about its history, success and competitors. *(About 150 words, in English.)*

b. Find examples of global exchanges or global economic activities which damage the environment and explain how they pose a threat. *(About 150 words, in English.)*

Lexical work

• to boom	être en expansion
• border	frontière
• to break into a market	pénétrer un marché
• comparative advantage	avantage comparatif
• to compete	concurrencer
• competitiveness	compétitivité
• competitor	un concurrent
• competition	concurrence
• containerised freight	du fret transporté en containers
• cross-border flows	flux transfrontaliers
• de-industrialisation	désindustrialisation
• to deregulate	déréglementer
• developed / developing countries	pays développés / en voie de développement
• economic prosperity	prospérité économique
• economical	qui ne revient pas cher
• economies of scale	économies d'échelle
• economy	l'économie en général
• export	marchandise exportée
• to export	exporter
• fair trade	commerce équitable
• fierce competition	concurrence féroce
• free market system	libéralisme économique
• free marketeer	partisan du libéralisme économique
• free trade	libre échange
• on a global scale	à l'échelle mondiale
• growth	la croissance
• living standard / standard of living	niveau de vie
• to lower	abaisser
• MNC (multinational corporation)	FMN (firme multinationale)
• offshoring	délocalisation
• to outsource / to source	sous-traiter *(par extension :* délocaliser*)*
• to produce	produire
• product	un produit
• production costs	coûts de production
• profitable	lucratif
• raise controversy	faire polémique
• range of products	gamme / variété de produits
• to ratchet up duties	augmenter des droits de douane
• raw materials	matières premières
• to reap benefits	récolter des avantages

• to rise	s'élever, se lever, monter
• to relocate (UK) / to relocate (US)	déménager, délocaliser
• relocating	déménagement, délocalisation
• to settle abroad	s'installer à l'étranger
• to ship goods	expédier des marchandises
• slowdown	ralentissement
• spare parts	pièces détachées
• to stagnate (UK) / to stagnate (US)	stagner
• standardisation	uniformisation
• steel and aluminium	l'acier et l'aluminium
• subcontractor	sous-traitant
• supply and demand	l'offre et la demande
• supply chain	chaîne d'approvisionnement
• to swamp the market	inonder le marché
• tax haven	paradis fiscal
• to threaten	menacer
• trade	le commerce
• trade talks	négociations commerciales
• worldwide	dans le monde entier
• WTO (World Trade Organisation)	OMC (Organisation mondiale du commerce)

Use the list

Fill in the gaps with the right word from each series (make the necessary changes). Then translate each sentence.

A *economical / economic / economy*

a. Since 2008, the global … has been in trouble in some sectors.
b. Drivers want … cars that do not use up too much petrol.
c. … prosperity is the main consequence of globalisation.

B *competition / competitor / competitive / competitiveness / compete*

a. Countries… with each other in order to gain market share.
b. When goods are at a … price, consumers tend to go for them.
c. MNCs provide greater … and quality.
d. By reducing costs, the company kept its … edge over its … .
e. … in business is supposed to benefit consumers.

C *produce / product / production*

a. This factory has been … smart cards for years.
b. China exports more and more consumer … like electronic goods.
c. The latest model will go into … by the end of the quarter.

Grammar work

L'article défini *the* ou ∅ ?

› Aide-mémoire grammatical, p. 163

Analysez et traduisez les exemples suivants.

1. MNCs usually offer lower prices and larger ranges of products.
2. The banks in this country have huge problems.
3. It is necessary to help the people who are starving in their country.
4. People benefit from globalisation in their everyday lives.
5. Poverty in a rich world must disappear.
6. Trade is always good for the economy but waste is a serious issue.

1 Utilisez l'article défini si nécessaire dans les phrases suivantes.

a. It is difficult to find a solution to … widespread poverty.
b. Nowadays, … competition is so fierce that many companies are cutting … jobs.
c. … global advertising means that some products are used worldwide.
d. Some people believe that … global trade is a recent phenomenon.
e. As … technology shrinks … world, we need to understand … other cultures.
f. All … trading partners usually benefit from … trade and … wealth it brings.
g. In some ways … world economy was just as globalised in … past as it is now.
h. … government has imposed … trade barriers.
i. … small businesses also benefit from … globalisation of … markets.

Les auxiliaires modaux *may* et *can*

› Aide-mémoire grammatical, p. 167

Analysez, puis traduisez les exemples suivants :

1. Poverty in developing countries may mean that people have to emigrate.
2. Some people think that globalisation may actually be better for the environment.
3. Thanks to international transport, migrants can cross some borders easily.
4. But they cannot always find good jobs in their host country.

2 Ajoutez *can*, *cannot* ou *may* selon le cas, puis traduisez les phrases.

a. These cheap goods from China … swamp the market, so some countries … retaliate by raising trade barriers to protect their workers.
b. Too many people … understand that protectionism … threaten the consumers' standard of living.
c. Global trade … reduce local or temporary shortages.
d. Some companies are too small and … compete on a global scale.

Les noms composés anglais

› Aide-mémoire grammatical, p. 187

Analysez et traduisez les exemples suivants :

1. There are fewer manufacturing jobs today.
2. Globalisation has favoured gender equality.
3. The luxury sector has boomed in recent years.
4. Clothes factories are numerous in Asia.

Remarque : Attention à l'ordre des termes des noms composés soulignés.

3 Complétez les phrases suivantes avec l'un des noms composés ci-dessous, puis traduisez les phrases.

carbon footprint – climate change – fashion industry – shopping habits – tax cuts – television channels

a. Textile production contributes to … .
b. With globalisation, you can watch … in many languages today.
c. Fast fashion has a very strong … .
d. Companies need … to face global competition.
e. The … gives rise to environmental degradation.
f. Young people's … have changed because of global exchanges.

Exercice de synthèse

4 Traduisez en anglais.

a. Les gouvernements ne peuvent pas toujours régler les problèmes économiques dus à la mondialisation.
b. La mondialisation peut créer du chômage mais aussi des richesses.
c. Les ouvriers pourraient avoir des accidents avec ces machines trop vieilles.
d. Le secteur automobile américain a souffert de la mondialisation.
e. Avec davantage d'échanges internationaux, nos habitudes de consommation ont changé.
f. Les gens savent parler plus de langues étrangères aujourd'hui.
g. Ils peuvent aller dans des écoles de langues pour progresser.
h. Les usines de voitures peuvent être délocalisées pour réduire les coûts.
i. Le changement climatique a des effets sur l'économie.
j. Ils ont délocalisé leur usine de voitures.
k. Ils veulent réduire leurs coûts de production.

Exam work

Document 1

Globalisation not to blame for rise in inequality research finds

Globalisation has stalled[1] over the past decade so it should not be blamed for the rise in inequality seen since the financial crisis, according to research by the OECD's former chief economist. Catherine Mann, now global chief economist at Citi, said her research, published by the investment bank on Sunday, showed that global integration had peaked[2] according to many measures some time ago. With public opinion becoming increasingly hostile to globalisation, even its proponents[3] have started to pay more attention to its ill-effects. World leaders, including US president Donald Trump and some economists, have blamed globalisation and international trade for rising inequality and job losses in many industries.

But Ms Mann's research supports the argument that globalisation makes countries richer in aggregate[4], and problems arise[5] because governments fail to share the gains fairly or to compensate those who lose out. Technology and the shift[6] in consumption from goods to services have played a bigger part in the loss of manufacturing jobs in advanced economies than globalisation has, the report found.

(...) The world's retreat from globalisation will lead to "a smaller [economic] pie[7], more poorly distributed," Ms Mann's report concluded. The unravelling[8] could make it harder for poorer countries to gain a foothold[9] in global trade and so raise their living standards, she said. Governments should aim to boost trade in services and open up fast-growing emerging markets, rather than closing markets in advanced economies, she recommended.

(...) Not all aspects of globalisation have gone into reverse[10], however. In contrast with trade and finance, the movement of people around the world is still rising, fuelling remittances[11]. Migration has more than doubled in the past 20 years, the report noted, with the bulk[12] of the increase over the past decade taking place within rich economies. Tourism, and the financial flows associated with it, have also been booming. Another big exception is digital globalisation, which is "skyrocketing"[13] according to measures of global IP traffic and the value of ecommerce, the report noted, although new barriers to digital trade erected by the EU and China could threaten this expansion.

By Delphine Strauss, *The Financial Times*, 25 August 2019.

1. to stall: *ralentir*. **2.** to peak: *atteindre son point le plus haut*. **3.** proponent: *partisan*. **4.** in aggregate: *dans l'ensemble*. **5.** to arise: *surgir*. **6.** shift: *changement*. **7.** pie: *gâteau*. **8.** unravelling: *effritement*. **9.** to gain a foothold: *trouver un point d'appui*. **10.** to go into reverse: *faire marche arrière*. **11.** to fuel remittances: *stimuler des envois d'argent*. **12.** bulk: *majeure partie*. **13.** to skyrocket: *monter en flèche*.

1 ***Compréhension.*** What does the writer want to explain to the critics of globalisation? *(About 150 words, in English.)*

Document 2

Making globalisation work for Africa

The current backlash[1] against globalization, most notably from working-class citizens in advanced economies who are worried about stagnant wages and insecure jobs, highlights how the benefits of global economic integration were oversold[2], and its costs undercounted. But the effects of globalization on Africa and its citizens have received far less attention, even though the continent is projected to account for[3] over 40 percent of the world's population by the end of this century. (...)

Ever since the First Industrial Revolution led to a surge[4] in international trade, Africa has remained largely on the sidelines[5] of the global economy. The main beneficiaries of early globalization were today's advanced economies, where industrial technologies emerged. This, in turn, led to the 'great divergence' in income levels between the Global North and South.

More recently, the advent[6] of new information and communications technology in the 1990s dramatically lowered the costs of distance and ushered in[7] another wave of globalization, characterized by the emergence of complex global value chains[8] (GVCs). These GVCs contributed to the 'great convergence' of recent decades by boosting industrial output[9] in countries such as China, India, Indonesia, Poland, South Korea, Taiwan, and Singapore, enabling them to narrow[10] the gap with advanced economies.

Yet African countries have remained excluded from this process. The continent's share of global merchandise trade has stagnated at around 3 percent, similar to its share of world manufacturing output. To be sure, globalization has brought benefits to Africa. Rising incomes elsewhere in the world have increased demand for African commodities and natural resources, boosting national economies. Globalization has also supported knowledge transfer, enabling African countries to improve living standards by 'leapfrogging'[11] to new technologies.

But myriad challenges have far outweighed[12] such benefits. For one thing, globalization has contributed to premature deindustrialization. Because advanced economies can now produce goods more cheaply, African countries have found it difficult to develop local industries that create jobs. Moreover, some multinational corporations operating in the region are dodging[13] taxes through sophisticated – and legal – accounting mechanisms such as profit shifting[14], depriving[15] governments of much-needed resources for economic development. Globalization is also contributing to climate change, which has a disproportionate effect on Africa despite the continent's limited contribution to the problem.

By Ngozi-Iweala and Brahima Coulibaly, www.project-syndicate.org, 30 May 2019.

1. backlash: *réaction négative.* **2.** to oversell: *exagérer.* **3.** to account for: *représenter.* **4.** a surge: *une hausse massive.* **5.** on the sidelines: *dans les coulisses.* **6.** advent: *avènement.* **7.** to usher in: *inaugurer.* **8.** complex global value chains: *des chaînes de valeur à échelle mondiale et plus complexes.* **9.** output: *production.* **10.** to narrow: *resserrer.* **11.** to leapfrog: *faire un très grand bond.* **12.** to outweigh: *l'emporter sur.* **13.** to dodge: *éviter de payer.* **14.** profit shifting: *détournement de bénéfices.* **15.** to deprive of: *priver de.*

2 ***Compréhension.*** Comment l'Afrique a-t-elle pu évoluer dans le processus de la mondialisation ? *(Environ 150 mots, en français.)*

Document 3

Globalisation boosts women – and tax cuts[1] could help even more, economists say

Free trade, tax cuts and slashing red tape[2] are all crucial to improving the lot[3] of poor women across the world, while threats to globalisation risk undoing crucial progress, economists have warned. Protectionism has become fashionable as a potential way to aid industries, boost local jobs and defend areas that are perceived to be threatened by foreign competition.

But this approach can only fail and instead risks harming[4] the most vulnerable, according to Niklas Potrafke at Ifo, the German economic institute. "These days, it is back in fashion to bad-mouth[5] globalisation. But if we limit the exchange of goods, we also limit the exchange of ideas – and that would be a step backwards in terms of the development of society in many countries," he said.

As well as promoting trade and investment, the globalisation of ideas has been crucial in challenging[6] traditional views of the place of women in society. "This has enabled them to influence the attitudes towards social roles prevailing[7] in their own country to their own benefit," said Mr Potrafke.

"Economic globalisation, meanwhile, has seen foreign trade and direct investments by foreign companies also importing models of social roles and paradigms[8] of western companies into developing countries."

Despite steps towards equality, women are still far less likely than men to be in work. More than two-thirds of men are in paid work, while just below half of women are in the same position, according to the International Labour Organisation (ILO). This amounts to a gap of 700m people, with 2bn men in employment but only 1.3bn women.

Solutions include scrapping[9] regulations that stop women working, and cutting taxes that harm incentives[10] to earn. "Achieving[11] gender equality in the world of work is possible if laws that discriminate against women and girls prior to entry into the labour market are repealed[12], as well as provisions preventing women from working at night or underground, or entering and progressing in a specific sector or occupation altogether," said the ILO in its report, *A Quantum Leap for Gender Equality*.

By Tim Wallace, *The Telegraph*, 7 March 2019.

1. tax cuts: *réductions d'impôts*. **2.** to slash red tape: *réduire la paperasserie*. **3.** lot: *sort*. **4.** to harm: *nuire à*. **5.** to bad-mouth: *critiquer*. **6.** to challenge: *remettre en question*. **7.** to prevail: *dominer*. **8.** paradigm: *modèle*. **9.** to scrap: *se débarrrasser de*. **10.** incentive: *incitation*. **11.** to achieve: *réaliser*. **12.** to repeal: *abroger*.

3 ***Compréhension.*** What benefit of globalisation does the author point out? What must be done to make sure it does not disappear? *(About 150 words, in English).*

4 ***Expression***. Would you say that the young benefit from globalisation or not? *(About 150 words, in English.)*

Document 4

Globalization may actually be better for the environment

The increasing pace[1] of globalization and how it affects the environment has been a major global concern. (…) Many strongly believe that increased globalization has been harmful[2] to the environment.

A large number of environmentalists who support this view base their arguments on the premise that globalization leads to an increase in global demand, resulting in increased production. This indirectly contributes to the exploitation of the environment and the depletion[3] of natural resources.

Amid[4] rising environmental concerns, an important question is whether deglobalization would have the opposite impact on the environment. Put differently, if globalization is harmful, then should we expect that the current deglobalization trend will be less harmful for the environment? (…)

But in fact, deglobalization may not necessarily translate into reduced emissions of harmful gases such as CO_2, SO_2, NO_2, but could actually worsen[5] it. Through what's known as the technique effect, we know globalization can trigger[6] environmentally friendly technological innovations that can be transferred from countries with strict environmental regulations to pollution havens[7].

Globalization doesn't just entail[8] the movement of manufactured goods, but also the transfer of intermediate, capital goods and technologies. That means multinational corporations with clean state-of-the-art[9] technologies can transfer their green know-how[10] to countries with low environmental standards.

It's widely recognized that multinational firms use cleaner types of energy than local firms, and therefore have more energy-efficient production processes. Deglobalization could mean these environmentally friendly technologies aren't passed on to countries that are trying to go green.

The rise of anti-globalization forces also means less specialization in sectors in which countries have comparative advantages. (…) If every country has to produce to meet its domestic demand, in other words, it could result in duplication in production processes and therefore an increase in local emissions.

By Sylvanus Kwaku Afesorgbor and Binyam Afewerk Demena, *The Conversation*, 24 April 2018.

1. pace: *rythme, vitesse.* **2.** harmful: *nocif.* **3.** depletion: *épuisement.* **4.** amid: *parmi.* **5.** to worsen: *aggraver.* **6.** to trigger: déclencher. **7.** haven: *lieu de prédilection.* **8.** to entail: *entraîner.* **9.** state-of-the-art: *à la pointe du progrès.* **10.** know-how: *savoir-faire.*

5 ***Compréhension.*** According to the authors, is globalisation good or bad for the environment? *(About 150 words, in English.)*

6 ***Expression.*** Do you agree with the opinions expressed in this text. Explain why or why not. *(About 150 words, in English.)*

Document 5

7 ***Expression.*** What paradox does this cartoon point to?

8 ***Synthèse.*** En vous appuyant sur les documents fournis, vous rédigerez en français une note qui répondra à la question suivante : quels sont les principaux effets de la mondialisation ? *(250 mots environ, en français.)*

9 ***Expression.* Rédigez un courrier en anglais** *(150 mots environ)*.

Vous travaillez pour un distributeur d'équipement sportif spécialisé dans le football, Soccer Paradise, situé à Londres. Vous souhaitez importer des chaussures *(boots)*, des tee-shirts *(jerseys)* et des ballons de football *(footballs)* fabriqués dans une usine en Chine (Wenzoufitness52687.cn). Présentez votre entreprise et assurez votre correspondant chinois de l'expérience et du sérieux de votre société.

Expliquez pourquoi vous avez choisi Wenzoufitness comme fournisseur (réputation, qualité des produits, etc.).

Vous souhaitez connaître entre autres le prix des articles, les matériaux utilisés pour les chaussures et vêtements, les délais de fabrication, les coûts de fret ainsi que les délais d'expédition de l'usine chinoise. Demandez des échantillons afin de faire votre choix pour une éventuelle commande. Vous leur demandez également s'ils ont un représentant en Europe.

Présentation et salutations d'usage.

CHAPITRE

11

The main regional trading areas

Les principaux espaces économiques régionaux

A regional trading area (RTA) is a group of countries where trading activities between its members are managed by an intergovernmental agreement. The four different types of RTAs, from the least to the most integrated ones, are:

- **free-trading areas** that have no internal trade-barriers, at least on certain goods or services: each country has trade-barriers against non-members and can negotiate its deals;
- **customs unions** which share trade-deals and have common tariffs against non-members;
- **common markets** that offer mutual freedom of movement for people, goods and investments;
- **economic unions** (the most fully integrated type) which have common laws, standards and regulations, political bodies and institutions, tax systems (to a certain extent), possibilities of technology transfers and sometimes a common currency.

The trading areas and the World Trade Organization (WTO)

All RTAs have to follow the WTO rules which guarantee free-trade and prevent protectionism, and must be notified by the countries to the WTO. In 2019 302 RTAs were in force, corresponding to 481 notifications (not all RTAs are active). They must be transparent and regulated by the WTO. Each continent has several RTAs. These trading areas or agreements often change. Some countries belong to several trading blocs, and only one belongs to none: Japan.

The main regional trading areas in the world

In Europe: The European Union. Starting with six countries in 1958 as the EEC (European Economic Community), the EU has become one of the world's largest economic and trade blocs, and the biggest exporter of goods. It has over 440 million inhabitants living in 27 countries and 24 official languages. It has 30% of the world's nominal GDP (Gross Domestic Product)[1], but there are big differences among the per capita[2] incomes and taxes, even VAT (Valued Added Tax) rates. The Single Market implemented in 1993 has created a real economic union among all member states, which must be democracies adhering to free trade and free enterprise[3]. It guarantees free movement of people, goods, services and capital among them and enforces common policies through Brussels' "directives" for trade, agriculture, fishing and regional development. By boosting exchanges in general and significant aid to poorer regions, the Single Market has improved citizens' living standards and conditions as never before. The euro is the currency[4] used by 19 countries. This system has helped cushion[5] several crises, as in 2008, but shown the need for fiscal and budgetary harmonisation in the eurozone. Political unity is still lacking[6] today on defence, the euro crisis, migration and fiscal harmonisation, with economic consequences. The United Kingdom left the European Union ("Brexit") in 2020. Since then, the future has become less clear.

In America: The USMCA (USA, Mexico, Canada) is a new free-trade agreement replacing NAFTA[7] signed between the USA, Canada and Mexico in 1994 (total population today: almost 500 million inhabitants), which had gradually eliminated tariff barriers in agriculture and industry, had increased cooperation in services and coordination of standards, regulations and performance objectives; but it was still limited. The USMCA has started reinforcing integration between the countries in 2020. For example, cars must now have 75% of their parts manufactured in one of these three countries to qualify for zero tariffs; all workers must be granted minimum wages and minimum protection, especially in Mexico; US farmers must have easier access to dairy[8] markets in Canada; digital trade and intellectual property are also better protected, etc.

In Asia: The Association of Southeast Asian Nations (ASEAN) is a group of 10 nations (Indonesia, the Philippines, Thailand, Cambodia, etc.) that work together to promote political, economic, cultural growth and solidarity. It has reduced its trade barriers and is probably the best-known of all Asian regional blocs.

In Africa: The African Continental Free-Trade Agreement (ACFTA) created in 2018, has been signed by all African Union countries except Erythrea. Tariffs have been removed from 90% of the goods, allowing free access to goods and services across the continent. This should boost intra-African trade by 52% by 2022. This RTA now is the world's largest in terms of participating countries.

Positive contributions and challenges

RTAs stimulate exchanges, economic growth opportunities, economies of scale, and job creations. They increase competition, which is good for consumers. They encourage investments and innovations because producers, especially in small countries, can enjoy bigger demand on the wider market created by the RTA. Some people see it as a barrier against globalisation because they are protected from countries outside their RTA. They help develop freedom of transport, raise living standards on the whole, and may help to reduce inequalities, especially in the poorer countries.

However, member nations lose some of their sovereignty (a major reason for Brexit). RTAs protect the trading blocs to the detriment of other countries. They boost large international companies and may threaten small national ones. They favour bilateralism over multilateralism which is enforced by the WTO. Inside the RTA, jobs may be displaced or switched to more competitive countries. That is why they can be controversial.

Now, will this trend last, since protectionism seems to be coming back?

1. GDP (Gross Domestic Product): *PIB (Produit Intérieur Brut).*
2. per capita: *par habitant.*
3. free enterprise: *libre entreprise, libéralisme.*
4. currency: *devise, monnaie d'un pays.*
5. to cushion: *amortir.*
6. to lack: *faire défaut.*
7. NAFTA: *ALENA (Accord de libre-échange nord-américain).*
8. dairy products: *produits laitiers.*
9. to outweigh: *l'emporter sur.*

Repérer les notions essentielles

Répondez aussi précisément que possible aux questions suivantes en français.

a. Qu'est-ce qu'un espace économique régional ?
b. Quels sont les quatre types d'espaces économiques régionaux ?
c. Comment s'appelle l'Organisation mondiale du commerce (OMC) en anglais ?
d. Quelles sont les principales fonctions de l'OMC ?
e. Tous les pays adhèrent-ils à un espace économique régional ?
f. Quelles sont les principales caractéristiques de l'Union européenne ?
g. Que pouvez-vous dire sur l'USMCA ?
h. Qu'est-ce que l'ASEAN ?

Résumer le texte en anglais

Summarise this text in about 150 words.

Approfondir

Select one of the RTAs mentioned in this document or any other RTA that you know of and carry out research about it on the Internet. Or research about the WTO.

Lexical work

• anti-dumping suit	procès pour pratiques de dumping
• to ban (an article)	interdire (une marchandise)
• border line	ligne de démarcation
• border/neighbour state	état limitrophe / voisin
• borderless	sans frontière
• boundary	limite ; frontière
• to break down barriers	faire tomber des barrières
• to cancel (an agreement / a deal)	annuler (un accord)
• to clear goods through customs	passer des marchandises en douane
• to comply with an obligation	respecter une obligation
• to consign / dispatch	expédier
• consignee ; consigner	destinataire ; expéditeur
• consignment	envoi
• customs clearance	dédouanement
• customs declaration	déclaration en douane
• customs house	poste de douane
• customs officer	douanier
• customs duty/tariff	droit de douane
• debt	endettement
• default	faillite
• to default	faire faillite, ne pas honorer un paiement
• to dismantle regulations	démanteler des règlements
• duty free goods	marchandises hors taxe / détaxées
• to endorse an agreement	approuver un accord
• export earnings	revenus de l'exportation
• exports and imports	exportations et importations
• freight	(transport de) marchandises
• (milk) glut	excédent (laitier)
• to glut a market	saturer un marché
• to go through customs	passer la douane
• to join a union / an organisation	adhérer à une union / une organisation
• to lift sanctions	lever des sanctions
• loose/close tie/link	lien lâche/étroit
• offset, to offset	compensation, compenser
• to overcome division	surmonter des divisions
• rating agency	agence de notation
• to remove borders	supprimer les frontières
• retaliatory measure	mesure de rétorsion

• to shape a new tie	former un nouveau lien
• sovereignty	souveraineté
• to strengthen border safety	renforcer la sécurité aux frontières
• to subsidise	subventionner
• subsidy	subvention
• to sue	poursuivre en justice
• tariff barrier	barrière douanière/tarifaire
• trade balance	balance commerciale
• trade surplus/deficit	excédent/déficit commercial
• to work out a joint constitution	élaborer une constitution commune

Use the list

1 Fill in the gaps with words from the list below, making the necessary changes. Then translate the sentences.

to lift – to cancel – retaliatory measure – customs duties – barrier (x2) – loose – ties – duty free – subsidy – border state – trade balance – to remove borders – regulations

a. In a free trade area where just reciprocal preferences for goods or services are exchanged, the … are … between member countries since different tariff … are imposed on imports from other countries.

b. Thanks to the USMCA, certain goods produced entirely in one of the three member states are sold … in the other two countries.

c. Brussels now controls all … given to a company by its national government.

d. Most but not all FTAs are between … .

e. In spite of the … there are still … between this union's member countries.

f. This year, our … is in deficit again.

g. Because of growing illegal immigration, a big concern in the EU today is whether it was a good idea … with the Shengen agreement.

h. When a country suddenly imposes new …, then other countries take… .

i. The agreement will be … if other countries do not … their sanctions.

2 Match the words below, add articles if necessary, and translate the expressions.

a. to cancel	b. to go through	c. to break down	d. to dismantle
e. customs	f. to join	g. tariff	h. rating
1. barrier	2. union	3. barriers	4. officer
5. regulations	6. customs	7. agreement.	8. agency

Grammar work

Le passif et « on »

› Aide-mémoire grammatical, p. 195

Analysez et traduisez les exemples.

1. This treaty <u>was signed</u> in 1998 <u>by</u> three countries.
   (= Three countries signed this treaty in 1998).
2. A joint constitution <u>is going to be worked out by</u> all the member nations.
3. Customers <u>will now be sold</u> duty free imports.
4. It is said that these measures <u>will be declared</u> illegal <u>by</u> the WTO.
5. The president <u>has been asked</u> to lift these trade barriers.
6. <u>It is well known</u> which country does not comply with its obligations.
7. We <u>have been sent</u> an email about the new regulation.
8. This agreement needs <u>to be discussed</u>.
9. <u>It is rumoured</u> that Belarus was to join the EU.
10. They <u>have been told</u> that tariffs will be imposed.

Remarque : Ces formes passives en anglais peuvent correspondre à des formes différentes en français : passif simple, construction avec « on », formes impersonnelles (voir fiche grammaticale, p. 195). Attention à respecter les temps.

1 Mettez les phrases suivantes au passif, en supprimant éventuellement le sujet de la forme active. Attention aux formes verbales, aux verbes irréguliers, et à l'ordre des mots. Puis traduisez les phrases.

Ex. : Three countries <u>ratified</u> this treaty in 1994.
→ *This treaty was ratified in 1994 (by three countries).*

a. This country made the worst trade deficit last year.
→ The worst trade deficit …

b. At the next summit meeting, they will discuss fair trade.
→ Fair trade …

c. We should anticipate customers' needs.
→ Customers'needs …

d. The government granted big subsidies to that company.
→ That company …

e. But the Brussels commission declared that the government had given them an illegal grant.
→ But it was … that an illegal grant …

f. Last year, they expected the increase in trade to reach 10%.
→ Last year, the increase in trade …

g. One should promote international transactions on equal terms for all nations.
→ International transactions …

Verbes pronominaux: les équivalents anglais

› Aide-mémoire grammatical, p. 209

Remarque : De nombreux verbes pronominaux français correspondent à des verbes actifs anglais. Il faut vérifier dans le dictionnaire.

Analysez et traduisez les exemples suivants en français en utilisant des verbes pronominaux pour les verbes soulignés.

1. I <u>wonder</u> if this trade agreement is really operational.
2. In a large economic union, it is difficult for small countries to <u>make themselves heard</u>.
3. The heads of state <u>have finally agreed</u> to put an end to their protectionist policies.
4. Everyone <u>got up</u> when the president came in.
5. When he <u>started</u> talking, they all <u>looked at one another/each other</u> <u>asking themselves</u> what he meant.
6. Following the meeting, two employees <u>made an appointment</u> the next day outside the office to discuss the issue.
7. Afterwards they <u>met</u> several times and <u>realised</u> that they had common objectives.

2 Traduisez les phrases suivantes.

a. Ces marchandises importées sans taxes se vendent très bien.
b. L'an dernier, notre pays s'est vu infliger une énorme amende par l'OMC pour sa politique protectionniste.
c. Dans un espace économique régional, les entreprises n'ont pas le droit de s'entendre sur les prix de vente de leurs marchandises.
d. Je me suis acheté une de ces belles voitures allemandes qui se vendent moins cher pour nous grâce au marché unique européen.
e. La directrice générale de la société s'est rendu à cette réunion internationale avant-hier.
f. Il s'est exprimé sur les nouveaux besoins de son entreprise.
g. Ces deux producteurs qui se concurrencent se poursuivent maintenant mutuellement en justice car ils s'accusent de s'être copiés pour leurs derniers produits.
h. Savez-vous ce qui se passe dans ce cas ?
i. Je me suis dit qu'un tel cas n'était pas facile à régler.
j. Elle voudrait s'offrir ce beau miroir pour s'y regarder.
k. Cette conférence s'est tenue à Washington l'an dernier.
l. Tu t'es bien amusée à la fête de Noël (*Christmas party*) de l'entreprise ?
m. Oui, mais ensuite je me suis sentie mal.

Exam work

Document 1

RTA currently in force (by year of entry into force), 1969-2020

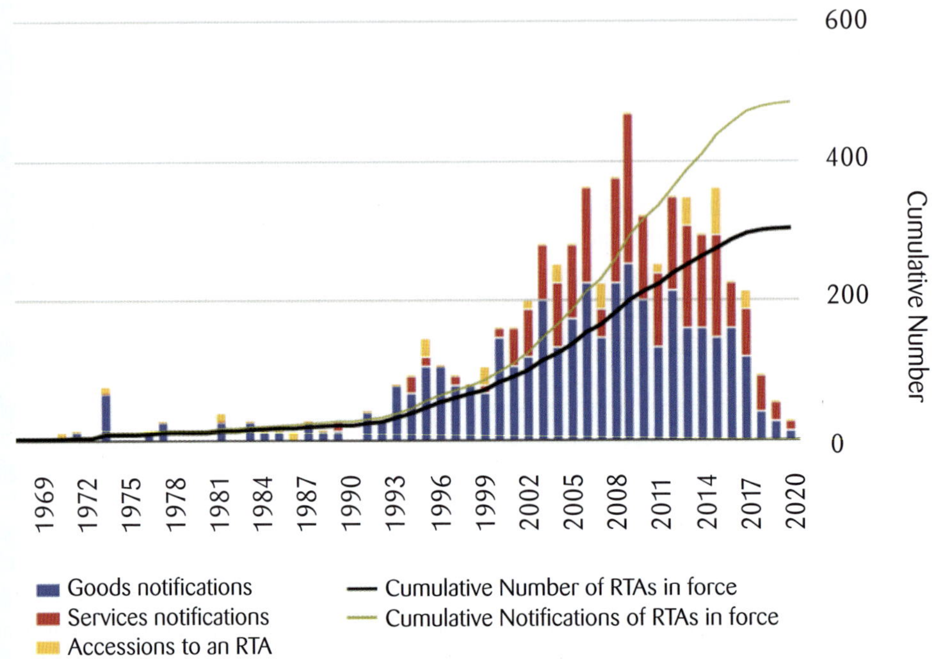

WTO members are bound[1] to notify the regional trade agreements (RTAs) in which they participate. Nearly all of the WTO's Members have notified participation in one or more RTAs (some Members are party to[2] twenty or more). Notifications may also refer to the accession of new parties to an agreement that already exists, e.g.[3] the notification of the accession of Croatia to the European Union Customs Union. Many WTO Members continue to be involved[4] in new RTA negotiations. Like agreements in force, most new negotiations are bilateral. However, a recent development has been negotiations among several WTO Members. The above chart[5] shows all RTAs notified to the GATT[6]/WTO (1969-2019), including inactive RTAs.

World Trade Organization Secretariat, November 2019.

1. to be bound to: *être obligé de*. **2**. to be party to: *être signataire de*. **3**. e.g.: *par exemple*. **4**. involved: *impliqué*. **5**. chart: *graphique*. **6**. GATT (General Agreement on Tariffs and Trade): *organisme antérieur à l'OMC*.

1 ***Compréhension.***

Analysez ce graphique avec l'aide du texte (source et date). Que représente-t-il ? Quels sont les différents types d'accords commerciaux régionaux et quel est l'historique de leur évolution ? *(En français, 100 mots environ.)*

Document 2

Africa's new free trade area is promising yet full of hurdles[1]

The Africa Continental Free Trade Agreement brings great prospects of growth and integration across the region, but it could also aggravate inequalities. How can citizens be confident that African integration will bring benefits to all?

While infrastructure has improved, there is still a long way to go to make trade easier between countries. You can't build a value chain across the continent when there are countless customs stamps, customs, signatures and certificates to simply move a container from one country to another. Logjams[2] and bureaucracy must be reduced.

"We need one-stop border posts and common rules and harmonious regulations to ensure that the flow of goods happens far more quickly and easily. Standardisation of regulations is going to be extremely important," said Patrick Khulekani Dlamini, Chief Executive Officer and Managing Director of the Development Bank of Southern Africa.

The African Union gave assurances this would happen: "We have got a very aggressive programme of trade facilitation, so that we minimize the number of documents that have to be signed for goods and services across borders," said Albert Mudenda Muchanga, Commissioner for Trade and Industry at the African Union Commission.

As global trade rules are being eroded in other regions, with (…) protectionism tightening its grip[3] in many countries, Africa has the opportunity to create a trade buffer[4] for itself. With all countries united in one giant bargaining[5] unit, it will hold far more sway[6] than before.

"Africa could stride[7] onto the trade negotiation stage as one enormous market. This could lead to a new engine of growth across the continent," said Ngaire Woods, Dean Blavatnik School of Government at the University of Oxford.

The continent will also be able to learn from the mistakes of other regions and start integration afresh[8], the speakers noted. Monitoring on a month-to-month basis will be important to see barriers are being dismantled and where gaps remain. (…) But with collaboration, starting 1 July 2020, this giant African market has great potential to be a new engine of growth across the continent.

By Kim Cloet, Official Writer, World Economic Forum on Africa, 6 September 2019.

1. hurdle: *obstacle*. **2.** logjam: *blocage*. **3.** to tighten one's grip: *resserrer son emprise*. **4.** buffer: *(ici) protection*. **5.** to bargain: *négocier*. **6.** to hold sway: *avoir de l'influence*. **7.** to stride: *arriver à grands pas*. **8.** afresh: *de nouveau*.

2 ***Compréhension.***

Summarise the text, pointing out to what extent Africa's new free-trading area is "promising", and what its "hurdles" are. *(Around 150 words, in English.)*

3 ***Expression (oral or in writing).***

Browse the net to find more information about the ACFTA today. How many years has it existed now, and what is its situation like today?

Document 3

Parts[1] with passports: how free trade drives GM's engines

Romulus, Mich. (…) Long before the pistons for General Motors Co V-6 engines reach the US No. 1 automaker's Romulus, Michigan plant, they are seasoned[2] international travellers (…) Powdered aluminum from Tennessee is shipped[3] to Pennsylvania and forged at high temperatures into connecting rods[4] for the pistons, which are then sent to Canada to be shaped and polished. They are then shipped to Mexico for sub-assembly and finally the finished pistons are loaded onto trucks bound for Romulus to become part of a GM V-6 engine. (…) The parts make four international border crossings in all, without a single tariff levied. (…) "They already have their passports," said Jim Bovenzi, GM's executive director of global supply chain on a recent tour of the Romulus plant. "We look at North America as a borderless region." (…) The Romulus-built V-6 uses 235 parts from 100 primary suppliers. Sixty-seven ship from factories in the United States, 13 from Mexico, 8 from Canada and 12 from elsewhere in the world. Most of the electronics come from Asia. (…) The Mexican parts are cheaper, GM's Bovenzi said, but using dual suppliers reduces the risk of relying on one plant for a critical part like the engine block. (…)

The more labor intensive[5] it is to make, the more likely a part is sourced from Mexico (…). The use of lower-cost countries for more labor intensive parts is now "part of the recipe to compete in the global market," said Kristin Dziczek, vice president of industry, labor and economics at the Center for Automotive Research (CAR) in Michigan (…). North American tariffs would force automakers to move sourcing of lower-cost parts from Mexico to other cheap markets like Vietnam, Dziczek said. (…) That would be bad for Mexican suppliers, but would also hurt US suppliers (…) as shuttling parts back and forth[6] between Asia and the United States would not be cost effective[7] (…).

By Nick Carey, *Reuters Business News*, 18 November 2019.

1. part: *pièce détachée.* **2.** seasoned: *chevronné.* **3.** to ship: *transporter.* **4.** connecting rod: *bielle.* **5.** labo(u)r intensive: *nécessitant beaucoup de main-d'œuvre.* **6.** to shuttle back and forth: *faire la navette/des allers-retours.* **7.** cost-effective: *rentable.*

4 ***Compréhension.***

Summarise this text, showing the advantages and difficulties for the USA, Mexico and Canada of free trading between them. *(About 100 words, in English.)*

Document 4

Three challenges for the new EU Trade Commissioner, Mr Hogan, expressed in his introductory speech

1. WTO reform, underlying[1] trade frictions and the role of the EU

Screening[2] foreign investment, especially from China, or the establishment of a new position of trade enforcer[3] are well-suited tools to defend European interests. Indeed, it is key to deal with some of the concerns that have long been expressed by the EU, such as forced technology transfer, intellectual property rights issues, and subsidies. But these tools cannot replace dialogue. The role of a manager also has to be that of actively reaching out[4] and pursuing to build consensus. (…)

2. Fostering increased and sustainable integration of European SMEs[6] in the global economy

In many regards, Europe enjoys a privileged position in global trade. (…) Yet, more can be done to make sure these benefits are equally shared among EU companies, especially given that SMEs tend to be underrepresented in international trade. For the future, it is vital to reduce inequalities across EU countries in terms of SMEs' capacity to contribute to total exports, value-added[7] and employment. Furthermore, recent data suggests that, especially for some Eastern European countries, an increased effort will be necessary to upgrade their participation in supply chains[8]. (...)

Moreover, to facilitate SMEs' transition towards sustainable production, these interventions could also involve a systematic matching with[9] lead[10] firms embracing environmentally friendly business practices (…).

3. Advancing trade integration while promoting EU values in a coherent way

One of the key messages of Mr Hogan's introductory speech is that his mandate will expand trade opportunities while at the same time also promoting EU values. (…) For example, the inclusion of sustainable development chapters in trade agreements, a practice that the EU has promoted since 2011, represents a strong commitment to protecting labor and environmental standards. Yet, this effort risks being shadowed[11] by EU member states' limited reaction in a major crisis (…).

Iacopo Monterosa and Philipp Lamprecht,
European Centre for International Political Economy, December 2019.

1. underlying: *sous-jacent.* **2.** to screen: *filtrer.* **3.** trade enforcer: *qui gouverne les échanges commerciaux.* **4.** to reach out: *tendre la main.* **5.** to foster: *encourager.* **6.** SME: *small and medium-size enterprise.* **7.** value-added: *valeur ajoutée (= value being added, somewhat different from added value = which is already added).* **8.** supply-chain: *chaîne globale d'approvisionnement.* **9.** to match with: *amener à la hauteur de.* **10.** lead: *leader.* **11.** to shadow: *assombrir.*

5 ***Compréhension.***

Résumez cet article en analysant les trois défis auxquels l'UE est maintenant confrontée en matière d'échanges commerciaux : rôle face à l'OMC et au commerce mondial, soutien aux PME, promotion des valeurs européennes. *(En 150 mots environ, en français.)*

Exam work

Document 5

* folks: *les gars.*

6 ***Compréhension.***

– Quel groupe de pays est représenté sur l'image de gauche de ce dessin et que réclament-ils ? (voir p. 128)

– Quel pays s'exprime à droite ? Qu'est-ce qui est « clair » ? Quel effet cela a-t-il sur le groupe ASEAN Business ?

– Que dénonce ce document ?

(Environ 100 mots, en français.)

7 ***Note de synthèse.***

Vous rédigerez une synthèse des cinq documents ci-dessus concernant certains grands espaces économiques régionaux, en dégageant leurs principales caractéristiques. *(Environ 250 mots, en français.)*

8 ***Expression.*** **Write a letter.**

Vous écrivez un courrier à Mr Hogan, commissaire européen (irlandais) pour le commerce extérieur (rue de la Loi 200, 1049 Bruxelles, Belgique) à la suite de la menace du président américain de doubler les taxes à l'importation des vins français aux États-Unis. En effet, votre entreprise, Prime French Wines International, y exporte tous les ans 200 000 bouteilles de grands vins très appréciés. Vous êtes déjà concurrencé par des vins venant du Chili, de Chine, d'Afrique du Sud, etc. à des prix très inférieurs grâce à leurs coûts de main-d'œuvre plus bas et aux subventions (interdites par l'OMC) de leurs gouvernements. Vous lui demandez d'agir pour défendre les vins français qui représentent des milliers d'emplois en France.

Présentation et formules d'usage. *(Environ 200 mots, en anglais.)*

CHAPITRE

12

Emerging countries

Les pays émergents

Definition

Broadly speaking emerging economies are not too rich, not too poor and not too closed to foreign capital. A more specific definition is that they are countries whose GDP1 per inhabitant is lower than that of developed countries, but which experience quick economic growth. Most of them are in Asia, but not just. The biggest ones today are China, India, Brazil, Mexico, Indonesia or South Africa. But there are others, among which are Russia, Bulgaria, the Philippines, Thailand, Turkey or even Peru, etc. All in all, 96 countries are viewed as "emerging", according to the IMF (International Monetary Fund).

Opportunities

Emerging countries are viewed as good places to invest and do business, especially as they have not only a cheaper labour force and an emerging middle class with a rising purchasing power[2] but also an upper class who is interested in purchasing luxury products from developed countries. Today a few emerging markets have become more mature and resistant, especially Brazil, Russia, India and China, known as the BRICs. Their long-term success is partly explained by attractive stock markets.

Challenges

Emerging countries do not merely experience economic growth and dynamism but can also become fragile because they are regularly faced with crises and slumps[3]. Numerous poor economies become "emerging markets" because they have grown quickly but they remain "emerging" because they have not managed to grow steadily. These countries face various challenges and sometimes have to ask for help from the IMF when their debt is too heavy. Moreover, political instability threatens some of these countries and financial fluctuations may put them at risk. Also, numerous emerging countries do not protect property rights, are affected by corruption, vote laws designed to hinder[4] international trade, and have weak financial systems.

Asia

China is now the second largest economy in the world. The trade war with the USA gives rise to uncertainty and escalating tensions. Added this, the country is experiencing an economic slowdown. Significant amounts of money are spent to develop the state sector and to invest in public organizations which are in debt.

The **Indian** economy started emerging when the government introduced policies meant to boost market competition in the 1990s. India has taken off[5] impressively. Services (half of India's production) represent a third of the labour force and are a source of economic growth thanks to an English-speaking, low-wage graduate workforce. It is now a buoyant[6] economy.

Indonesia, the largest Muslim country in the world and the world's fourth most populous nation, developed rapidly in the 1990s. Around half its population is under 30 years old, making it a dynamic economy. **Thailand**'s economic growth has been exceptional, rising from a low-income country to an upper-income country in just one generation. It is an export-oriented emerging economy. Manufacturing is a highly developed sector in the country.

Vietnam emerges as a vibrant economy. It is the most export-oriented economy in the area. Samsung's factory in Vietnam produces half of Samsung's smartphones and accounts for 25 per cent of Vietnam's exports.

Latin America

Brazil has shown impressive growth. However, its political decisions pose a threat to its development and hamper[7] growth expectations. **Mexico** is the second largest economy in Latin America. Even though it suffered from the 2008 crisis, it is a thriving economy, but it mainly depends on exports to the USA. **Peru**'s economy is attractive and booming because of its liberal trade policies. Its primary industry sectors, which are anchovy[8] fishing and hydrocarbon production, are doing well.

Europe

Russia started experiencing stronger growth when the government defaulted on[9] the post-Soviet era debt in 1998. It also re-emerged thanks to high global petrol prices in 1999. It benefits from its exports of natural gas but also from EU subsidies. **Poland**'s very competitive economy also does well and is viewed as a growth champion.

North Africa and the Middle East

Turkey's economy has faced recessions and is vulnerable financially-speaking, but it is a promising economy. **Morocco**'s GDP growth is forecast to accelerate in the coming years as it has become a strategic hub, with political stability.

Sub-Saharan Africa

It is the next big market ready for unprecedented growth in the coming years. Sub-Saharan countries have 800 million inhabitants and now 29 of its 48 countries have stock markets. **South Africa** is the leading force on the African continent in terms of potential investment in business even if it suffers downturns[10]. **Nigeria** is a major emerging country on the continent, but it still suffers from a recession which took place in 2016. **Rwanda** has recovered[11] from the 1994 genocide and now experiences steady economic growth. **Ethiopia** is now emerging from troubled times with an incredible GPD growth rate thanks to food exports but also economic policies, cheap electricity and industrial parks which attract foreign investors.

1. GDP (Gross Domestic Product): *PIB (produit intérieur brut).*
2. purchasing power: *pouvoir d'achat.*
3. slump: *depression.*
4. to hinder: *entraver.*
5. to take off: *décoller.*
6. buoyant: *dynamique.*
7. to hamper: *freiner.*
8. anchovy: *anchois.*
9. to default on: *ne pas payer.*
10. downturn: *récession.*
11. to recover: *se remettre.*

Repérer les notions essentielles

Answer the following questions.

a. What defines an emerging economy?
b. Explain what kind of difficulties emerging countries sometimes face.
c. Which Asian economies are thriving today and why?
d. What problems do Latin American emerging economies face?
e. Why are Mexico's economic prospects threatened?
f. Why do oil-producing countries face growth problems today?
g. Why is Sub-Saharan Africa such a good opportunity for business?

Résumer le texte en français

Faites un résumé de ce texte en *150 mots environ*, en mettant en valeur les éléments qui stimulent ou freinent les économies émergentes.

Approfondir

Choose one emerging country and find information about it. You can draw up a fact sheet about its characteristics (capital, official language, head of state, population numbers, birth and death rates, surface area, GDP per capita, GDP growth, imports and exports, industries, inflation rate, literacy rate, etc.)

Pair work: Present your work to your partner and then compare the countries you have chosen.

Class presentation: Present your work to your class with a slide show.

Lexical work

billion	milliard
to benefit an economy	profiter à une économie
boom	expansion, essor
to boost	stimuler
to bring about	avoir pour conséquence, entraîner
buoyant	prospère
capital-intensive	à forte intensité capitalistique
cutting-edge	à la pointe du progrès
double-digit	à deux chiffres
to drop	chuter
English-speaking	anglophone
to evolve	évoluer
export-driven	basé sur les exportations
to face problems	faire face à des difficultés
fast-growing	à croissance rapide
foreign-produced	produit à l'étranger
to foster competition	favoriser la concurrence
to fuel	alimenter
GDP growth	croissance du PIB
ground-breaking	innovant
growth rate	taux de croissance
to implement a policy	mettre en place une politique
innovation-based	basé sur l'innovation
investment	investissement
knowledge-based	basé sur la maîtrise de connaissances
labour-intensive	nécessitant une main-d'œuvre abondante
to lag (behind)	être à la traîne
manufacturing-based	basé sur l'industrie
to overcome hurdles	surmonter des obstacles
to prevent	empêcher
rebound	rebondir
to recover from	se remettre de
service-oriented	basé sur les services
to soar	monter en flèche
to solve	résoudre
standard of living	niveau de vie
steady	stable
strain	tension
to strengthen	renforcer

Lexical work

• to sustain growth	faire durer la croissance
• to take off	décoller
• technology-intensive	à forte intensité technologique
• to threaten	menacer
• to thrive	prospérer
• up-and-coming	prometteur
• to weaken	affaiblir
• well-educated	qui a fait des études supérieures
• to worsen	empirer

Use the list

1 Fill in the gaps with compound adjectives taken from the list. A definition of each adjective is given to help you.

a. Ethiopia's ... sectors are textiles and garments, leather, sugar, flowers and cement. (*which requires numerous workers)*

b. African firms largely lag behind because they lack … sectors. (*which uses or produces new technologies*)

c. Even if Malaysian workers are …, firms have trouble finding employees with the right skills. (*who have a university diploma*)

d. Africa must digitise its economies and aim for … growth according to a UN report. (*said of a number with two figures*)

e. Morocco has … activities, like agro-processing, textile and leather. (*which is specialised in exports*)

f. Egypt is often viewed as an … emerging market. (*promising and rising*)

g. Firms in … regions of Southern and East Africa have a competitive edge. (*who speak English*)

2 Use verbs from the list to translate the following sentences.

a. Ces pays doivent faire face à des conflits politiques.

b. Le Brésil ne s'est pas remis de la dernière crise.

c. Les pays pauvres doivent surmonter divers obstacles.

d. Le gouvernement met en place des réformes économiques.

e. Cela stimule la concurrence et profite à l'économie.

f. Les investissements entraînent davantage de croissance.

g. La situation politique a empiré.

h. Quelques pays sont à la traîne et ne décollent pas.

Grammar work

Les différents emplois de *as*

› Aide-mémoire grammatical, p. 166

Analysez et traduisez les exemples suivants :

1. Countries such as Malaysia and the Philippines have developed recently.
2. Thailand is now viewed as a source of cheap products.
3. As India lacks good roads, farmers find it difficult to sell their products.
4. As India becomes richer, so the gap between the poor and the rich is growing.

■ **Dans ces phrases, *as* est-il une préposition (qui introduit un groupe nominal) ou une conjonction (qui introduit une proposition) ? Quels sont ses différents sens ?**

1 **Complétez les phrases suivantes en traduisant l'expression donne entre paranthèses à l'aide de *as*.**

a. The advent of China … is a challenge for all countries. *(comme puissance mondiale)*
b. … are overcrowded, roads are congested all the time. *(Étant donné que les grands villes asiatiques)*
c. … Lagos have grown significantly. *(Des capitals telles que)*
d. India's young graduates may work … … they speak English fluently. *(comme employés de centre d'appel / puisque)*
e. … is developing at great speed, banks are lending more and more money to its entrepreneurs. *(Tandis que le Maroc)*

Since, for, ago, during, while

› Aide-mémoire grammatical, p. 180

Analysez et traduisez les exemples suivants en observant particulièrement les temps utilisés, puis traduisez-les.

1. China has been the second biggest economy in the world for a few years now.
2. Economic growth in sub-Saharan Africa has averaged 3.6% since 2018.
3. A few years ago, China became the world's leading emitter of CO_2.
4. Brazil's economy greatly suffered during the recession.
5. We visited a shipbuilding site while we were in Peru.
6. They stayed in Turkey for three weeks.

■ **Que remarquez-vous au sujet de la traduction de *for* ?**

2 **Complétez les phrases suivantes avec la traduction en anglais des expressions entre parenthèses.**

a. …, Bulgaria was one of the world's poorest countries. *(Il y a 20 ans)*
b. Vietnam's high-tech firms will enjoy a boom … . *(pendant de nombreuses années)*
c. … greenhouses in Ethiopia have boosted this country's exports of fresh cut flowers. *(Depuis 2012)*
d. … is setting up trade barriers, African leaders are launching an African free-trade zone. *(Pendant que les États-Unis)*
e. … the economic and political crisis in Colombia in 2018, people fled the country. *(Au cours de)*

3 **Complétez les phrases suivantes en utilisant *for*, *since* ou *ago*, combiné avec le repère proposé entre parenthèses.**

a. China has produced inexpensive goods … now. *(many years)*
b. Vietnamese smartphone brands have been competing Samsung with cheaper products … . *(2014)*
c. Thailand started reforming its economy more than … . *(two decades)*
d. Ethiopia's economy has been based on agriculture … . *(a long time)*
e. Brazil's economy has lagged behind … . *(the 2014-2017 crisis)*

4 **Posez une question commençant par *How long* ou *How long ago* sur chaque phrase de l'exercice précédent, et traduisez le tout.**

Exemples de questions : *How long has India been independent?*
How long ago did India become independent?

5 **Traduisez en anglais les phrases suivantes.**

a. Leur PIB a augmenté de 6 % au cours des trois dernières décennies.
b. – Depuis combien de temps la Bulgarie fait-elle partie de l'UE ?
– Depuis plusieurs années.
c. Depuis les années 2000, des pays comme le Ghana connaissent un essor important.
d. Il n'y a pas très longtemps, comme tous ces pays étaient très pauvres, les enfants ne pouvaient pas aller à l'école.
e. Pendant dix ans, notre fournisseur égyptien nous a vendu ce coton comme étant le meilleur.
f. – Cela fait combien de temps que la Pologne est entrée dans l'UE ?
– 16 ans.

Exam work

Document 1

Looking for growth? Emerging Asia is the present and future

Emerging Asia accounts for two-thirds of global growth currently. The world's middle class is at a tipping point[1] – by 2020, a majority of the world population will be classified as middle class or above, according to the Brookings Institute. Asia will lead the increase in middle-class populations, as those in the West stagnate. The domestic consumption story is compelling[2]. We forecast global growth at 3.4%. Without emerging Asia's contribution, it would be closer to 1.1%, the weakest performance in decades (with the exception of 2009). Even excluding China and India, emerging Asia's contribution to world growth today already exceeds that of the US and is three times the size of the euro area. (…)

The region's outperformance[3] reflects its reduced growth dependence on Western economies and its boost to domestic demand instead. China-ASEAN [Association of South-East Asian Nations] has been one of the world's fastest-growing trade corridors. Asia's rising middle class will offer a growing pool[4] of consumer demand to counter the weakening trend in the West for many years to come. A growing middle class will also mean greater south-south or intra-EM *(emerging market)* trade.

(…) In a world of stagnating growth, the contrast with emerging Asia stands out. We expect selected Asian economies to grow by at least 7% in the coming years – roughly the pace[5] at which an economy can double in size every decade. The region's likely '7% Club' members in the 2020s include India, Bangladesh, Vietnam and the Philippines. (…)

There are risks to the growth outlook[6], however. Ageing populations in advanced economies and some Asian economies will increasingly weigh[7] on global growth. However, the growing global middle class is likely to at least practically offset[8] this demographic drag[9].

Countries in South Asia still enjoy a demographic dividend. For them, the threat from rising anti-globalisation sentiment and the increase in factory automation are key concerns. However, the world is turning more service-oriented, with the services sector now accounting for around 65% of total world GDP – and countries that focus on upgrading skills will have an edge[10]. Malaysia, the Philippines and Indonesia are doing well on skills indicators, while India, Thailand and countries need to focus more on this.

David Mann, *Standard Chartered*, 16 August 2019.

1. tipping point: *tournant*. 2. compelling: *impressionnant*. 3. outperformance: *performance extraordinaire*. 4. pool: *réservoir*. 5. pace: *vitesse*. 6. outlook: *perspective*. 7. to weigh: *peser*. 8. to offset: *compenser*. 9. drag: *lenteur*. 10. edge: *avantage*.

1 ***Compréhension.*** Qu'est-ce que l'auteur, qui est analyste financier, explique au sujet de la situation économique des pays émergents asiatiques ? *(Environ 150 mots, en français.)*

Document 2

Africa needs to seize this golden chance

(...) Significant progress has been achieved in Africa over the past decade (...). In countries such as Ethiopia, people are urging[1] their governments to push forward with ambitious reforms. The spread of new technologies and smarter financial regulation, notably in Kenya, has opened opportunities for digital financial services, providing millions more people, including women and small-scale entrepreneurs, with economic opportunities. Low-carbon energy investments (...) can help unleash[2] growth. (...)

Countries need rules of law[3] that encourage competition and are enforced[4]. Sound money, spending discipline, clean water and dependable[5] electricity are all required for progress. Taxes and regulation must be balanced and encourage sustainable growth—with an early focus on more productive, market-based agricultural sectors. Adequate capital is important, and human capital is the most valuable. (...)

Many countries in Africa have a long way to go to create these conditions. Too often, top-down[6] and unfocused policies and programmes leave space for vested interests[7]—both domestic and foreign—to further[8] their own agendas and resist opening markets, making Africa's business environment less attractive for investment. Policy planners are too often influenced by these vested interests. This has held back development, leaving fragility and conflict for many millions of people.

A key obstacle to foreign investment is that some of Africa's biggest economies—for example, Nigeria, South Africa, and Angola—have not performed well in recent years. Another challenge is that cross-border trade and investment, which is vital for growth, isn't making enough progress to lift Africa's average growth rate. (...)

Four areas need urgent attention. First, reforming state-owned enterprises and de-monopolising markets for greater competition. (...) Second, Africa needs to reduce barriers to cross-border trade. Red tape[9] and excessive regulation keep goods, services, ideas, and resources from flowing freely among countries. (...) Third, government debts and investments need to be more transparent. This will give people more voice in the contracts and commitments[10] made by their governments. (...) Fourth, the region must address "learning poverty". Our recent study reported on children's ability at the age of 10 to read a basic story. In some African countries, as many as 80 per cent can't do this. (...)

By David Malpass, blogs.worldbank.org, 20 January 2020.

1. to urge: *pousser*. **2.** to unleash: *stimuler*. **3.** rules of law: *règles de droit*. **4.** to enforce: *faire appliquer*. **5.** dependable: *fiable*. **6.** top-down: *qui vient d'en haut*. **7.** vested interests: *intérêts particuliers*. **8.** to further: *promouvoir*. **9.** red tape: *paperasse*. **10.** commitment: *engagement*.

2 ***Compréhension.*** What is necessary for African economies to develop and what obstacles have to be faced?

Document 3

Latin America's 'missing middles'

Once the world's most prosperous emerging-market region, Latin America is in danger of being overtaken[1] by its peers, owing to its sluggish[2] and unevenly distributed growth. To break that pattern and make growth more dynamic and inclusive, Latin American economies must fill two "missing middles": a lack of medium-size firms that can foster[3] competition, and too few middle-class consumers whose spending could create much-needed demand. (...)

Despite reform initiatives and poverty reduction, the region's economies are struggling. GDP growth in the region averaged just 2.8% per year between 2000 and 2016, well below the 4.8% average rate in 56 other emerging economies. Moreover, labor-force expansion accounted for 72% of Latin America's growth over that period. As fertility rates fall, the region will need to increase productivity to compensate.

Although Latin America is home to some highly productive global companies, it lacks the backbone[4] of midsize firms that drive innovation and competition – and create productive, well-paying jobs – in more vibrant economies. (...) Compounding[5] the problem, many Latin American economies have a long tail of[6] small, often informal companies that collectively employ millions, but that hold back growth because of their low productivity.

Because weak productivity keeps wages low, Latin America also has too few upwardly mobile consumers whose rising disposable income[7] could help drive demand and investment on a sustainable basis. In addition, high indirect taxes further[8] reduce people's purchasing power by making consumer goods more expensive. (...)

Worse, economically vulnerable groups have limited ability to borrow and save. Less than half of the population in Mexico and Colombia has access to a bank account, and the lack of consumer credit across the region significantly affects consumption patterns. (...)

The dearth[9] of middle-class consumers limits demand and growth opportunities for domestic businesses, which provide the majority of jobs in a modern economy. It also delays[10] the development of more complex or differentiated goods and services, which are typically characterized by higher value added and productivity.

By Jaana Remes and Homi Kharas,
Project Syndicate, 21 August 2019.

1. overtaken: *dépassé.* **2.** sluggish: *morose.* **3.** to foster: *favoriser.* **4.** backbone: *colonne vertébrale.* **5.** to compound: *aggraver.* **6.** a long tail of: *toute une série de.* **7.** income: *revenu.* **8.** further: *davantage.* **9.** dearth: *pénurie.* **10.** to delay: *retarder.*

3 ***Compréhension.*** Explain what the "missing middles" are in Latin America. Why do they pose a problem? *(About 150 word, in English.)*

Document 4

How Poland's 'golden age' of economic growth is going unreported

During the current global economic slow-down, Poland stands out as a European growth champion. With an uninterrupted pace[1] of high growth averaging 4.2% per annum between 1992-2019, Poland is steadily catching up with[2] Western Europe and has become the seventh largest economy in the EU with a total GDP of €524 billion. (…)

The strength and resilience[3] of the Polish economy can be attributed to its large domestic market, early and deep economic reforms and prudent policies, with consistent[4] EU strategy being the top priority, serving as an important discipline for political and economic integration. A vibrant entrepreneurial landscape of small and medium-sized enterprises (SMEs) benefiting from a large domestic market and strong competitive advantages in neighbouring European countries is also an important source of growth. Large inflows[5] of immigrants from Ukraine and Commonwealth of Independent States (CIS) countries have supported the labour market, exports' competitiveness, the real estate[6] market and domestic consumption. Poland's resilience was proven during the financial crisis of 2008/09 when it was the only EU country to avoid recession. (…)

In terms of infrastructure investments, Poland has been the biggest beneficiary of EU funds from 2007 to 2013 and from 2014 to 2020, with €102 billion and €106 billion of funds received and to be received respectively for each period. (…)

The construction and real estate sectors are booming, driven by infrastructure projects as well as growing business activities and expansion of global service centres in Poland, with international companies such as IBM, Citi Group, Credit Swiss and Capgemini relocating[7] part of their operations to Poland. (…)

Poland also managed to find robust innovative sources of growth in the 'New economy.' One of the fastest growing sectors is video game development. The success of CD Projekt, now a company with a market capitalisation of over €5bn surging[8] almost ten-fold[9] over the last three years, triggered[10] an impressive growth in the number of video game developers in the country. Currently, there are over 300 game developing companies operating in Poland and over 20 are listed[11] on the Warsaw Stock Exchange.

By Eglé Fredriksson, *Euronews*, 25 June 2019.

1. pace: *rythme.* **2.** to catch up with: *rattraper.* **3.** resilience: *résistance.* **4.** consistent: *cohérent.* **5.** inflow: *afflux.* **6.** real estate: immobilier. **7.** to relocate: *délocaliser.* **8.** to surge: *augmenter fortement.* **9.** tenfold: *multiplié par dix.* **10.** to trigger: *déclencher.* **11.** listed: *coté.*

4 ***Compréhension.*** Quelles sont les caractéristiques de la croissance économique de la Pologne ? *(150 mots environ, en français.)*

Document 5

Paresh Nath, *"BRICS Economies"*, politicalcartoons.com, March 2015.

5 ***Expression.*** Describe the cartoon and say why, according to this cartoon, BRIC countries have difficulty taking off. *(About 100 words, in English.)*

6 ***Compréhension.*** En vous appuyant sur les documents 1 à 5, vous ferez une synthèse dans laquelle vous dégagerez les défis et les opportunités des pays émergents aujourd'hui. *(250 mots environ, en français.)*

7 ***Expression.* Write a letter.**

Vous êtes importateur de fleurs en gros (Flower-Direct). Pour la Saint-Valentin, vous devez fournir en roses rouges les boutiques de vos distributeurs fleuristes.

Vous écrivez un courrier en anglais à une ferme horticole *Rosebud Farm* (Adresse : Rosebud Farm, P.O. box 2541, Addis Abeba, Ethiopia). Vous expliquez que votre choix s'est porté sur cette exploitation pour ses pratiques éthiques et écologiques. Vous commandez 800 cartons de 10 sachets de 20 roses, dont la moitié contiendra des roses avec de longues tiges (*stems*) ; les épines (*thorns*) et les pétales (*petals*) disgracieux seront coupés et les roses doivent être expédiées le 12 février.

Vous indiquez l'aéroport de la livraison : Heathrow Cargo Terminal, Longford TW6, UK, et le nom de la société réceptrice du chargement (Compact Freight).

Présentation et formules d'usage.

(150 mots environ dans le corps de la lettre, en anglais.)

CHAPITRE

13

Social protection and demography

La protection sociale et la démographie

Social protection

Social protection concerns healthcare, retirement, unemployment and family needs. Welfare programmes help people cope with[1] poverty, housing problems, unemployment and health issues but also retirement. This protection is provided by the state, companies and/or charities.

Demographic evolutions

Today's world is ageing quickly. The share of people over 65 is increasing. Better access to birth control had led to falling fertility rates. Medical advances have increased life expectancy. Soon, the elderly will outnumber[2] the young and not only in rich countries. Even in China, there are more people over 60 than under 15. The consequence of this demographic time bomb is a growing concern[3] for governments. As people live longer, it poses new challenges in terms of pension funding.

Healthcare in the USA and in the UK

Social protection is not as extensive in the USA as in other large economies. Healthcare insurance is provided by the federal state, private medical insurance companies, and employers. Private insurance has become extremely expensive because of high medical costs. *Medicare* is free medical insurance for people over 65 and *Medicaid* for low-income families. President Obama's administration's *Affordable Care Act*, which made it compulsory[4] for all Americans to get private, reasonably-priced health insurance, is threatened. Health insurance has become a nightmare. In 2018, 30.4 million Americans had no health coverage at all. One in four people decided not to see a doctor for cost reasons.

In the UK, the National Health Service (NHS) provides all British citizens with free medical care, paid for by income tax. In order to face the pressure these growing costs create, successive governments have recently encouraged greater participation from the private sector and charities. With an aging population, the system is increasingly strained[5], giving rise to crises in hospitals which cannot admit all patients. The problem is who will foot the bill[6] for long-term care in an ageing society. Over the past 15 years, the British welfare system has cut spending on working-age, low-income families, and spent more on pensioners. This has given rise to poverty. As a result, 4.1 million children live in relative poverty.

Unemployment protection in the USA and in the UK

In the USA, workers who become unemployed through no fault of their own can benefit from unemployment compensation. The federal government provides money thanks to taxes but conditions vary by state. Most Americans are employed but many jobs are not well-paid. Employees have lost so much bargaining power[7] that wages do not rise enough. A new social class has appeared: the working poor.

In the UK, *Universal Credit* is a system which supports those who work on a low income or are out of work. The unemployment rate in Britain is ultra-low, but wages have remained low for many years. However, today wages are rising again. Austerity policies have made the conditions to get job seekers' allowances more difficult. The authorities want to demonstrate they are tough on benefit claimants and so have organized a complex set of penalties. These penalties have been blamed for causing stress, ill-health, hunger and food-bank dependency among vulnerable job seekers.

Pensions in the USA and in the UK

Over the last thirty years, many countries and companies have altered[8] the way they fund pensions. *Defined benefit schemes* (DB), which are predetermined plans offered by employers, are now replaced by *defined contribution schemes* (DC) that depend on how much workers saved in investment funds. Also, social security plans are less generous on the whole and governments have raised the retirement age.

In the USA, *Social Security* is a federal system that provides pensions for Americans from age 62. However, the federal government is facing a huge funding gap for pensions and so most Americans rely on[9] private and company retirement accounts and work longer to be able to afford their expenses. Some companies offer no pension funds at all. The retirement age is now 67 but if workers retire earlier, payments are reduced. On the whole, workers work longer than thirty years ago and mortality rates for American men in their 60s have declined by 40% since 1980. For women, they have fallen by 30%. There are more and more elderly workers in this country.

Actually[10] 20% of over-65 workers can't afford to retire, often the less educated. They even have difficulty finding qualified jobs as companies prefer young workers. This form of discrimination is called "ageism".

In the UK, retirees benefit from three sources for their pensions: state pensions, individual funds and company funds. The state pension age is set at 66. You need 35 years of contributions to get a full state pension. You also have the option of postponing[11] your state pension to get more later. If workers have contributed enough money in the different schemes, they can retire earlier. But many British people actually retire later. The retirement age will continue to rise and those in their 20s will probably retire when they are 70. There might not be state pensions left[12] by that time.

Calculating pension

It is complicated for workers to calculate at what age they will eventually be able to retire. They use online calculators to do so and they must also keep track of all the company plans they contributed to. This is especially important since people will have different jobs in their working lives. Also, it has been calculated that a third of self-employed workers have no provisions for retirement. If they are not careful, they are at a risk of poverty in old age. This is an alarming prospect.

1. to cope with: *faire face à.*
2. to outnumber: *surpasser en nombre.*
3. concern: *inquiétude.*
4. compulsory: *obligatoire.*
5. strained: *sous tension.*
6. to foot the bill: *payer la facture.*
7. bargaining power: *pouvoir de négociation.*
8. to alter: *transformer.*
9. to rely on: *dépendre de.*
10. actually: *en fait.*
11. to postpone: *repousser à plus tard.*
12. left: *qui restent.*

Repérer les notions essentielles

Answer the following questions.

a. What is the aim of social protection?
b. Why do we talk about a demographic time bomb?
c. What characterises the health care system in the USA?
d. What are the problems with the British and American healthcare systems?
e. What characterises unemployment protection in the UK and in the USA?
f. Why do people increasingly have to work after 65?
g. Why is it complicated for people to find out how much pension they will get?

Résumer le texte en français

Résumez ce texte en *150 mots environ*.

Approfondir

Browse the web to find information about the consequences of ageing populations in terms of economic, political, cultural and social impacts. Write quick notes in English.

Lexical work

• to age	vieillir
• ageism, age discrimination	âgisme, discrimination par l'âge
• benefit	avantage social, allocation
• birth rate	taux de natalité
• to be badly off / well off	être pauvre / riche
• to be entitled to	avoir droit à
• to be on the dole	toucher des allocations chômage
• to be on welfare	recevoir de l'aide sociale
• burden	fardeau
• care	soin(s)
• census	recensement
• claimant	ayant droit
• compensation, benefit	indemnité, allocation
• to contribute	cotiser
• to cope with	faire face à, affronter
• cost of living	coût de la vie
• death rate	taux de mortalité
• to die	mourir
• disablement pension	pension d'invalidité
• disease, illness	maladie
• to draw a pension	toucher une retraite
• elderly people	personnes âgées
• family allowance	allocations familiales
• to fund	financer
• GP (general practitioner)	médecin généraliste
• holiday with pay	congé payé
• income tax	impôt sur le revenu
• labour shortage	pénurie de main-d'œuvre
• life expectancy	espérance de vie
• life span	durée de vie
• maternity/paternity/sick leave	congé maternité/paternité/maladie
• means-tested	indexé sur les revenus
• minimum wage	salaire minimum
• nursing home	maison de retraite médicalisée
• of child-bearing age	en âge de procréer
• the old	les personnes âgées
• overpopulation	surpopulation
• to pay contributions	verser des cotisations
• pensioner / retiree	retraité
• pension scheme/plan	régime/système de retraite

Lexical work

• poverty	pauvreté
• to protect/guarantee sb's rights	protéger les droits de qqn
• purchasing/buying power	pouvoir d'achat
• to retire	partir à la retraite
• retirement age	l'âge de la retraite
• savings	épargne
• senior citizen / elderly person	personne âgée
• to shelter	arbiter, protéger
• sickness benefit	prestation maladie
• social worker	assistant(e) social(e)
• standard of living	niveau de vie
• to stay healthy	rester en bonne santé
• to take early retirement	partir en pré-retraite
• tax allowance/rebate	abattement fiscal
• the haves and the have-nots	les riches et les pauvres
• the homeless	les sans-abris, les sans domicile fixe
• unemployment benefit / compensation	allocation chômage
• universal health coverage	CMU
• volunteer work	bénévolat
• welfare state	État providence
• the young	les jeunes

Use the list

1 Make 10 different compound nouns by matching the following nouns together and translate them. Mind the word order.

age – age – birth – compensation – discrimination – volunteer – home – leave – life – maternity – nursing – power – purchasing – rate – rebate – retirement – span – tax – unemployment – work

2 Match the verbs from the list on the left with the words from the list on the right and translate the expressions.

a. to be	1. holidays with pay
b. to cope with	2. on welfare
c. to be entitled to	3. healthy
d. to contribute to	4. poverty
e. to stay	5. a pension scheme

Grammar work

Exprimer une rupture entre présent et passé, avec sujet + *used to* + base verbale (V)

› Aide-mémoire grammatical, p. 208

Analysez et traduisez les exemples suivants :

1. People used to work long hours for very little pay.
2. Before the implementation of Roosevelt's New Deal, American children did not use to be protected by the federal state.
3. What financial aid did poor people use to get before the creation of the welfare state?

1 Transformez les phrases suivantes en utilisant la structure sujet + *used to* + V, puis traduisez-les.

a. … *(old people's homes / to be)* much worse?
b. Mary says that for old people … *(things / to be)* much worse a hundred years ago.
c. … *(They / not to have)* state pensions, so … *(many of them / to work)* until they died.
d. … *(Fertility rates / be)* much higher a century ago.
e. … (*People / to die*) at a younger age a hundred years ago?
f. Before 1929, … (*Americans / not to get*) federal pensions.
g. … (*There / to be*) fewer old people in China in the 20th century.
h. … (*Women / to work*) during the Second World War?
i. … (*Most women / not to have*) maternity leaves in the 1970s in the UK.

Le cas possessif

› Aide-mémoire grammatical, p. 172

Analysez et traduisez les exemples suivants :

1. "Where is Ann's medical file?"
   "I think this one is hers."
   "No, it is mine."
2. The secretary mixed up my colleagues' pension documents with the manager's.
3. The company's pension policy has changed.
4. Wednesday's meeting will be held in room 8.
5. "Whose decision is that?"
   "It was Mr. Hadley's."

- **Quelles formes d'expression de la possession apparaissent ici ?**

2 Écrivez une nouvelle phrase en mettant les mots soulignés au cas possessif.

Ex.: The talks last week were very useful. ➡ Last week's talks were very useful.

a. The meeting next month has been postponed.
b. The social policy of the government has been criticised.
c. The success of both systems is the result of good thinking.
d. The treatments we ordered for elderly patients are very efficient.
e. The needs and complaints of pensioners should be taken into consideration.
f. The questions sent in by Mr. James must be answered at once.
g. For the conference of this year, we will discuss family allowances.
h. The hospital bills of these children will be refunded.

Exercice de synthèse

3 Traduisez en anglais les phrases ci-dessous. Veiller à utiliser « *used to* + base verbale » pour les actions révolues.

a. Avant le licenciement de sa femme, il se levait tous les matins pour préparer le café.
b. La dette des jeunes est trop élevée.
c. Est-ce que les gens partaient à la retraite plus jeunes autrefois ?
d. Il faut écouter les remarques des employés.
e. Le taux de pauvreté a baissé. Autrefois, il était plus élevé.
f. La conférence de demain portera sur les retraites.
g. Autrefois, il y avait assez d'argent pour payer les retraites.
h. Il y a longtemps, les personnes âgées dépendaient de leurs enfants.
i. Les employés de la maison de retraite sont en grève.
j. La population du Japon vieillit.
k. Autrefois, les gens n'avaient pas de congés maladie.
l. Les allocations ne sont plus ce qu'elles étaient.
m. Les Américains ont moins de protection sociale qu'avant.
n. Son allocation chômage a été payée. Celle de sa femme aussi.

Exam work

Document 1

Millennials urged to[1] consider[2] pension saving

Millennials spend £1,770 a month on average, more than twice as much as the annual state pension allowance they are likely to get, according to research. Pension adviser *Profile Pensions* found millennials spent the equivalent of 242 per cent of the monthly state pension allowance each month, with a chunk[3] of this going towards takeaways or a night out. (…)

If millennials cut the amount spent on nights out by half they would have an extra £100 each month that they could put into a private pension instead, the adviser stated.

The research showed, on average, the largest proportion of millennials' spending went on rent[4] (£772). This was followed by nights out (£212), groceries[5] (£206), and utility bills[6] (£143). (…)

Michelle Gribbin, chief investment officer at *Profile Pensions*, said: "Although monthly expenses can vary from generation to generation, we wanted to showcase[7] to those still climbing the career ladder[8] the necessity of preparing for their financial future early, by highlighting just how much of their current lifestyles they would have to change in order to live comfortably in retirement."

Kay Ingram, director of public policy at LEBC, said there needs to be a balance between saving for retirement but also enjoying life and paying for other expenses[9]. She said: "If we were to advise all our millennials clients to stop going out and not have any takeaways but instead to save this money into a pension scheme, then life would be very boring.

"Instead millennials could cut back on one night out each month and consider putting the money saved towards their pension or even to save for a deposit[10] on a house." She added people need to think about saving for retirement sooner rather than later, as in later life when they have more money to save, pension tax rules could hinder how much they can contribute to their pension pot[11].

"The money individuals put in their pension pot now will earn them a lot more in compound interest[12] than the money contributed in their 50s," she explained.

"Due to pension legislation, it would be a mistake for someone to put off[13] saving into a pension until they are much older and earning a higher wage."

By Amy Austin, *The Financial Times*, 10 May 2019.

1. urged to: *poussé à*. **2.** to consider: *envisager*. **3.** chunk: *part*. **4.** rent: *loyer*. **5.** groceries: *produits alimentaires*. **6.** utility bills: *factures d'eau, d'électricité, etc.* **7.** to showcase: *mettre en avant*. **8.** career ladder: *échelons dans l'entreprise*. **9.** expense: *dépense*. **10.** deposit: *(ici) apport pour un achat immobilier*. **11.** pension pot: *épargne retraite*. **12.** compound interest: *intérêt incorporé au capital*. **13.** to put off: *remettre à plus tard*.

1 ***Compréhension.*** How do millennials spend their money and how should they use it instead according to the writer? Why? *(About 150 words, in English.)*

2 ***Expression.*** Do some research about student debt today and explain why it is a problem. *(Write about 80 words, in English.)*

Document 2

Retirement should not mean hardship[1] – but many older Americans live in poverty

(…) Elderly poverty was supposed to be a thing of the past. Social security supposedly wiped out[2] the scourge[3] of old-age penury, signaling one of the great social-policy triumphs of the modern era. But this is far from the whole story. Inequality, which has grown markedly in Europe and North America since the 1970s, has widened the gap[4] between the secure and insecure in all age groups, and has exposed American seniors to financial distress in ways that often go unnoticed. According to research from the University of Massachusetts Boston, material hardship bedevils[5] millions of Americans (…) who are over 65. (…)

In the US, the poverty line was set by the Department of Agriculture as a multiple of the price of a typical "food basket" in the 1960s. It has been updated and benchmarked[6] for family size every year since. The incidence of poverty for Americans over 65 has declined significantly, even further if measured against the poverty rate in the 1930s and 40s. Social security expenditures[7] have played a crucial role in bringing about this improvement. As this safety net spread and the benefits available increased, poverty moved decisively downward.

We tend to think of inequality as shaping the lives of children and working-age adults, depending on their educational attainment[8]. But the trajectory of inequality powerfully affects older people as well. Their lives in old age are a natural extension of their experiences in the prime working years. Social security is, in the end, insufficient to protect a surprisingly large number of older Americans from poverty.

The US is an outlier[9] in terms of elderly poverty – in the wrong direction. Retirement expert Teresa Ghilarducci, a professor at the New School, points out that a higher proportion of older Americans are below the threshold[10] set by the Organization for Economic Cooperation and Development than all other advanced economies in the world except for Australia and Switzerland.

By Katherine Newman, *The Guardian*, 24 May 2019.

1. hardship: *épreuve*. **2.** to wipe out: *éliminer*. **3.** scourge: *fléau*. **4.** to widen the gap: *élargir le fossé*. **5.** to bedevil: *rendre infernal*. **6.** to benchmark: *comparer à*. **7.** expenditure: *dépense*. **8.** educational attainment: *niveau d'étude*. **9.** outlier: *cas particulier*. **10.** threshold (of poverty): *seuil (de pauvreté)*.

3 ***Compréhension.*** What is the situation like for some American retirees today? *(About 150 words, in English.)*

Document 3

Age is no bar[1] in the modern world of work

As life expectancy rises, embracing older workers is going to be the next big thing in business

The three phases of life are increasingly a thing of the past. Where once[2] working lives slotted neatly into[3] the model of education, employment and then retirement, the simplicity of that segmentation is being challenged by changing norms of the workforce.

Increasing numbers of workers, nearing[4] their long-imagined transition into retirement, seem to be actively postponing[5] the moment at which they down tools[6]. Newly released figures[7] from the Office for National Statistics (ONS) have shown that there are over a million more over 50s in part-time work than a decade ago. And with nine out of 10 employers reporting difficulties hiring workers, there's likely to be a growing market for their talents as bosses extend their searches to older people, including those who are willing[8] to take on part-time responsibilities.

The ending of the three phases of working life isn't simply down to[9] people living longer or financial necessity – though those are certainly important factors – but also to an increasing desire to maintain a purposeful[10] life. One survey of British retirees over 50 found that 85 per cent of them felt they'd retired too young – stopping working had left a void[11] that they subsequently regretted. (…)

Already, we are seeing people in their 50s and 60s looking ahead to[12] a retirement lasting 30 years, choosing instead to build second careers that they can maintain into their 70s or beyond. Freed from the financial burden of young children, they can prioritise flexibility, shorter working hours or more rewarding[13] jobs in areas such as charity work or teaching. Many do it for no money at all, volunteering[14] behind the till[15] in charity shops or showing people round National Trust properties.

However, it's the next generation where the effect of living longer will really be felt, and the financial imperative will start to bite[16]. In the West, more than half of the children born in 2016 have a life expectancy of more than 100 years. Then there is the oft-repeated claim[17] that young people today are the first generation to be poorer than their parents. Certainly property prices are changing the way they plan for the future. It is why 44 per cent of under 30s say they expect to be working well into their 70s[18].

By Bruce Daisley, abridged from *The Daily Telegraph*, 9 July 2019.

1. bar: *obstacle*. **2.** once: *autrefois*. **3.** slotted neatly into: *bien calé dans*. **4.** to near: *approcher*. **5.** to postpone: *retarder*. **6.** to down tools: *cesser le travail*. **7.** figure: *chiffre*. **8.** willing: *désireux*. **9.** to be down to: *être dû à*. **10.** purposeful: *utile*. **11.** void: *vide*. **12.** to look ahead to: *anticiper*. **13.** rewarding: *gratifiant*. **14.** to volunteer: *faire du bénévolat*. **15.** till: *caisse*. **16.** to bite: *faire mal*. **17.** oft-repeated claim: *affirmation souvent répétée*. **18.** well into their 70s: *bien après 70 ans*.

4 ***Compréhension.*** Is the future dark for elderly workers according to the writer of this article? Using information from this article, explain why or why not. *(About 150 words, in English.)*

Document 4

While the UK dithers over[1] social care, China is starting to deliver[2]

(…) China is experiencing rapid ageing as life expectancy rises and, due to the one-child policy, birth rates have fallen. As a result, there are more people over the age of 60 than under 15. Within the next three decades, China will have the oldest population on the planet: by 2050, 39% of Chinese people will be over 65.

At both national and provincial level, the government has embarked on a massive expansion of care provision[3] to support family care and help people remain[4] in their own homes. The policy is to grow the homecare and community care market. (…) In the past three or four years the Chinese care sector has seen explosive growth in services from homecare to retirement communities. One example is a network of more than 200 care hubs[5] that has been established across Shanghai.

The hubs provide social activities and connections, rehabilitation[6], information and advice as well as respite and early stage dementia care. Publicly funded and owned but privately operated, they are playing a key role in supporting older people in their own homes.

Technology is also an important part of China's plans. That might include things like smart beds that can monitor[7] sleeping patterns, and enable social connections via a screen that can be used for Skype and other communications; screening[8] and rehabilitation equipment; and greater use of motion detectors and AI, to analyse how people walk, or facial analysis, to identify potential risks of falls or stroke[9]. (…)

Here in the UK, most people think social care is like the NHS and will be free when they need it. (…) It comes as a shock when people find out that care is means-tested[10] and not free at the point of need. Before any reforms can be sold to the public, it is necessary to tell the truth about the rotten[11] system we have today, which is complex, dysfunctional and underfunded.

Our system is too complicated when it comes to[12] working out who gets help and who pays for it. And it is dysfunctional because chronic underfunding inhibits investment in prevention that could improve people's quality of life and help manage the increasing demand that puts such pressure on our health and care system.

By Paul Burstow, *The Guardian*,
10 April 2019.

1. to dither over: *hésiter au sujet de.* **2.** to deliver: *assurer, tenir ses promesses.* **3.** provision: *prestation.* **4.** to remain: *rester.* **5.** hub: *plateforme.* **6.** rehabilitation: *rééducation.* **7.** to monitor: *surveiller.* **8.** screening: *diagnostic.* **9.** stroke: *attaque cérébrale.* **10.** means-tested: *indexé en fonction du revenu.* **11.** rotten: *dysfonctionnel.* **12.** when it comes to: *quand il s'agit de.*

5 ***Compréhension.*** How is China preparing for the future concerning care for the elderly? Then compare China's plan with the UK's. *(About 150 words, in English.)*

Document 5

6 ***Compréhension.*** Describe and explain this cartoon in English. *(About 150 words.)*

7 ***Compréhension.*** En tenant compte des documents 1 à 5, rédigez en français une synthèse qui dégage la problématique relative à l'ensemble du dossier. *(Environ 250 mots.)*

8 ***Expression.*** Rédigez la lettre suivante adressée à Mr Trevor Dixon, CEO of Applied Web Systems, 772 Colusa Avenue, El Cerrito, CA 94530-2392, USA, dans le cadre de négociations d'embauche dans sa société.

Vous le remerciez de l'offre de salaire intéressante qu'il vous a faite pour un emploi qui vous tente *a priori*. Toutefois, avant d'accepter définitivement, vous voulez connaître les avantages sociaux auxquels vous aurez droit : assurance maladie, accident du travail et décès, plan de retraite complémentaire à capitalisation ou revenus garantis (de quelle caisse de retraite *(pension fund)* s'agit-il, et comment elle est gérée (*managed*), conditions de travail (congés rémunérés, éventuellement crèche d'entreprise *(company creche)* et services proposés sur le lieu de travail, etc.), aide au logement *(housing benefit)*, voiture de fonction *(company car)*, stock-options, etc.

Salutations et formules d'usage. *(150 mots environ, en anglais.)*

Aide-mémoire grammatical

REMARQUE

∅ = mot absent en anglais correspondant à un mot présent en français. Ceci concerne surtout les articles et certains relatifs.

V = base verbale

V*ed* = prétérit

V*en* = participe passé

V*ing* = gérondif ou participe présent ou conjugaison en *be* + V*ing*

FICHE 1 Articles

1. L'article défini : *THE*

▸ L'article ***THE*** a une valeur déterminante, voire démonstrative et s'emploie devant des noms dans un **sens déterminé**.

• Sens déterminé **explicitement par le contexte** :

The oil crisis of 1973 triggered inflation.
Le choc pétrolier de 1973 a provoqué de l'inflation.

The articles which are on sale in this shop are out of fashion.
Les articles qui sont en vente dans ce magasin sont démodés.

• Sens déterminé **implicitement par le contexte** :

The manager wants to know where you have stored the files.
Le directeur veut savoir où vous avez rangé les dossiers.

▸ Certains **noms** sont **toujours précédés de *THE***.

• Seuls quelques **noms de pays** prennent l'article :

the United States of America – the United Kingdom – the Netherlands.

• Les **adjectifs substantivés** (c'est-à-dire des adjectifs employés comme noms) permettent de désigner des catégories de personnes déterminées. Ils ne prennent pas la marque du pluriel :

the poor – the rich – the unemployed – the British.

• Les **inventions** et des lieux d'activités :

the Internet – the radio – the cinema – the theatre – the train – the plane – the office, sauf ∅ *television* (*the television* désigne le poste de télévision).

• D'autres **noms courants précédés de *THE*** :

the environment – the economy – the consumer society – the world – the climate – the weather.

2. L'article ∅

L'**article défini français** (« le / la / les ») permet de désigner les choses de manière déterminée, mais aussi générale. Dans ce dernier cas, l'anglais a recours à ∅.

- **Les indénombrables :**

∅ Business is ∅ business.
Les affaires sont les affaires.

∅ Unemployment is an economic and social issue.
Le chômage est un problème économique et social.

Everyone has to adapt to ∅ modern society.
Tout le monde doit s'adapter à la société moderne.

- Les **dénombrables au pluriel** :

∅ Employees should be well paid.
Les employés devraient être bien payés.

∅ Companies have to make a profit.
Les entreprises doivent faire du bénéfice / des bénéfices.

Un groupe nominal incluant un nom propre de personne :

∅ Queen Elizabeth was crowned in 1953.
La Reine Elizabeth a été couronnée en 1953.

∅ General Smith's order has been sent.
On a envoyé la commande du Général Smith.

Les expressions de lieux familiers suivants : *home, church, hospital*

Many people now work from home.
Beaucoup de gens travaillent depuis leur domicile maintenant.

REMARQUE S'il s'agit d'un bâtiment et non d'un lieu familier, on emploiera l'article :
The church of that village needs to be repaired.
L'église de ce village a besoin d'être réparée.

3. L'article indéfini : *A / AN*

A / AN est toujours suivi d'un nom dénombrable au singulier.

- Il permet de désigner **les choses de manière générale** (au singulier) :

A merger consists in joining several companies.
Une fusion consiste à regrouper plusieurs entreprises.

- Il a une **fonction numérique** (= *one*) :

  We spent a week, on the report.
  Nous avons passé une semaine (et non deux) sur le rapport.

- On le trouve **après une préposition** (+ nom dénombrable au singulier) :

  It is difficult to invest without a loan.
  Sans prêt, il est difficile d'investir.

- On le trouve **devant les noms de profession** :

  She is an accountant.
  Elle est comptable.

REMARQUE Si la fonction est unique et introduite dans un attribut, on omet l'article :

He was appointed ∅ sales manager.
Il a été nommé directeur des ventes.

- On le trouve dans les **exclamatives** (+ nom dénombrable au singulier) :

  What a relief when we heard the delivery had arrived in time!
  Quel soulagement quand nous avons appris que la livraison avait été faite à temps !

- On le trouve dans les **expressions de fréquence** :

  He checks the price of our shares twice a day.
  Il vérifie le prix de nos actions deux fois par jour.

REMARQUE L'article ∅ + dénombrable au pluriel peut correspondre à « les » ou « des » selon le contexte.

∅ People came to visit the factory yesterday.
Des personnes sont venues visiter l'usine hier.

∅ People usually want ∅ lower prices.
Les gens veulent généralement des prix plus bas.

4. SOME / ANY / NO

SOME, *ANY* et *NO* permettent *de* **traduire l'article partitif (« de / du / des ») français** (voir aussi fiche 22, p. 204).

We sent some brochures to our customers.
Nous avons envoyé des / quelques brochures à nos clients.

They did not lend us any money.
Ils ne nous ont pas prêté d'argent.

There is no social policy in this company.
Il n'y a pas de politique sociale dans cette entreprise.

FICHE 2 *As* ou *LIKE*

AS et *LIKE* sont souvent des équivalents de « comme », mais il ne faut pas les confondre car en principe ils se construisent différemment, et *AS* a bien d'autres emplois que *LIKE*.

1. *AS*

AS a de nombreuses constructions.

- ***AS* conjonction (+ sujet éventuel) + verbe**

  As you know, he is an accountant.
  Comme vous savez, il est comptable.

  We can organise our work as we like.
  Nous pouvons organiser notre travail comme il nous plaît.

  He paid the bill immediately, as (was) required.
  Il a payé la facture immédiatement, comme (c'est) demandé.

  She received a phone call just as she was leaving.
  Elle a reçu un appel téléphonique comme / au moment précis où elle partait.

  As the company developed, (so) they needed more capital.
  Comme / À mesure que la société se développait, ils ont eu besoin de plus de capitaux.

  Things are not organised here as (they were) in my previous company.
  L'organisation ici n'est pas comme dans mon ancienne société.

- ***AS* préposition + groupe nominal**

  As an accountant, he is very efficient.
  Comme / En tant que comptable, il est très efficace. (Notez l'emploi de l'article indéfini en anglais.)

  Accountancy is considered as a complex job.
  La comptabilité est considérée comme un travail complexe.

REMARQUE

On trouve aussi *AS* exprimant la comparaison après *THE SAME* et pour former un comparatif d'égalité :

Working hours in France are not the same as in the UK.
Les horaires de travail en France ne sont pas les mêmes qu'au Royaume-Uni.

Their products are not as good as ours.
Leurs produits ne sont pas aussi bons que les nôtres.

2. *LIKE*

En principe, *LIKE*, toujours préposition, **ne peut être suivi que d'un nom ou d'un pronom.**

- *LIKE* peut introduire une comparaison :

  He is a bookkeeper, like her.
  Il est comptable, comme elle.

  There are going to be job cuts, like last year.
  Il va y avoir des suppressions d'emplois, comme l'an dernier.

  Working hours in France are not like those in the UK.
  Les horaires de travail en France ne sont pas comme ceux du Royaume-Uni.

- *LIKE* peut introduire un exemple :

  A bank like HSBC would never have done that.
  Une banque comme HSBC n'aurait jamais fait cela.

REMARQUES

1. On peut aussi dire *SUCH AS* pour introduire un exemple :

A bank such as / like Citibank…

2. Dans la langue parlée (américaine surtout), on entend souvent *LIKE* à la place de *AS* ; cette construction est à éviter dans la langue soignée, surtout à l'écrit.

Like I said, he is very successful.
Comme je l'ai dit, il réussit très bien.

As I said est nettement préférable.

FICHE 3 Auxiliaires modaux : *CAN, COULD, MAY, MIGHT, MUST, SHALL, SHOULD, WILL, WOULD*

1. Généralités

- Les auxiliaires modaux, très fréquents en anglais, indiquent des modalités de la pensée, des sentiments ou des opinions de l'énonciateur.
- Ils ne prennent pas de *s* à la 3e personne du singulier.
- Ils s'utilisent sans *do / does / did*, à la forme négative ou interrogative.
- Ils sont suivis de la base verbale (V).
- Ils sont parfois remplacés par d'autres formes verbales.
- On ne peut pas utiliser deux modaux dans le même groupe verbal.

2. *CAN / CANNOT*

Ils peuvent exprimer :

- la **possibilité** (*CAN*) et **l'impossibilité** (*CANNOT/CAN'T*).

  I can finish drawing up this cost estimate by Friday.
  Je peux finir d'établir ce devis pour/d'ici vendredi.

  But I cannot/can't finish it before that date.
  Mais je ne peux pas le finir avant cette date.

REMARQUE

CANNOT/CAN'T s'emploient fréquemment avec les verbes de perception.

Can you see our new office, from here?
Vous voyez notre nouveau bureau, d'ici ?

Speak up please: I can't hear you.
Parlez plus fort, s'il vous plaît : je ne vous entends pas.

- la **capacité** (*CAN*) et l'**incapacité** (*CANNOT/CAN'T*) :

  She can speak Russian, but she can't read or write it.
  Elle parle russe, mais elle ne sait ni le lire, ni l'écrire.

- la **permission** (*CAN*) et l'**interdiction** (*CAN'T*) :

  The workers can clock in at 7 or 8, but they can't clock in any later.
  Les ouvriers peuvent pointer à 7 ou 8 h, mais ils ne peuvent pas pointer plus tard.

- une **action effectuée malgré une impossibilité quasi-totale** (*CAN'T HAVE* + **Ven**) :

  She can't have done all that just by herself!
  Il est impossible qu'elle ait fait tout cela à elle seule ! [Sous-entendu : mais elle l'a fait]

3. *COULD / COULD NOT*

- ***COULD / COULD NOT*** peuvent exprimer une simple **capacité au passé**.

  Susan could speak three languages fluently when she was a child.
  Susan savait/pouvait parler trois langues couramment quand elle était enfant.

- ***COULD / COULD NOT*** peuvent aussi exprimer une **possibilité incertaine au présent**.

  I suppose she could do it if she really tried.
  Je suppose qu'elle pourrait/saurait le faire si elle essayait vraiment.

I could never do all that for tomorrow, even if I really tried: it is much too long.
Je ne pourrais jamais faire tout cela pour demain, même si j'essayais vraiment : c'est bien trop long.

- ***COULD (NOT) HAVE* + Ven** exprime une **possibilité incertaine au passé.**

  I couldn't have done it, even if I had tried.
  Je n'aurais pas pu le faire, même si j'avais essayé.

REMARQUE *COULD* est remplacé par *was able to / managed to* pour exprimer une action que l'on a pu accomplir malgré des difficultés.

We were able to / managed to send the order on time.
Nous avons pu / avons réussi à envoyer la commande à la date prévue.

4. *MAY / MIGHT*

MAY / MIGHT sont parfois interchangeables, avec des nuances de sens légèrement différentes. Ils peuvent indiquer :

- l'**éventualité**, l'**incertitude**, voire le **risque**, au présent ou au futur : ***MAY / MIGHT***

  The goods may / might be delivered as early as tomorrow. (*Might* exprime une incertitude plus grande que *may*)
  Il se peut / se pourrait que les marchandises soient livrées dès demain.

  I have not seen them yet: they may / might be late.
  Je ne les ai pas encore vus : ils sont peut-être en retard.

  His company is in trouble: he may / might lose his job.
  Sa société connaît des difficultés : il risque de perdre son emploi.

- une **éventualité au passé** : ***MAY / MIGHT HAVE* + Ven**

  They may have missed the train.
  Ils ont peut-être manqué le train.

  They might have missed their train if they had not left home early.
  Ils auraient pu manquer leur train s'ils n'étaient pas partis en avance de chez eux.

- la **permission** : ***MAY***

  May I have a day off, please? (*Can / could* est possible ici, dans une langue plus courante.)
  Puis-je prendre un jour de congé, s'il vous plaît ?

- la **suggestion** : ***MIGHT***

  You might ask your supplier to send us the goods more rapidly.
  Vous pourriez peut-être demander à votre fournisseur de nous envoyer les marchandises plus vite.

5. *MUST*

MUST a des sens différents selon les cas. Il peut exprimer :

• une **obligation** ou une **nécessité :**

I must remember to call him back.
Il faut que je pense à le rappeler.

You must go on this training course.
Il faut absolument que vous suiviez ce stage de formation.

• une **déduction** d'après des faits ou indices :

That company has developed very quickly: the CEO must be very efficient.
Cette société s'est développée très vite : le PDG doit être très efficace.

• une **obligation négative** ou une **interdiction** : ***MUST NOT*** (sens plus fort que ***CANNOT***)

We must not forget to pay this bill promptly. (Ici *cannot* est impossible.)
Nous ne devons pas oublier de payer cette facture rapidement/immédiatement.

You must not use this product immediately. (Ici *cannot* est possible.)
Vous ne devez pas utilisez ce produit tout de suite.

REMARQUES

1. ***MUST*** exprimant l'obligation ou la nécessité peut être remplacé par ***HAVE (GOT) TO*** au présent, au passé ou au futur (obligatoire dans ces deux derniers cas).

We have to move: this office is too small for us now.
Nous devons/sommes obligés de déménager : ce bureau est trop petit pour nous maintenant.

You will have to start working on this project as soon as possible.
Il vous faudra commencer à travailler sur ce projet dès que possible.

They had to work out a cost estimate quickly.
Ils ont dû établir un devis rapidement.

2. ***HAVE GOT TO*** + V, employé uniquement au présent, est plutôt réservé à la langue parlée.

I have got to go now.
Il faut que je parte maintenant.

3. ***MUST HAVE*** + **Ven** s'emploie pour exprimer la déduction concernant une action ou une situation passée.

They are very successful: they must have been extremely well organized.
Ils ont très bien réussi : ils ont dû/devaient être extrêmement bien organisés.

4. ***DO NOT HAVE TO / DO NOT NEED TO*** exprime l'absence d'obligation.

Our customers do not have to / do not need to pay a deposit when they place an order.
Nos clients ne sont pas obligés de verser un acompte lorsqu'ils passent une commande.

If you don't have to use that product, don't use it.
Si vous n'êtes pas obligé d'utiliser ce produit, ne l'utilisez pas.

À ne pas confondre avec l'interdiction :

You mustn't use this product immediately.
Vous ne devez pas utiliser ce produit tout de suite.

6. *SHOULD*

Très fréquent, il s'emploie dans des contextes variés. Il peut exprimer :

- un **conseil**, une **recommandation** au présent (équivalent de ***OUGHT TO***) :

  They ought to / should do more marketing research.
  Il faudrait qu'ils fassent davantage de recherche marketing.

- une **probabilité** au présent :

  The file should be in the top drawer.
  Le dossier devrait se trouver dans le tiroir du haut.

- un **regret** ou une **probabilité** au passé : ***SHOULD HAVE* + Ven :**

  He should have explained that this job entailed long hours. (Regret ou reproche)
  Il aurait dû expliquer que cet emploi impliquait de longues journées de travail.

  You should have received our report by now. (Probabilité)
  Vous devriez avoir reçu notre rapport, à présent.

7. *WILL et SHALL*

Ces deux modaux sont étudiés dans la fiche 10, p. 183 (futur).

8. *WOULD et WOULD HAVE*

Ils ont des usages et des sens très variés :

- **équivalent d'un conditionnel** en français (il n'y a pas de conjugaison propre au conditionnel en anglais) :

  I would not do it if I were you.
  Je ne le ferais pas si j'étais à ta place.

I would have done it if I had had time.
Je l'aurais fait si j'en avais eu le temps.

He wouldn't have thought it possible.
Il n'aurait pas pensé que c'était possible.

- **discours indirect** (voir fiche 6, p. 177) :

- expression d'une forme de **volonté,** surtout à la forme négative :

I asked him to come earlier, but he wouldn't.
Je lui ai demandé de venir plus tôt, mais il a refusé.

- **demande polie comme en français :**

We would like to meet you when you next come to London.
Nous aimerions faire votre connaissance la prochaine fois que vous viendrez à Londres.

- **désir, souhait :**

He would love to set up his own business.
Il aimerait bien créer sa propre affaire.

We would have liked to talk with you about that project.
Nous aurions aimé parler de ce projet avec vous.

FICHE 4 Cas possessif et expression de la possession

1. L'emploi

On emploie le cas possessif surtout avec les **êtres vivants, groupes** et **collectivités** *:*

my assistant's office	*the firms' policy premises*	*London's architecture*
le bureau de mon assistant	les locaux des intreprises	l'architecture de Londres

On utilise le cas possessif aussi avec des indications de **date** ou **durée** :

today's newspaper	*last month's results*	*a three hours' wait*
le journal d'aujourd'hui	les résultats du mois dernier	une attente de trois heures

REMARQUE Il ne faut pas abuser de l'utilisation du cas possessif.

2. La formation

- **+ *'s* après un nom singulier, un pluriel irrégulier, un nom de famille au pluriel :**
  John's book – the women's bags – the Jones's car

- **+ '(*s*) après un nom singulier en -*s* :**
  James'(s) camera

- **+ *'s* après une expression comportant plusieurs mots :**
  the Prime Minister's speech

- **+ *'s* lorsqu'il y a plusieurs possesseurs d'un seul objet :**
  Bill and Mary's telephone
  le téléphone de Bill et Mary

- **+ *'s* + *'s* lorsqu'il y a plusieurs possesseurs et plusieurs objets :**
  Bill's and Mary's mobiles
  les portables de Bill et Mary

  Do you know Bill's phone number, and Mary's?
  Connaissez-vous le numéro de téléphone de Bill, et celui de Mary ?

- **+ ' (sans *s*) après un pluriel en -*s***
  our employees' salaries
  les salaires de nos employés

3. Les adjectifs possessifs (suivis d'un nom ou d'un groupe nominal)

my – your – his / her / its – our – your – their

- Les adjectifs possessifs sont suivis d'un nom ou d'un groupe nominal.
- Le choix entre *his* / *her* / *its* dépend du possesseur :
  ***He** has lost his job, and **she** has lost her job too.*
  Il a perdu son emploi et elle a perdu son emploi aussi.

  ***This building** is very modern – its windows are round.*
  Ce bâtiment est très moderne – ses fenêtres sont rondes.

4. Les pronoms possessifs qui remplacent un nom

mine – yours – his / hers / its – ours – yours – theirs

▸ Les pronoms possessifs remplacent un nom.

His salary is higher than hers. Mine is even higher!
Son salaire (à lui) est plus élevé que le sien (à elle). Le mien est encore plus élevé.

a friend of mine	*a colleague of hers*	*a colleague of Peter's*
un de mes amis	un(e) de ses collègues (à elle)	un collègue de Peter

REMARQUE Ne pas confondre *their* (adjectif) et *theirs* (pronom).

5. *WHOSE*

WHOSE indique ou demande à qui appartient un objet, ou quelle est la relation entre deux personnes :

Whose colleague is he? He is Jane's (colleague).
De qui est-il le collègue ? Il est le collègue de Jane. / C'est celui de Jane.

Whose papers are these? They are hers / theirs.
À qui sont ces papiers ? Ils sont à elle / eux / elles. / Ce sont les siens / leurs.

The employee whose report has disappeared is angry.
L'employé dont le rapport a disparu est en colère.

REMARQUE Notez l'absence d'article après un cas possessif, et après *WHOSE* :
Jane's papers… – The employee whose report…

FICHE 5 Comparatifs et superlatifs

1. Les comparatifs et superlatifs de supériorité

▸ **Adjectifs** ou **adverbes courts** (une syllabe, parfois deux syllabes) :

Comparatif : adjectif + -ER + THAN

Superlatif : THE + adjectif + -EST

B&A is a smaller firm than C&D, but it is better for us because it is closer.
B&A est une entreprise plus petite que C&D, mais elle est mieux pour nous car elle est plus proche.

Mr Abbott is <u>the oldest</u> employee in / of the company.
M. Abbott est le salarié le plus ancien de la société.

We have <u>fewer</u> branches than them / they do.
Nous avons moins de succursales qu'eux.

Flying is <u>faster</u> than sailing.
L'avion est plus rapide que le bateau.

Adjectifs ou **adverbes longs** (deux syllabes et plus) :

<u>Comparatif</u> : *MORE + adjectif / adverbe + THAN*

<u>Superlatif</u> : *THE MOST + adjectif /adverbe*

His mobile is <u>more expensive than</u> mine.
Son téléphone portable vaut plus cher que le mien.

This laptop is <u>the most efficient</u> of all, in my opinion.
Cet ordinateur portable est le plus efficace de tous, à mon avis.

REMARQUES

1. Le second élément d'un comparatif de supériorité est toujours introduit par *THAN*.

2. Court ou long ? Les adjectifs / adverbes de deux syllabes sont longs, sauf s'ils se terminent en *-e*, *-y*, *-er*, *-ow* :
close / closer – friendly / friendlier – clever / cleverer – narrow / narrower.

Adjectifs irréguliers

- *Good / Well* → *better, the best.*
- *Bad / Ill* → *worse, the worst.*
- *Far* → *farther, the farthest* (« loin »), ou *further / the furthest* (souvent employé dans un sens figuré).

I shall not go any <u>further</u> into the matter.
Je n'irai pas plus loin sur ce sujet.

Do you need any <u>further</u> details?
Avez-vous besoin d'autres détails ?

- *Many* → *more, the most*

He has <u>many</u> customers / <u>more</u> customers than her / <u>the most</u> customers.
Il a beaucoup de clients / plus de clients qu'elle / le plus de clients.

- *Little* → *less, the least*

It is Sylvia who earns <u>the least</u> money.
C'est Sylvia qui gagne le moins d'argent.

Ces règles de formation s'appliquent au **comparatif progressif** *:*
Prices are getting <u>higher and higher</u>.
Les prix sont de plus en plus élevés.

Cars are more and more expensive.
Les voitures coûtent de plus en plus cher.

The situation is changing more and more rapidly / faster and faster.
La situation change de plus en plus rapidement.

- Le **double comparatif :**

The harder they work, the more money they earn.
Plus ils travaillent, plus ils gagnent d'argent.

2. Les comparatifs d'égalité

- Le **comparatif d'égalité positif** se forme avec *AS* + adjectif / adverbe + *AS*. *AS* s'emploie aussi après *THE SAME*.

My new office is as pleasant as my old one.
Mon nouveau bureau est aussi agréable que l'ancien.

She gets the same salary as he does / him.
Elle a le même salaire que lui.

REMARQUE Le pronom complément *him* est plus familier qu'une proposition sujet + auxiliaire.

- Le **comparatif d'égalité négatif** se forme avec *NOT AS / SO … AS* :

I do not earn as much money as (I did) before.
Je ne gagne pas autant d'argent qu'avant.

My new job is not as interesting as my former one.
Mon nouvel emploi n'est pas aussi intéressant que le précédent.

3. Les comparatifs d'infériorité

- Les **comparatifs d'infériorité** se forment avec *LESS / FEWER … THAN* :

I have less work to do and fewer responsibilities than before.
J'ai moins de travail, et moins de responsabilités qu'avant.

REMARQUES **1.** ***LESS*** s'emploie avec un indénombrable ou, comme adverbe, avec un verbe, et ***FEWER*** s'emploie avec un dénombrable au pluriel,

It takes less time to warm up.
Elle met moins de temps à chauffer.

We use the machine less than we used to.
Nous utilisons moins la machine qu'autrefois.

Fewer customers go to fast-food outlets.
Moins de clients vont dans les fast-foods.

We now have fewer people at the office.
Nous avons maintenant moins de personnes au bureau.

2. Le comparatif d'égalité négatif *NOT AS … AS* est beaucoup plus courant que *LESS … THAN* :

The new accountant is not as / so competent as the previous one (plus courant que *less competent than*).
Le nouveau comptable n'est pas aussi compétent que l'ancien.

FICHE 6 « Dire » : traductions, constructions et équivalents

1. *SAY* ou *TELL* ?

• ***SAY*** est employé pour **rapporter les paroles d'une personne** directement ou indirectement, généralement **sans mentionner la personne à qui on s'adresse**.

He said (that) it would be done by the next day. (Discours indirect)
Il a dit que ce serait fait dès le lendemain.

"Well done," he said (to me). (Discours direct)
« Bon travail », m'a t-il dit.

• ***TELL*** est utilisé **quand on mentionne la personne à qui l'on parle**.
He told us (that) a very important visitor was coming the next day.
Il nous a dit qu'un visiteur très important venait le lendemain.

2. Discours direct ou indirect

▸ Le **discours direct** désigne des paroles dites ou écrites « en direct ».
"This report is inaccurate. John will have to do it all over again."
« Ce rapport est inexact. John devra le refaire entièrement. »

▸ Le **discours indirect** consiste à rapporter des paroles après coup. L'action est perçue du point de vue de celui qui rapporte les paroles.

• On peut rapporter ces paroles avec un **verbe au présent**.
He says (that) this report is inaccurate and (that) John will have to do it all over again.
Il dit que ce rapport est inexact et que John devra le refaire entièrement.

Dans ce cas, le temps des verbes n'est pas modifié.

• On peut rapporter ces paroles avec un **verbe au passé**.
He said (that) the report was inaccurate and (that) John would have to do it all over again.
Il a dit que ce rapport était inexact et que John devrait le refaire entièrement.

Dans ce cas, les verbes sont modifiés en fonction des règles suivantes :

Discours direct	Discours indirect
Présent	Prétérit
Prétérit	*Past perfect*
Present perfect	*Past perfect*
will / can / may	*would / could / might*
would / could / might / should	*would / could / might / should*
must / need (modal)	*must / need*
Impératif	Infinitif

• Une action considérée comme étant toujours valide quand on la rapporte peut rester au même temps :

"We <u>want</u> to merge with some competitors."
→ *They declared that they <u>want</u> to merge with some competitors.*

• On conserve le prétérit modal lors du passage au discours indirect :

"If the company <u>had</u> more customers, it <u>would make</u> more profit."
→ *He said that if the company <u>had</u> more customers, it <u>would make</u> more profit.*

• D'autres modifications interviennent, dues aux changements de repères spatiaux et temporels :

Discours direct	Discours indirect
"here"	*there*
"this / these"	*that / those*
"today"	*that (same) day*
"yesterday"	*the day before*
"next week"	*the next week / the following week*
"last week"	*the week before / the previous week*
"now"	*then*

"<u>These</u> documents can be filed here until <u>next week</u>."
→ *He said that <u>those</u> documents could be filed there until <u>the following week</u>.*

• Des **changements de pronoms personnels et de possessifs** interviennent en fonction du point de vue de celui qui rapporte les paroles :

"<u>I</u>'ll give <u>you</u> <u>my</u> point of view," he (= Mr Jones) said to her (= Helen).
→ *Mr Jones said <u>he</u> would give <u>her</u> <u>his</u> point of view.*

Le choix des pronoms se fait en fonction de la ou des personnes désignées dans le contexte précis.

▸ L'ordre des termes dans une interrogative directe et dans une interrogative indirecte en anglais est différent.

"Where are all the files?" → *He asked where all the files were.*
Où sont tous les dossiers ? → *Il a demandé où étaient tous les dossiers.*

▸ Les formes contractées

Elles sont réservées à l'oral ; à l'écrit, il faut utiliser les formes entières :

"I wouldn't have ordered so many samples if I'd known."
« Je n'aurais pas commandé autant d'échantillons si j'avais su. »

→ *He said he would not have ordered so many samples if he had known.*
Il a dit qu'il n'aurait pas commandé autant d'échantillons s'il avait su.

3. Autres verbes déclaratifs se construisant différemment de *SAY* et *TELL* : *TO DECLARE (TO SB), TO ANNOUNCE (TO SB), TO EXPLAIN (TO SB)*

He has just announced (to his team) (that) he is going to resign.
Il vient d'annoncer (à son équipe) qu'il va démissionner.

Don't sign anything until your lawyer has explained the contract (to you).
Ne signez rien tant que votre avocat ne vous aura pas expliqué ce contrat.

FICHE 7 « Dont / Ce dont » : équivalents anglais

• « Dont » peut être un relatif complément de nom : il correspond alors à ***WHOSE***.

A manager whose assistant can speak several languages will be more efficient.
(Remarquez l'absence d'article après whose en anglais)
Un directeur dont l'assistant pratique plusieurs langues sera plus efficace.

Companies whose workers often go on strike lose money.
Les entreprises dont les ouvriers se mettent souvent en grève perdent de l'argent.

• « Dont » peut être complément d'un verbe suivi d'une préposition : il peut correspondre à ***WHICH, WHO, WHOM, THAT, ∅***, selon la nature et la fonction de l'antécédent (c'est-à-dire le mot auquel il se rapporte), et le niveau de langue.

The company that / ∅ / which we talked about yesterday is very profitable. (langue parlée)
The company about which we talked yesterday is very profitable. (langue soignée)
La société dont nous avons parlé hier est très rentable.

He is just the kind of accountant whom / ∅ / that we need.
C'est exactement le type de comptable dont nous avons besoin.

- « Dont » peut introduire des éléments d'un ensemble : il s'emploiera avec ***WHOM / WHOSE*** pour les personnes et ***WHICH*** pour les choses (attention aux virgules).

  These firms, several of which export to South Africa, are going to face difficulties.
  Ces entreprises, dont plusieurs exportent en Afrique du Sud, vont avoir des difficultés.

  Our employees, many of whom do not speak any foreign language, have applied for a language course.
  Nos employés, dont beaucoup ne parlent aucune langue étrangère, ont demandé un stage linguistique.

  This insurance company, some of whose managers can speak Chinese, is booming in China.
  Cette compagnie d'assurance, dont quelques directeurs savent parler chinois, connaît actuellement un fort développement en Chine.

- « Ce dont » : ***WHICH*** ou ***WHAT*** ?

  He can learn quickly, which I suspected. (Remarquez la virgule avant *which*.)
  Il peut apprendre vite, ce dont je me doutais.

  What I remember is that he is very competent. (Introduit une proposition.)
  Ce dont je me souviens, c'est qu'il est très compétent.

- « ***Ce qui / ce que*** » se traduisent différemment selon leur fonction.

WHAT sert à introduire ou à annoncer quelque chose (sans antécédent) :

I didn't understand what he was saying.
Je n'ai pas compris ce qu'il disait.

WHICH, après une virgule, sert à reprendre quelque chose :

They sent us a few samples, which was a good idea.
Ils nous ont envoyé quelques échantillons, ce qui était une bonne idée.

FICHE 8 *During, while, for, since* suivis d'une expression de durée ou de date

Quoique généralement (mais pas toujours) équivalents de « pendant » ou « depuis », il ne faut pas confondre *DURING*, *WHILE*, *FOR* et *SINCE*, et il faut faire attention aux temps des verbes qui les accompagnent.

1. *During*

DURING indique à quelle période de temps une action a lieu :

She works / worked / as a trainee during her holidays / the summer months.
Elle travaille / a travaillé comme stagiaire pendant ses vacances / les mois d'été.
(Remarquez l'emploi du prétérit (V ed) au passé car c'est terminé au moment où l'on parle.)

2. While

- *WHILE* s'emploie au début d'une proposition de temps :

  It happened while Dave was travelling.

  C'est arrivé pendant que Dave voyageait. (Remarquez l'emploi du prétérit.)

- *WHILE* ne peut pas être suivi de *WILL* dans un contexte futur :

  The goods will arrive while we are away.

  Les marchandises arriveront pendant que nous serons partis.

3. For

- *FOR* équivalent de « pendant » est suivi d'une indication de durée :

  We exported that product to Sweden for years.

  Nous avons exporté ce produit en Suède pendant des années.

  (Remarquez le prétérit au passé : l'action est maintenant terminée.)

- *FOR* équivalent de « depuis » :

  We have been importing gas from Norway for years.

  Cela fait des années que / Depuis des années nous importons du gaz de Norvège.

  (Remarquez le *present perfect* en anglais, et le présent en français : l'action continue au moment où l'on parle.)

4. Since

Équivalent de « depuis », *SINCE* est suivi d'une indication de date, même s'il introduit une idée de durée :

We have been waiting for that payment since February 1st / last month / they received the goods.

Nous attendons ce règlement depuis le 1er février / le mois dernier / qu'ils ont reçu les marchandises.

(Remarquez le *present perfect* en anglais correspondant à un présent en français.)

REMARQUES

1. *SINCE* peut également avoir le sens de « comme », « étant donné que » et être alors suivi du présent :

Please ignore this letter since your account is closed.

Veuillez ne pas tenir compte de cette lettre étant donné que votre compte est fermé.

2. *AGO*, souvent présenté avec *FOR* et *SINCE*, car il introduit aussi une information temporelle, est traité avec le prétérit, Fiche 19.

FICHE 9 « Faire faire »

1. Traductions de « faire faire quelque chose à quelqu'un »

- Sens le plus courant avec une notion de contrainte forte se traduit par *to get somebody to do something.*

  We are going to get a supplier to come and change our equipment.
  Nous allons faire venir un fournisseur pour qu'il change nos équipements.

- Construction un peu moins fréquente, sans notion de contrainte : *to have somebody do something*

  Are you going to have Smith and Co install it for you?
  Allez-vous les faire installer par Smith and Co ?

- Sens d'« obliger » : *to make somebody do*

  The new manager made the employees work overtime.
  Le nouveau directeur a fait faire des heures supplémentaires aux employés.

- Sens de « causer » : *to make somebody do*

  His jokes do not make us laugh at all.
  Ses plaisanteries ne nous font pas du tout rire.

- « Se faire faire » : *to make oneself* + Ven

  Did I make myself understood?
  Me suis-je bien fait comprendre ?

  The connection was so bad she could not make herself heard.
  La connexion était si mauvaise qu'elle ne pouvait se faire entendre.

2. Traduction de « faire faire quelque chose (par quelqu'un) »

On utilise : *to have / get sth done (by sb)* :

We had / got the new machine installed yesterday (by a specialist).
Nous avons fait installer la nouvelle machine hier (par un spécialiste).

FICHE 10 Futur et expression de l'avenir

La langue anglaise n'a pas de conjugaison propre au futur : l'avenir est exprimé de façons différentes selon l'énonciateur ou le contexte.

1. *WILL* ou *SHALL* + V ou *BE* + V *ING*

▸ Les modaux ***WILL*** (ou ***SHALL***, moins courant) + **V ou *be* + *Ving*** permettent de prédire une simple action future.

Co-op bank clean-up will take three more years.
L'assainissement de la banque Co-op prendra trois années de plus.

When will Mr Ferguson arrive?
Quand est-ce que Mr Ferguson arrivera ?

We will be working 12 hours a day while you are away on holiday.
Nous travaillerons 12 heures par jour pendant que tu seras en vacances.
(La forme en V*ing* est une forme d'insistance sur la durée.)

REMARQUES

1. *WILL*, auxiliaire modal, peut aussi avoir un sens de volonté ou d'habitude ; il n'exprime donc pas nécessairement le futur :

Any bank will do it for us.
N'importe quelle banque le fera / acceptera de le faire pour nous.

The new boss will talk all the time.
Le nouveau patron ne peut s'empêcher de parler tout le temps.

2. La forme négative, *WILL NOT*, s'emploie souvent pour exprimer un refus :

I have told him to apply for that job but he won't (will not).
Je lui ai dit de poser sa candidature pour ce poste mais il refuse.

▸ *SHALL* s'emploie surtout à la **forme interrogative** lorsqu'on demande un avis ou une autorisation et que l'on demande à son interlocuteur de décider :

Shall I invite Richard to the meeting next Thursday?
Voulez-vous que j'invite Richard à la réunion de jeudi prochain ?

▸ Comparez :

Shall I change the date of the conference?
Voulez-vous que je change la date du colloque ?

Will you cancel the conference, please?
Pourrez-vous annuler le colloque, s'il vous plaît ?

- On n'emploie jamais *WILL* après les conjonctions de temps telles que *WHILE, WHEN, AS SOON AS, AS LONG AS*, même dans un contexte futur :

  When the construction of the factory is finally completed next May, 300 people will be employed there.
  Quand la construction de l'usine sera enfin terminée en mai prochain, 300 personnes y seront employées.

  We will send them the payment as soon as we receive the goods.
  Nous leur enverrons le règlement dès que nous recevrons les marchandises.

2. Le présent simple ou en *BE* + V*ING*

Ils peuvent indiquer un futur avec des marqueurs de temps se référant à l'avenir (*tomorrow, next week, later, soon, in a few days, etc.*), dans le cas d'un programme ou d'un horaire, ou simplement grâce au contexte. La forme ***be* + Ving** exprime une sorte de commentaire par rapport au présent simple.

I am going to Japan next week and I am staying at the same hotel as last year.
Je pars au Japon la semaine prochaine et je séjourne(rai) au même hôtel que l'an dernier.

Our plane leaves at 3 pm and arrives two and a half hours later.
Notre avion part à 15 h et arrive deux heures et demie après.

The Birmingham train is leaving at 5.16 sharp: hurry up. (La forme en *be* + Ving ajoute une notion d'insistance par rapport à la forme simple ci-dessus.)
Le train de Birmingham part à 17 h 16 pile : dépêchez-vous. (Remarquez les différences d'écriture des horaires entre le français et l'anglais.)

When do you start work on the international project?
Quand commencerez-vous le travail sur ce projet international ?

3. *TO BE GOING TO* + V

Cette forme annonce une intention ou une conséquence prévisible.

We are going to invest in some new top quality office furniture.
Nous allons investir dans du nouveau mobilier de bureau haut de gamme.

The economic situation is not too good and is going to get worse.
La situation économique n'est pas très bonne et va s'aggraver.

4. *TO BE TO* + V

Cette forme indique un futur programmé, donc quasi-obligatoire mais moins impératif que ***MUST*** ou ***HAVE TO***.

The goods are to be delivered no later than January 31.
Les marchandises sont à livrer / doivent être livrées d'ici le 31 janvier au plus tard.

5. *TO BE ABOUT TO* + V

Cette forme indique un futur très proche.

The new head of department is about to be appointed.
Le nouveau chef de service est sur le point d'être nommé.

FICHE 11 Infinitif ou gérondif ?

1. Certains verbes régissent toujours l'infinitif (*TO* + V)

afford	*deserve*	*intend*	*promise*
agree	*enable*	*manage*	*refuse*
allow	*expect*	*offer*	*seem*
aim	*fail*	*plan*	*wish*
ask	*hesitate*	*prepare*	*would like*
decide	*hope*	*pretend*	etc.

They have decided to review this year's sales.
Ils ont décidé de faire le point sur les ventes de cette année.

2. Certains verbes régissent toujours le gérondif (V*ING*)

admit	*dislike*	*go on*	*practice*
avoid	*enjoy*	*can't help*	*recommend*
consider	*feel like*	*keep*	*risk*
delay	*finish*	*mind*	*can't stand*
deny	*give up*	*miss*	etc.

They considered outsourcing production.
Ils ont envisagé de délocaliser la production.

3. Autres cas

▸ Certains verbes sont suivis **soit de l'infinitif *to* + V, soit du gérondif V*ing*** en entraînant des **modifications de sens**. Il s'agit de : *regret*, *remember*, *step*, *try*.

They stopped to think about the strategy.
Ils ont arrêté pour réfléchir à la stratégie.

They have stopped selling cars.
Ils ont arrêté de vendre des voitures.

I regret to announce such news.
J'ai le regret d'annoncer une telle nouvelle.

I regret sending the letter.
Je regrette d'avoir envoyé la lettre.

Remember to post the letter.
N'oubliez pas de poster la lettre.

I can't remember posting the parcel.
Je ne me rappelle pas avoir posté le paquet.

I'm trying to understand the message.
J'essaie (en faisant un effort) de comprendre le message.

Try phoning them at 6am.
Essaie (pour voir) de les appeler à 6 heures du matin.

▸ Certains verbes sont suivis de l'**infinitif (*to* + V) ou** du **gérondif (V*ing*), sans** entraîner de **modifications de sens.** Il s'agit de : *start, begin, continue, like, hate, love.*

Have they started advertising / to advertise yet?
Ont-ils déjà commencé à faire de la publicité ?

▸ Certaines **expressions comportant un nom** entraînent un gérondif :

It is not worth sending the catalogues too early.
Cela ne vaut pas la peine d'envoyer les catalogues trop tôt.

They spend their time answering the phone.
Ils passent leur temps à répondre au téléphone.

It is no use typing that report all over again.
Cela ne sert à rien de taper tout ce rapport à nouveau.

They had trouble finding the address.
Ils ont eu du mal à trouver l'adresse.

▸ Quand **un verbe suit une préposition**, il est toujours au gérondif (V*ing*). Attention à la préposition *TO* dans : *look forward to* (« avoir hâte de, se réjouir à l'idée de »), *contribute to, when it comes to* (« lorsqu'il s'agit de »), *be / get used to* (« être habitué à / s'habituer à »), qu'il ne faut pas confondre avec la marque de l'infinitif (*to* + V).

*The commission reproached him **with cooking** the books.*
La commission lui a reproché de truquer les comptes.

*CO_2 emissions contribute **to** warming up the atmosphere.*
Les émissions de CO_2 contribuent à réchauffer l'atmosphère.

*I look forward **to** hearing from you soon.*
J'espère avoir bientôt de vos nouvelles.

*You could photocopy the report instead **of** copying it out by hand.*
Vous pourriez photocopier le rapport au lieu de le recopier à la main.

- L'**infinitif** (*to* + V) correspond plutôt à des **actions qui vont avoir lieu ou qui commencent juste** :

  Pleased to meet you.
  Enchanté(e) (de vous rencontrer).

Le **gérondif** correspond plutôt à des **actions qui ont déjà eu lieu** :

  It was a pleasure meeting you.
  Ravi(e) d'avoir fait votre connaissance.

- ***NEED*** suivi du gérondif entraîne un sens passif :

  The offices need repainting. (ou : *The offices need to be repainted.)*
  Les bureaux ont besoin d'être repeints.

FICHE 12 Mots composés

1. Les noms composés

- Les noms composés anglais sont bâtis « de droite à gauche » ; le mot le plus important est déterminé ou modulé par tous ceux qui le précèdent :

a car race	*a race car*
une course de voitures	une voiture de course

Plusieurs noms peuvent ainsi se suivre :

London property values	*an employment research organisation*
les prix de l'immobilier à Londres	un organisme de recherche d'emploi

- Au pluriel, seul le nom le plus important (le plus à droite) se met au pluriel :

a car factory	*car factories*
une usine de voitures	des usines de voitures

- Tous les noms composés anglais ne se traduisent pas automatiquement par un nom composé en français :

a wage earner	*a phone call*
un salarié	un appel téléphonique

2. Les adjectifs composés

Ce type d'adjectif n'existe pas en français et requiert une traduction parfois analytique. Comme tous les adjectifs anglais, l'adjectif composé est invariable et placé à gauche du nom qu'il détermine :

a full-time position	*a London-based company*
un poste à plein temps	une entreprise située à Londres

capital-intensive activities
des activités à forte intensité capitalistique

ground-breaking innovations
des innovations révolutionnaires

a time-saving device
un appareil qui fait gagner du temps

a short-term contract
un contrat à durée déterminée

FICHE 13 Noms dénombrables et indénombrables

Les noms en anglais sont divisés en deux catégories :

– les **dénombrables** (***countable***) qui ont une forme au singulier et une au pluriel ;

– les **indénombrables** (***uncountable***) qui n'ont qu'une forme au singulier.

Certains noms peuvent appartenir aux **deux catégories** avec des sens plus ou moins différents.

1. Les noms dénombrables

Les noms dénombrables désignent des êtres, des objets, des événements, etc. que l'on peut dénombrer. Ils peuvent être précédés de l'article défini ***THE*** ou indéfini ***A / AN / SOME***, d'un quantificateur : ***(A) FEW, MANY, SOME*** ou d'un nombre.

the / a / one / four / some lawyer(s)
l' / un / quatre / quelques avocat(s)

We have five offices, one on the ground floor and the others on the first floor.
Nous avons cinq bureaux, l'un au rez-de-chaussée et les autres au premier étage.

REMARQUE

Certains noms dénombrables s'emploient sans article quand l'accent est mis sur l'idée et non sur l'objet physique.
Exemples : *school, church, hospital, town, market, prison, college, cinema, television.*

In the USA, more young people go to college than in France.
Aux États-Unis, davantage de jeunes fréquentent un établissement d'enseignement supérieur / font des études supérieures qu'en France.

City College of San Francisco is one of the biggest colleges in the nation.
Le City College de San Francisco est l'un des plus gros établissements d'enseignement supérieur du pays.

2. Les noms indénombrables

Les noms indénombrables désignent des **substances**, des **concepts**, etc., qui ne peuvent pas se diviser en éléments séparés, donc qui n'ont pas de pluriel, ne sont jamais précédés d'un nombre, et s'emploient souvent sans article. Ils peuvent être précédés de ***MUCH***, ***A LOT OF***, ***(A) LITTLE***, ***SOME***. Ils peuvent correspondre à un pluriel en français.

Par exemple : *milk*, *advice*, *information*, *furniture*, *luggage*, *work*, *equipment*, *transport*, *money*.

We are always pleased to get good advice; you gave us some very good advice yesterday.
Nous sommes toujours contents de recevoir un / de bons conseil(s) ; vous nous avez donné un / de très bon conseil(s) hier.

We have not got much money left.
Il ne nous reste pas beaucoup d'argent.

REMARQUE

Certains indénombrables peuvent être précédés de l'article indéfini dans les expressions ***WHAT A / SUCH A***, ou dans certaines expressions idiomatiques :

What a pity / shame you lost your position!
Quel dommage que vous ayez perdu votre poste !

It was such a relief to hear you have found another one!
Quel soulagement de savoir que vous en avez trouvé un autre !

Why are you are making such a fuss?
Pourquoi faites-vous tant d'histoires ?

He is in a hurry.
Il est pressé.

3. Les noms tantôt dénombrables tantôt indénombrables

Certains noms sont **dénombrables** quand ils sont utilisés dans un **contexte précis** ou concret, et sont **indénombrables** quand ils sont utilisés dans un **contexte général** ou abstrait ; le nom change alors de sens :

business	*a business*
les affaires	une entreprise / affaire

Advertising plays a very important role in business.
La publicité joue un rôle très important dans les affaires.

The company was a family business.
L'entreprise était une affaire de famille.

Many people believe that work is the key to <u>success</u>.
Beaucoup de gens pensent que le travail est la clé du succès.

The book about globalization became <u>a commercial success</u>.
Le livre sur la mondialisation est devenu un succès commercial.

Our company made <u>a big profit</u> last year.
Notre société a fait de gros bénéfices l'an dernier.

There will not be <u>much profit</u> in doing that.
Nous ne gagnerons pas grand-chose à faire cela.

REMARQUE Le dictionnaire indique généralement si le nom est dénombrable (C : *countable*) ou indénombrable (U : *uncountable* / NonC : *non-countable*).

FICHE 14 Négatifs et semi-négatifs : équivalents de « ne plus », « non plus », « presque plus / pas » : *NO MORE / NOT ANY MORE, NO LONGER / NOT ANY LONGER, NOT EITHER / NEITHER / NOR, HARDLY (ANY) / BARELY (ANY) / SCARCELY (ANY)*

Ces expressions indiquent qu'une action ou un état n'est pas vrai, plus vrai ou quasiment pas vrai, mais elles ne sont pas toujours équivalentes.

1. « Ne plus » dans un sens quantitatif ou temporel : *NO / NOT ANY MORE*

We have <u>not</u> got <u>any more</u> of these products.
Nous n'avons plus ces produits.

Mrs Colson does <u>not</u> live in Swindon <u>any more</u>.
Mrs Colson n'habite plus à Swindon.

There is <u>no more</u> left.
Il n'en reste plus.

2. « Ne plus » dans un sens temporel uniquement : *NO / NOT ANY LONGER*

David Ashton is <u>no longer</u> with us.
David Ashton n'est plus chez nous.

We can<u>not</u> stay <u>any longer</u>.
Nous ne pouvons plus rester.

We <u>no longer</u> sell those products.
Nous ne vendons plus ces produits.

3. « Ne plus » après une phrase négative : *NOT EITHER / NEITHER / NOR*

I cannot wait any more / longer. – Neither can I./Nor can I. / I can't either.
Je ne peux plus attendre – Et moi non plus. **(Attention à l'ordre des mots !)**

4. « Presque plus / presque pas » (semi-négatif)

We hardly have any of these articles left.
Il ne nous reste presque plus aucun de ces articles.

They barely had any customers yesterday.
Ils n'ont presque pas eu de clients hier.

Scarcely any mail arrived this morning.
Presqu'aucun courrier n'est arrivé ce matin. / Il n'est arrivé pratiquement aucune lettre ce matin.

REMARQUE

Il ne faut pas confondre ***HARDLY*** et ***HARD***.

He hardly works.
Il ne travaille presque pas.

He works hard.
Il travaille dur / beaucoup.

Remarquez leur place (voir aussi Fiche 16 sur la place des adverbes)

FICHE 15 « On » : ses équivalents anglais

1. Différents équivalents de « on »

- Dans un **registre soutenu**, pour exprimer une **généralité** : *one*
  One should never leave one's handbag in an empty office.
  On ne devrait jamais laisser son sac à main dans un bureau vide.

- Dans un **registre plus courant**, pour exprimer une **généralité** : *you*
  If you are laid-off, you will get unemployment benefits.
  Si on est licencié, on reçoit des indemnités de chômage.

- Quand « on » signifie « **nous** » : *we*
  In our company, we are not allowed to drink coffee near a computer.
  Dans notre entreprise, on n'a pas le droit de boire un café à proximité d'un ordinateur.

▸ Quand « on » signifie **les autres / les gens** : *they / people*

In that department, they are allowed to have a short nap.
Dans ce service, on a le droit de faire une petite sieste.

People imagine accountancy is boring.
On croit que la comptabilité est ennuyeuse.

▸ Quand « on » correspond à quelqu'un d'inconnu ou de non identifié : *someone*

Someone called while you were out.
On a appelé pendant que vous étiez sorti.

▸ Des **tournures impersonnelles** permettent de traduire « on » quand il correspond à un peu tout le monde.

It is possible to find all the employees' names in this directory.
On peut trouver les noms de tous les employés dans ce répertoire.

2. « On » correspond souvent à un passif en anglais

- Avec les verbes d'opinion :

The new manager is said to be very authoritarian.
On dit que le nouveau directeur est très autoritaire.

It was reported that some board members were disappointed with the company's performance.
On a raconté que certains membres du conseil d'administration ont été déçus des résultats de la société.

He is believed to have undertaken illegal operations.
On pense qu'il s'est lancé dans des opérations illégales.

- Avec *to be sent / given / told / sold / taught*, etc.

Mr Pritchett was given a beautiful painting when he retired.
On a offert une belle peinture à M. Pritchett pour son départ en retraite.

The trainees will be taught basic knowledge about the workings of their department.
On donnera des notions de base aux stagiaires sur le fonctionnement de leur service.

Voir aussi la Fiche 17 sur le passif en anglais, p. 195.

FICHE 16 Ordre des mots

1. La place des adjectifs

• Les adjectifs qualificatifs épithètes se placent tous avant le nom dans un ordre variable, parfois délicat à déterminer. En général, l'adjectif le plus près du nom est celui qui dépend le moins de l'appréciation de l'énonciateur, parce qu'il décrit une caractéristique plus permanente.

Advanced manufacturing methods
Des méthodes de fabrication avancées

Incredible low prices
Des prix bas incroyables

A polluting old industrial firm
Une vieille entreprise industrielle polluante

An even bigger future fiscal problem
Un futur problème fiscal encore plus grave

A sleek, big, black Bentley
Une grosse Bentley noire et élégante

A well-known, prosperous, large public British company
Une grosse société britannique prospère, bien connue, cotée en Bourse

• Les adjectifs ordinaux (*first, second, third*, etc.), ainsi que *last, next, other*, se placent avant le chiffre ou le quantificateur :

the first two months — les deux premiers mois
the last few days — les derniers jours
the other two figures — les deux autres chiffres

2. La place des adverbes ou expressions adverbiales

En principe, l'adverbe ne doit pas séparer le verbe du complément d'objet direct.

He managed his company very well.
Il a très bien géré sa société.

He speaks German fluently.
Il parle couramment l'allemand.

L'adverbe se place généralement devant le mot sur lequel il porte (adjectif, verbe ou autre adverbe) :

He works very hard.
Il travaille très dur.

We hardly ever use this machine.
Nous n'utilisons pratiquement jamais cette machine.

S'il porte sur une phrase ou proposition, l'adverbe se place, selon les cas, au début, au milieu ou à la fin de la proposition ou de la phrase. On peut parfois avoir le choix.

Au début (forme d'insistance)

- Adverbes de **liaison :**

  Our sales dropped last year; consequently we had to advertise.
  Nos ventes ont baissé l'année dernière; par conséquent, nous avons dû faire de la publicité.

- Adverbes de **lieu** et/ou de **temps :**

  Afterwards, our turnover rose.
  Après, notre chiffre d'affaires a augmenté.

  Over there, business is exciting.
  Là-bas, travailler dans les affaires est passionnant.

- Adverbes indiquant un **jugement :**

  Fortunately, his business improved.
  Heureusement, ses affaires se sont améliorées.

Au milieu

En principe, les adverbes suivants précèdent immédiatement le verbe à un temps simple, ou se mettent après l'auxiliaire ou après le premier verbe s'il y en a plusieurs.

- Adverbes **négatifs** ou **semi-négatifs**, de **temps imprécis**, de **fréquence**, ainsi que ***ALSO***. Attention à l'ordre des mots !

  We had rarely / never experienced such a serious situation.
  Nous avions rarement / Nous n'avions jamais connu une situation aussi grave.

  Have you ever met them?
  Les avez-vous déjà rencontrés ?

  We barely / hardly know them.
  Nous les connaissons à peine.

  She will soon have finished typing her letter.
  Elle aura bientôt fini de taper sa lettre.

  Your remittance still has not arrived.
  Votre versement n'est toujours pas arrivé.

  People often commute by public transport.
  Les gens vont souvent au travail par les transports en commun.

  We also sell spare parts for German cars.
  Nous vendons aussi des pièces détachées pour voitures allemandes.

- ***NOT*** suivi d'un adjectif + nom, sujet du verbe.

  Not all laws are fair.
  Toutes les lois ne sont pas équitables.

• Adverbes de **manière** : placés après le dernier auxiliaire (ou en fin de proposition)

The report has been very carefully typed (very carefully).
Le rapport a été tapé très soigneusement.

À la fin

Les adverbes qui se mettent au début peuvent aussi souvent venir à la fin, selon l'intention du locuteur, le style, ou la construction du reste de la phrase :

Yesterday, I sent him an e-mail (yesterday).
Hier, je lui ai envoyé un mail (hier).

Unfortunately, the goods arrived late (unfortunately).
Malheureusement, les marchandises sont arrivées en retard (malheureusement).

FICHE 17 Passif

1. Formation

Un groupe verbal au passif est composé de *BE* conjugué au temps désiré ou mis à la forme désirée, suivi du participe passé du verbe choisi.

• Présent simple :

Offices are usually painted in pale colours.
Les bureaux sont généralement peints en couleurs claires.

• Présent en *be* + V*ing* :

Our office is being repainted.
Notre bureau est en train d'être repeint.

• Prétérit simple :

My office was painted dark blue.
Mon bureau était peint en bleu foncé.

• Prétérit en *be* + V*ing* :

While my office was being repainted, I worked in another one.
Pendant que l'on repeignait mon bureau, j'ai travaillé dans un autre.

• *Present perfect (have / has been + Ven) :*

My office has been renovated.
Mon bureau a été rénové.

• Plus-que-parfait *(had been + Ven)*

My office had been renovated when I arrived.
Mon bureau avait été rénové quand je suis arrivé.

- Avec un modal :

  Your office will be renovated next year.
  Votre bureau sera rénové l'an prochain.

- Avec un infinitif (*to* + V) :

  Your office needs to be renovated.
  Votre bureau a besoin d'être rénové.

- Avec un gérondif :

  Your office needs renovating.
  Votre bureau a besoin d'être rénové.

Ici, il s'agit d'un sens passif avec un verbe à la forme active.

2. Utilisation

- Le passif est une construction verbale plus fréquente en anglais qu'en français. Comme en français, il permet de mettre en valeur le sujet grammatical et de mettre au second rang, voire de passer sous silence, l'agent de l'action.

  These boxes have been sent back by dissatisfied customers.
  Ces boîtes ont été renvoyées par des clients mécontents.
  (Le sujet grammatical est mis en valeur.)

  These boxes were sent back yesterday.
  Ces boîtes ont été renvoyées hier. (Peu importe par qui.)

REMARQUE

Notez les deux constructions possibles et leurs nuances de sens.

A report of the meeting was sent to the shareholders. (L'important ici, c'est le compte rendu, et non autre chose.)
Un compte rendu de la réunion a été envoyé aux actionnaires.

The shareholders were sent a report of the meeting. (L'important ici, ce sont les actionnaires à qui on a envoyé le compte rendu).
On a envoyé un compte rendu de la réunion aux actionnaires.

- Il peut correspondre à certains verbes pronominaux en français (voir Fiche 25).

- Il peut être équivalent à « on » (voir Fiche 15).

  The new manager is said to be very efficient.
  On dit que le nouveau directeur est très efficace.

▸ *Say*, *report*, *consider*, *believe*, *think* permettent d'exprimer ce qui se dit à propos du sujet grammatical (réputations, rumeurs) :

  The new manager is said to be efficient.
  On dit que le nouveau directeur est efficace.

FICHE 18 Présent simple ou présent en *BE* + V*ING*

1. Le présent simple

Le présent simple sert à indiquer :

• une **information simple**, non située dans le temps :

Julian Freeman works in a start-up.
Julian Freeman travaille dans une startup.

That company produces generic medicines.
Cette entreprise produit des médicaments génériques.

This document explains how the WTO operates.
Ce document explique comment fonctionne l'OMC.

Worries grow over global warming. (Titre de presse.)
Les inquiétudes grandissent au sujet du réchauffement climatique.

• une **action habituelle ou répétée** *:*

He always reads his paper when he commutes in the morning.
Il lit toujours le journal en se rendant à son travail le matin.

• un **jugement**, une **perception**, une **opinion** :

I think this bank is very reliable.
Je pense que cette banque est très solide.

Do you understand / see what I mean?
Tu comprends ce que je veux dire ?

I agree with you on this point.
Je suis d'accord avec vous sur ce point.

Their proposal sounds very attractive.
Leur proposition semble très séduisante.

• un **événement programmé** (voir aussi Fiche 10, p. 183) :

The meeting starts at 4 pm.
La réunion commence à 16 h.

Attention : Lorsque *think* est employé au présent en *be* + V*ing*, son sens est légèrement différent (voir « Remarque » paragraphe 2, p. 198).

• une **action ou un événement introduit par *when, as soon as, as long as, while, once***, même si le verbe principal est au futur :

We will send you our payment as soon as we get the invoice.
Nous vous enverrons notre réglement dès que nous aurons reçu la facture.

I will pay a visit to Mr Han when I am next in Shanghai.
Je rendrai visite à M. Han la prochaine fois que je serai à Shanghaï.

I am sure my mobile phone will start ringing while I am busy.
Je suis sûr(e) que mon mobile se mettra à sonner pendant que je serai occupé(e).

2. Le présent en *BE* + V*ING*

C'est une forme d'insistance, presque un commentaire, qui exprime :

- une **action en cours** au moment où l'on parle :

Please be quiet: they are listening to the manager's speech.
Veuillez ne pas faire de bruit : (en ce moment) ils écoutent le discours du directeur.

We are selling this new product very well.
Pour l'instant, nous vendons très bien ce nouveau produit.

What is he saying? I can't believe it!
Qu'est-ce qu'il dit, là ? Je n'arrive pas à le croire !

- une action en cours, mais pas nécessairement au moment où l'on parle :

He is learning German as well as English.
Actuellement, il apprend l'allemand ainsi que l'anglais.

- une **action répétée** sur laquelle on insiste car elle agace :

That customer is always complaining.
Ce client n'arrête pas de se plaindre.

- un programme, une intention :

Today, we are closing at 4pm.
Aujourd'hui, nous fermons à 16 h.

REMARQUE

To think, comme certains autres verbes, change de sens selon qu'il est au présent simple ou au présent en *be* +V*ing*.

He thinks he has a very good job.
Il pense qu'il a un très bon emploi.

I am thinking of changing jobs.
J'envisage de changer d'emploi.

FICHE 19 Prétérit et *present perfect*

Ces deux temps expriment le passé selon un système différent des temps du passé en français.

1. Le prétérit

Le prétérit simple (V*ed*)

• Il exprime un **passé révolu**, coupé du présent. Le contexte passé peut être précisé explicitement ou implicitement par une date ou un lieu :

*We received the consignment **yesterday**.* (Date)
Nous avons reçu cet envoi hier.

*He phoned me **two days ago**.* (*ago* s'emploie avec une expression de durée, mais exprime une date).
Il m'a téléphoné il y a deux jours.

*I bought this watch (when I was) **in Geneva**.* (Lieu)
J'ai acheté cette montre (quand j'étais) à Genève.

***When** did you last go to Chicago?*
Quand êtes-vous allé à Chicago pour la dernière fois ?

*He worked in that company **for years**.*
Il a travaillé dans cette société pendant des années.

• Le prétérit simple s'emploie aussi lorsqu'il s'agit d'une action répétée au passé :

*He commuted to London **every day**.*
Il se rendait à son travail à Londres tous les jours.

Le prétérit en *be* + V*ing*

Il a à peu près les mêmes caractéristiques que le présent en *be* + V*ing* et s'emploie pour exprimer une action qui a duré au passé, souvent interrompue par un événement soudain exprimé au prétérit simple :

*She was telephoning on her mobile **when her fixed line phone rang**.*
Elle téléphonait sur son portable quand son téléphone fixe a sonné.

2. Le *PRESENT PERFECT*

Le *present perfect* relie passé et présent. Il s'emploie pour un événement ou une action à cheval sur le présent et le passé. Il peut correspondre à un temps présent ou passé en français, selon le contexte. Comparez l'anglais et le français dans les exemples suivants :

Le *present perfect* simple (*have* + *Ven*)

On s'intéresse au résultat de l'action.

I have lost key data on my computer.
J'ai perdu des données essentielles sur mon ordinateur.
(J'en subis les conséquences encore maintenant.)

It has happened many times before.
C'est arrivé de nombreuses fois auparavant. (Et cela peut encore se produire.)

I have finally recovered them.
Je les ai enfin récupérées.

I have tried to understand why again and again – but I still can't.
J'ai essayé de comprendre pourquoi de nombreuses fois, mais je n'y arrive toujours pas.

He has not answered our e-mail ***so far / yet****.*
Il n'a pas répondu à notre mail jusqu'ici / encore.

We have ***just*** *received an answer.*
Nous venons de recevoir une réponse.
(Notez la différence avec le français : « je viens de » = passé proche.)

You have ***already*** *met them.*
Vous les avez déjà rencontrés.

We have had business dealings with them ***for years / since 2000*** *perhaps.*
Nous sommes en affaires avec eux depuis des années / peut-être depuis 2000.

We have known them ***for years and years****.*
Cela fait des années et des années qu'on les connaît.

How often *have you talked to them?*
Combien de fois leur avez-vous parlé ?

Have they ***ever*** *replied?*
Ont-ils jamais répondu ?

REMARQUE

1. En américain, *EVER* et *NEVER* s'emploient toujours avec le prétérit :

They never replied.
Ils n'ont jamais répondu.

2. À la différence du français qui emploie le présent, on emploie le *present perfect* après *It is the first time* :

It is the first time *I have heard about this event.*
C'est la première fois que j'entends parler de cet événement.

Le *present perfect* en *be* + V*ing*

On insiste sur cette action commencée au passé et se prolongeant au présent, ainsi que sur sa durée :

*Our company has been trading with China **for years*** (durée), ***since 2000*** (date).
Cela fait des années que notre société a des relations commerciales avec la Chine, depuis 2000.

*We have been negotiating **for over a week** now.*
Cela fait plus d'une semaine que nous négocions.

***How long** have they been talking?*
Cela fait combien de temps qu'ils discutent ?

That customer has been complaining again!
Ce client s'est encore plaint !

FICHE 20 Pronoms relatifs

1. Les pronoms relatifs

Ce sont : *who(m), which, that, ∅, whose, when, where, what*. On les choisit en fonction de deux facteurs :

la **nature de l'antécédent** (mots auxquels ils se rapportent) :

– être humain ou personnifié (*workers, Mr Jones, secretary, my cat…*) :
who, that, ∅, whose ;

– non humain (*factory, job, advice, animals…*) :
which, that, ∅, whose.

la **fonction grammaticale du pronom relatif** : sujet, complément d'objet ou complément de nom.

• Pronom relatif **sujet de la relative :**

A man who / that works too much can become ill. (Antécédent animé)
Un homme qui travaille trop peut tomber malade.

A job which / that pays well would be my dream. (Antécédent animé)
Un travail qui paie bien serait mon rêve.

• Pronom relatif **complément d'objet du verbe de la relative :**

The visitor who(m) / that / ∅ you saw is Indian. (Antécédent animé)
Le visiteur que vous avez vu est indien.

The machine which / that / ∅ we bought works well. (Antécédent animé)
La machine que nous avons achetée fonctionne bien.

REMARQUES

1. ***THAT*** et ∅ sont rares dans une langue soignée (langue des affaires, rapports, correspondance commerciale). Toutefois ***THAT*** et ∅ sont obligatoires après ***SOMETHING, EVERYTHING, ALL, THE LAST, THE FIRST, THE ONLY***, les superlatifs et les quantifieurs.

Everything *that / ∅ I told you is true.*
Tout ce que je t'ai dit est vrai.

It is ***the best proposal*** *that we have received.*
C'est la meilleure proposition que nous avons reçue.

All the parcels *that / ∅ we received were damaged.*
Tous les colis que nous avons reçus étaient endommagés.

There is not much *that can be done.* (Ici *that* est obligatoire car sujet du verbe.)
Il n'y a pas grand-chose à faire.

The last person *that left was the CEO.*
La dernière personne qui est partie était le directeur général.

2. Ne jamais séparer ***THAT*** de son antécédent par une virgule.

The customers that / who were angry wrote a letter of complaint.
Les clients qui étaient mécontents ont écrit une lettre de réclamation.

Our customers, who are mainly in China, are placing large orders.
Nos clients, qui sont surtout en Chine, passent de grosses commandes.

FICHE 21 Propositions infinitives

1. La proposition infinitive : verbe + nom ou pronom complément + *TO* + V (infinitif)

Elle s'emploie après des verbes qui expriment :

• une **volonté**, un **ordre**, un **désir**, une **interdiction**, une **intention** ou une **préférence** :

want	*hate*	*compel*	*mean*
like	*prefer*	*forbid*	*order*
love	*force*	*intend*	*urge*, etc.

The manager wants his employees to work every other Saturday.
Le directeur veut que ses employés travaillent un samedi sur deux.

He would also like them to arrive very early in the morning.
Il voudrait aussi qu'ils arrivent très tôt le matin.

The chief accountant ordered the bank to refund the sum at once.
Le chef comptable a donné l'ordre à la banque de rembourser la somme immédiatement.

• une **invitation à agir** :

ask	*advise*	*require*	*remind*
beg	*warn*	*teach*	*help*
request	*tell*	*allow*	*challenge*
persuade	*invite*	*enable*	*dare*, etc.

The young man asked the job centre to help him (to) find a job.
Le jeune homme a demandé au pôle emploi de l'aider à trouver un emploi.

The company lawyer has advised the manager to revise their equal opportunities policy.
L'avocat de l'entreprise a conseillé au directeur de revoir leur politique d'égalité des chances.

• une **attente** :

wait for	*depend on*	*trust*	*call on*
expect	*rely on*	*count on*	etc.

He has always counted on his personal assistant to remind him to go to a meeting.
Il a toujours compté sur son assistant personnel pour lui rappeler d'aller à une réunion.

They expected the manager to show his appreciation of their work.
Ils s'attendaient à ce que le directeur leur montre comme il appréciait leur travail.

They waited for him to congratulate them, in vain!
Ils ont attendu qu'il les félicite, en vain !

REMARQUE

TO RECOMMEND a plusieurs constructions possibles :

The committee recommended that the CEO should resign.
Le conseil d'administration a recommandé que le PDG démissionne.

The instructions recommend using this product in small quantities only.
La notice recommande de n'utiliser ce produit qu'en très petite quantité.

2. La proposition infinitive avec *FOR* + nom / pronom + *TO* + V (infinitif)

Elle s'emploie :

• lorsque la phrase exprime un **but** et que les **deux sujets sont différents :**

He organised the meeting on Tuesday for them all to be able to be present.
Il a organisé la réunion pour mardi afin qu'ils puissent tous être présents.

I have brought this report for you to read.
J'ai apporté ce rapport pour que vous le lisiez.

• **après certains adjectifs** précédés de *it is / was* : *important, necessary, easy, difficult, impossible, unusual* et après l'expression *It is time.*

***It is necessary** for you to have a plan of action if you want to win the competition.*
Il faut que vous ayez un plan d'action si vous voulez gagner le concours.

***It was impossible** for me to agree with their marketing policy.*
Il m'était impossible d'être d'accord avec leur politique marketing.

***It is time** for you to increase your ethical commitments.*
Il est temps que vous intensifiez vos engagements éthiques.

FICHE 22 Quantificateurs : expression de la quantité

1. *SOME, ANY, NOT ANY, NO*

▸ ***SOME*** s'emploie dans des phrases affirmatives ou interrogatives pour exprimer une quantité peu précise :

We have had some staff problems recently.
Nous avons eu quelques problèmes de personnel récemment.

They have bought some wine.
Ils ont acheté du vin.

Would you like some papers to read?
Voulez-vous des journaux à lire ? **(C'est une proposition.)**

▸ ***ANY*** s'emploie dans des phrases négatives ou interrogatives :

We have not had any news of the construction plan.
Nous n'avons pas reçu de nouvelles du projet de construction.

Have you got any books to read?
Avez-vous des livres à lire ? **(C'est une question.)**

REMARQUES

1. ***ANY*** par lui-même n'est pas négatif mais a le sens de « quelque / n'importe » dans une phrase affirmative :

Any date will do.
N'importe quelle date conviendra.

2. Les composés *SOMETHING*, *SOMEBODY*, *NOTHING*, *NOBODY*, *ANYTHING* et *ANYBODY* s'emploient de la même façon.

- ***NO*** s'emploie surtout avec un sujet.

  No shops are open on Sundays here.
  Il n'y a aucune boutique ouverte le dimanche ici.
  (*No* s'emploie surtout avec un sujet.)

2. *Much*

MUCH + nom indénombrable s'emploie surtout dans les phrases négatives ou interrogatives :

We haven't got much mail to do.
Nous n'avons pas beaucoup de courrier à faire.

How much time have we got?
Combien de temps avons-nous ?

3. *Many*

MANY + nom au pluriel peut s'employer dans tout type de phrase :

We have had / have not had many opportunities to travel. Have you had many?
Nous avons eu / n'avons pas eu beaucoup d'occasions de voyager. Et vous ?

How many times has he called us?
Combien de fois nous a-t-il appelés ?

4. *A lot of / lots of / plenty of*

Ils peuvent s'utiliser avec un nom indénombrable ou un nom au pluriel :

The manager has a lot of / lots of / plenty of time / help / employees to prepare the exhibition.
Le directeur a beaucoup de temps / d'aide / d'employés pour préparer l'exposition.

5. *Too much* + indénombrable, *too many* + pluriel, *too* + adjectif

Some people have <u>too much work</u>, others have <u>too many days off</u>, some firms are <u>too big</u>.
Certaines personnes ont trop de travail, d'autres ont trop de journées de congé, certaines entreprises sont trop grosses.

6. *Most* + nom

- Idée générale : ***MOST*** **+ nom.**

<u>Most workers</u> look forward to going on holiday.
La plupart des travailleurs attendent impatiemment le moment de partir en vacances.

- Idée spécifique : ***MOST OF*** **+ *THE*** **+ nom** ou ***MOST OF*** **+ pronom**

<u>Most of the employees in my firm</u> also look forward to the weekend.
La plupart des employés dans mon entreprise attendent impatiemment le week-end aussi.

<u>Most of them get along well with</u> the management
La plupart d'entre eux s'entendent bien avec la direction.

7. *(A) little* + nom indénombrable

« (Un) peu de »

We have <u>very little time</u> for sporting activities.
Nous avons très peu de temps à consacrer aux activités sportives.

We have <u>a little time</u> to spend on golf.
Nous avons un peu de temps pour le golf.

8. *(A) few* + nom pluriel

« Quelques / peu de »

They have <u>very few</u> skilled technicians.
Ils ont très peu de techniciens qualifiés.

They have <u>a few</u> skilled workers.
Ils ont quelques ouvriers qualifiés.

REMARQUE *LITTLE* et *FEW* sont souvent précédés de *VERY et TOO.*

9. Les nombres

Seuls les nombres cardinaux sont des quantificateurs.

Hundred, thousand, million et ***billion*** ne prennent jamais de *-s* s'ils sont précédés d'un nombre ou de *a few / several*, et ils sont suivis immédiatement du nom sur lequel ils portent (sauf pour les sommes d'argent). Attention aux différences entre ce qui se dit et ce qui s'écrit !

That project cost us over £3m ("three million pounds") / $2bn ("two billion dollars").
Ce projet nous a coûté plus de 3 millions de livres / 2 milliards de dollars.

He is in charge of 135 people ("one hundred and thirty-five").
Il a la responsabilité de 135 personnes.

REMARQUE

On dira ***hundreds / thousands / millions / billions of*** s'ils ne sont pas précédés d'un nombre car ils sont alors substantivés :

Renovating the building will probably cost hundreds of thousands of euros.
La rénovation de ce bâtiment s'élèvera probablement à des centaines de milliers d'euros.

FICHE 23 Subordonnées de but

1. *To* + V (infinitif)

C'est la construction la plus courante :

The two firms merged to make savings of scale.
Les deux entreprises ont fusionné pour faire des économies d'échelle.

2. *In order to* + V / *so as to* + V

Forme d'insistance, ou plus formelle, et que l'on trouve souvent en début de phrase :

In order to get compensation for their losses, they filed a lawsuit.
Afin d'obtenir un dédommagement pour leurs pertes, ils ont déposé une plainte.

3. *In order not to* + V / *so as not to* + V

Ces deux constructions sont plus courantes que la simple forme *NOT TO* :

The department has been completely reorganized so as not to become less competitive.
Le service a été totalement restructuré pour ne pas devenir moins performant.

4. *So that* + sujet + auxiliaire modal

SO THAT + auxiliaire modal (*CAN / WILL / MAY / SHOULD / WOULD / MIGHT*, etc.) est employé lorsque les deux sujets sont différents :

We have patented the new device so that it will not be copied.
Nous avons breveté le nouveau procédé afin qu'il ne soit pas copié.

REMARQUE Lorsque les **deux sujets** sont différents, on peut aussi avoir un infinitif avec la construction suivante (voir Fiche 21, p. 202) :

I e-mailed Jane the information right away for her to make a rapid decision.
J'ai envoyé les renseignements à Jane par mail immédiatement pour qu'elle prenne une décision rapide.

FICHE 24 *USED TO* + V (passé révolu) et *TO BE / GET USED TO* + V*ING* (expression de l'habitude)

Il ne faut pas confondre ***USED TO*** **+ V** et ***TO BE / GET USED TO*** **+ V*ing***.

1. *USED TO* + V

Cette forme verbale fréquente indique un passé révolu contrastant avec le présent, souvent indiqué en français par « autrefois », « dans le passé », etc.

Our head office used to be in Manchester – now it is in Liverpool.
Notre siège social était autrefois situé à Manchester ; maintenant il est à Liverpool.

REMARQUE Notez les formes interrogatives et négatives.

Did you use to commute by bus?
Alliez-vous travailler en bus autrefois ?

Our goods did not use to be shipped by road, as they are now.
Dans le passé, les marchandises n'étaient pas expédiées par la route, comme elles le sont maintenant.

They never used to be late.
Elles n'étaient jamais en retard autrefois.

2. *TO BE / GET USED TO* + NOM OU V*ING*

Cette tournure exprime une habitude acquise ou en cours d'acquisition.

He is used to commuting by train now.
Maintenant, il est habitué à aller à son travail en train.

The new employee will have to get used to shift work.
Le nouvel employé devra s'habituer à faire les 3 x 8.

Robert has finally got used to (using) his new smartphone.
Robert s'est enfin habitué à (utiliser) son nouveau smartphone.

Has she got used to working late at night?
S'est-elle habituée à travailler tard le soir ?

REMARQUE

Une habitude peut aussi être exprimée avec un adverbe : *usually, generally*.

He generally calls / He is used to calling his clients early in the afternoon.
Il a l'habitude de téléphoner à ses clients en début d'après-midi.

The English usually have / are used to having a mid-morning coffee or tea-break.
Les Anglais ont l'habitude de prendre une pause thé ou café en milieu de matinée.

He generally commutes / is used to commuting by bike.
Il a l'habitude de venir au travail en vélo.

FICHE 25 Verbes pronominaux : équivalents en anglais

1. L'utilisation de verbes simples

Là où la langue française utilise des verbes pronominaux, le plus souvent l'anglais utilise des verbes simples : *get up* (se lever), *hurry* (se dépêcher), *hide* (se cacher), *wonder* (se demander), *remember* (se rappeler), *apologize* (s'excuser), *meet* (se rencontrer), *agree* (se mettre d'accord), *sell well* (bien se vendre). En cas de doute, vérifiez dans le dictionnaire.

Je me demande quand la réunion va commencer.
I wonder when the meeting will begin.

Nous nous sommes mis à travailler à 8 h du matin.
We started to work at 8 am.

Nos produits se sont-ils bien vendus ?
Have our products sold well?

Cet événement s'est produit l'an dernier.
This event happened last year.

Le comptable s'est vu confier une lourde tâche.
The accountant was given / assigned a difficult task.

2. L'utilisation du pronom réfléchi

Quand le sujet fait l'action sur ou pour lui-même, on peut utiliser un pronom réfléchi, qui est toujours accordé avec le sujet grammatical.

Le candidat s'est regardé dans le miroir avant l'entretien.
The applicant looked at himself in the mirror before the interview.

Mettez-vous à l'aise en attendant notre directeur.
Make yourselves comfortable while you are waiting for our manager.

Le client coréen ne parvenait pas à se faire comprendre.
The Korean customer could not make himself understood.

Vous êtes-vous bien amusé/amusés à la fête de Noël de l'entreprise ?
Did you enjoy yourself / yourselves at the company's Christmas party?

3. ONE ANOTHER / EACH OTHER

Quand il y a un sens réciproque (mutuel) on a recours à *ONE ANOTHER* ou *EACH OTHER*.

Ils travaillent en équipe en s'envoyant des mails.
They work in teams by sending e-mails to one another.

Nous nous téléphonons tous les lundi matins.
We call each other every Monday morning.

4. Équivalents à un passif en anglais (voir fiche 17)

- Notez en plus quelques constructions parmi d'autres :

Ils se sont vus interdire l'exportation de ces produits de haute technologie.
They were borbidden to export these high-tech products.

Cette augmentation de prix ne se sentira pas, à mon avis.
That price increase will not be felt, in my opinion.

Principaux verbes irréguliers

• **arise**	arose	arisen	*survenir ; se produire*
• **awake**	awoke	awoken	*(se) réveiller*
• **be**	was, were	been	*être*
• **beat**	beat	beaten	*battre*
• **become**	became	become	*devenir*
• **begin**	began	begun	*commencer*
• **break**	broke	broken	*casser*
• **bring**	brought	brought	*apporter*
• **broadcast**	broadcast	broadcast	*diffuser / émettre*
• **build**	built	built	*construire*
• **burn**	burnt	burnt	*brûler*
• **burst**	burst	burst	*éclater*
• **buy**	bought	bought	*acheter*
• **catch**	caught	caught	*attraper*
• **choose**	chose	chosen	*choisir*
• **cling**	clung	clung	*s'accrocher*
• **come**	came	come	*venir*
• **cost**	cost	cost	*coûter*
• **cut**	cut	cut	*couper*
• **deal**	dealt	dealt	*distribuer*
• **do**	did	done	*faire*
• **draw**	drew	drawn	*dessiner / tirer*
• **dream**	dreamt / dreamed	dreamt / dreamed	*rêver*
• **drink**	drank	drunk	*boire*
• **drive**	drove	driven	*conduire, aller en voiture*
• **eat**	ate	eaten	*manger*
• **fall**	fell	fallen	*tomber*
• **feel**	felt	felt	*se sentir / ressentir*
• **fight**	fought	fought	*combattre / se battre*
• **find**	found	found	*trouver*
• **fly**	flew	flown	*voler*
• **forbid**	forbade	forbidden	*interdire*
• **forecast**	forecast	forecast	*prévoir*
• **forget**	forgot	forgotten	*oublier*
• **get**	got	gotten / got (US)	*obtenir*
• **give**	gave	given	*donner*
• **go**	went	gone	*aller*
• **grow**	grew	grown	*grandir / pousser*
• **have**	had	had	*avoir*
• **hear**	heard	heard	*entendre*
• **hide**	hid	hidden	*cacher*
• **hit**	hit	hit	*frapper*
• **hold**	held	held	*tenir / détenir*
• **hurt**	hurt	hurt	*blesser / faire mal*
• **keep**	kept	kept	*garder*
• **know**	knew	known	*connaître / savoir*

• **lay**	laid	laid	*poser*
• **lead**	led	led	*mener / guider*
• **learn**	learnt	learnt	*apprendre*
• **leave**	left	left	*laisser / quitter / partir*
• **lend**	lent	lent	*prêter*
• **let**	let	let	*permettre / louer / laisser*
• **lie**	lay	lain	*être allongé*
• **lose**	lost	lost	*perdre*
• **make**	made	made	*fabriquer*
• **mean**	meant	meant	*signifier / vouloir dire*
• **meet**	met	met	*rencontrer*
• **pay**	paid	paid	*payer*
• **put**	put	put	*mettre*
• **read**	read	read	*lire*
• **ride**	rode	ridden	*monter (vélo, cheval)*
• **rise**	rose	risen	*se lever*
• **run**	ran	run	*courir*
• **say**	said	said	*dire*
• **see**	saw	seen	*voir*
• **sell**	sold	sold	*vendre*
• **send**	sent	sent	*envoyer*
• **set**	set	set	*placer / fixer*
• **shake**	shook	shaken	*secouer*
• **show**	showed	shown	*montrer*
• **shut**	shut	shut	*fermer*
• **sing**	sang	sung	*chanter*
• **sit**	sat	sat	*s'asseoir*
• **sleep**	slept	slept	*dormir*
• **smell**	smelt	smelt	*sentir (avec le nez)*
• **speak**	spoke	spoken	*parler*
• **spend**	spent	spent	*dépenser / passer du temps*
• **split**	split	split	*fendre / diviser*
• **spread**	spread	spread	*étaler / répandre*
• **stand**	stood	stood	*être debout*
• **steal**	stole	stolen	*voler / dérober*
• **stick**	stuck	stuck	*coller*
• **strike**	struck	stricken / struck	*frapper / impressionner / faire grève*
• **swear**	swore	sworn	*jurer*
• **sweep**	swept	swept	*balayer / emporter*
• **swell**	swelled	swollen / swelled	*gonfler / enfler*
• **swim**	swam	swum	*nager*
• **take**	took	taken	*prendre*
• **teach**	taught	taught	*enseigner*
• **tell**	told	told	*dire / raconter*
• **think**	thought	thought	*penser*
• **throw**	threw	thrown	*jeter*
• **understand**	understood	understood	*comprendre*
• **wear**	wore	worn	*porter (avoir sur soi)*
• **weep**	wept	wept	*pleurer*
• **win**	won	won	*gagner*
• **write**	wrote	written	*écrire*

Méthodes

Expression écrite

Conseils de base

Lisez bien l'énoncé d'un sujet d'expression écrite pour cerner ce qui est précisément demandé et donner une réponse pertinente.

Rédigez un brouillon aéré. Cela permet d'améliorer la copie finale.

Changez de paragraphe quand vous changez d'idée.

Relisez-vous toujours pour éliminer des erreurs qui vous auraient échappé (orthographe, faux amis, groupe verbale, place de l'adjectif, singuliers et pluriels, etc.)

Mobilisez vos connaissances en grammaire anglaise pour éviter les erreurs classiques. En effet, les plus grosses erreurs sont celles que l'on commet en calquant la grammaire française.

Commencez toujours une phrase par une majuscule et terminez-la par un point, sans oublier la ponctuation intermédiaire.

Enfin, soignez votre écriture, car une copie peu lisible sera pénalisée.

Orthographe

1 Voyelles

Des mots proches du français peuvent donner lieu à des erreurs.

*for ex**a**mple*	par ex**e**mple
*depend**ent** on*	dépend**a**nt de
*exp**e**nsive*	cher
*exp**a**nsive*	vaste
*respons**i**ble*	respons**a**ble
*med**i**cine*	méd**e**cine / médicament
*compar**i**son*	compar**ai**son
environment	environn**e**ment
*g**o**vernment*	g**ou**vern**e**ment

La lettre « i » se place avant la lettre « e », sauf après un « c ».

*a **pie**ce*

*to be**lie**ve*

*to re**cei**ve*

*a **cei**ling*

2 Consonnes

Les doubles consonnes sont plus rares en anglais. Observez les différences.

developed	développé
personal	personnel
consumer	consommateur

Voici quelques mots avec des doubles consonnes à connaître :

address	adresse
to disappear	disparaître
current	actuel
committee	comité

Quand doubler une consonne ?

Avec l'ordre **consonne + voyelle + consonne**, dans une syllabe accentuée, on double la consonne finale.

begin	*beginning*
deter	*deterrent*
equip	*equipped*

Dans tous les autres cas, on ne double pas la consonne.

wide	*widen*
happen	*happening*
open	*opening*
transition	*transitional*

Alors que le mot « *full* » prend deux « l », le suffixe « *-ful* » ne prend qu'un seul « *l* ».

full	plein, rempli
useful	utile

Quand on ajoute le suffixe « *-ly* » :

- à un mot qui se termine par un « *-y* », « *y* » devient « *i* » :
  - *happy* → *happily*
  - *easy* → *easily*
- à un mot qui se termine par un « *-l* », on double le « *l* ».
  - *global* → *globally*
  - *real* → *really*

3 Majuscules

Les noms et adjectifs de nationalité, les pays et les langues commencent toujours par une majuscule.

Nationalités	*French*	*British*	*Chinese*
Pays	*China*	*Italy*	*Greece*

Les jours et le mois prennent toujours une majuscule.
Monday, Tuesday, etc. *January, February, etc.*

Les organismes officiels, les titres officiels, les noms propres de lieux, etc. prennent une majuscule sur chaque mot porteur de sens (même les adjectifs, à la différence du français.)
the European Commission : la Commission européenne
Mitsubishi Motors Corp : la société Mitsubishi Motors
the World Economic Forum : le Forum économique mondial
New York City : la ville de New York
the International Energy Agency : l'Agence internationale de l'énergie

Attention, certains noms propres ne se traduisent pas en français.
Silicon Valley : la Silicon Valley *Loch Ness* : Loch Ness

4 Divers

Les mots qui se terminent par la lettre « *-y* » subissent une modification orthographique quand on ajoute un « *-s* ».

- « *-s* » marqueur du pluriel :

a reply	→	*replies*	(une réponse / des réponses)
technology	→	*technologies*	

- « *-s* » marqueur de la 3ᵉ personne du singulier au présent :

to carry	→	*he carries*	(porter / il porte)

Une différence sur une seule lettre peut modifier le sens d'un mot. Il ne faut pas confondre :

to fund (financer)	et	*found* (trouvé)
to lose (perdre)	et	*loose* (ample)
through (au travers de)	et	*though* (bien que)
a means (un moyen)	et	*to mean* (signifier)

people (gens)	et	*peoples* (peuples)
to advise (conseiller)	et	*advice* (conseil(s))
silicon (silicium)	et	*silicone* (silicone)

Certains mots sont contractés en anglais.

another	un / une autre
cannot	ne peux/peut pas

Mots qui posent parfois des problèmes d'orthographe :

to conclude	conclure
necessary	nécessaire
future	avenir
company	entreprise

Les acronymes, invariables en français, se mettent au pluriel en anglais :

des OGM	*GMOs*
des PDG	*CEOs*
des ONG	*NGOs*

Quelques difficultés classiques

1 Les faux amis

Ces mots faussement transparents sont nombreux. Voici les plus courants dans le lexique des affaires :

- *to achieve* : réaliser
- *actually* : en réalité
- *an agenda* : un programme / ordre du jour
- *an application* : une candidature
- *an appointment* : un rendez-vous
- *to attend* : assister à
- *a benefit* : un avantage, une allocation
- *to charge* : faire payer
- *a commodity* : une marchandise
- *a copy* : un exemplaire
- *currently* : actuellement
- *a delay* : un retard
- *to deliver* : livrer
- *an issue* : une question, un problème
- *a location* : un emplacement / lieu
- *to prevent* : empêcher
- *to realize* : se rendre compte
- *to rely on* : dépendre de
- *to resign* : démissionner
- *to survey* : examiner

2 Les noms composés

Les noms composés anglais sont bâtis de droite à gauche. Pour les comprendre, on les déchiffre généralement en commençant par le nom le plus à droite (voir Fiche 12 de l'Aide-mémoire grammatical) :

- *a public awareness campaign* → une campagne de sensibilisation du public
  a brand image → une image de marque
  a market share → une part de marché

3 Les titres de civilité et noms propres

Les titres de civilité sont traduits pour les personnes réelles.

- *Mr and Mrs Smith, who live in London, are moving to Belgium.*
  → Monsieur et Madame (ou M. et Mme) Smith, qui vivent à Londres, vont déménager en Belgique.

On ne traduit pas les noms propres sauf s'il existe une traduction reconnue.

- *Doctor Stephen Jones works for the WHO (World Health Organization).*
  → Le docteur Stephen Jones travaille pour l'OMS (Organisation mondiale de la santé).
- *London is the capital of the United Kingdom.*
  → Londres est la capitale du Royaume-Uni.
- *She works for the CIA.*
  → Elle travaille pour la CIA.

2 Les devises ou monnaies

Elles ne sont pas traduites, mais sont écrites différemment.

- *It will cost a record $5m.* (Prononcer « *five million dollars.* »)
  → Cela va coûter la somme record de 5 millions de dollars.
- *It cost £50,000* (prononcer « *fifty thousand pounds* »), *not £50.50!* (prononcer « *fifty pounds point fifty* »).
  → Cela a coûté 50 000 livres, pas 50,50 livres !
- *This is worth €3bn.* (Prononcer « *three billion euros.* »)
  → Cela vaut trois milliards d'euros.

REMARQUE Les chiffres ne s'écrivent pas de la même façon en français et en anglais. Attention aux différences de ponctuation.

Traduction

Méthode générale

1 Comprendre

Lisez le texte à traduire entièrement, voire tout le texte d'où est tiré le passage à traduire, pour le comprendre globalement. Puis analysez chaque phrase pour repérer sa construction : sujet, verbe, complément(s), pronom(s), mot(s) de liaisons, subordonnée(s), etc.

Observez les phrases suivantes et leur traduction :

- *Most of the people found the new product very easy to use.* (*found* est ici à la voix active, indiquée par le contexte.)
  → La plupart des gens ont trouvé que le nouveau produit était très facile à utiliser.
- *But most of the people found working in appalling conditions were underpaid.* (*found* est ici au passif, indiqué par le contexte.)
  → Mais la plupart des personnes qu'on a trouvées en train de travailler dans des conditions épouvantables étaient sous-payées.

2 Premier jet

Traduisez les phrases une à une sur un brouillon aéré afin de pouvoir y noter plusieurs solutions de traduction. Cherchez des synonymes, le mot juste, l'expression exacte dans la langue d'arrivée. Même si vous n'avez pas d'épreuve de traduction à l'examen, vous aurez probablement à en faire au cours de votre vie professionnelle, et les conseils de technique, présentées page 220, vous seront utiles.

3 Relecture critique

Reprenez votre brouillon et opérez des choix définitifs.

Tenez compte :

– du contexte ;

– du niveau de langue ;

– des règles de grammaire en vigueur dans la langue d'arrivée.

Prenez du recul pour ne pas écrire de phrases absurdes.

4 Rédaction finale

Mettez au propre en vérifiant l'orthographe et la ponctuation.

Vérifiez aussi les majuscules (parfois différentes entre les deux langues) et le découpage des paragraphes.

Relisez une dernière fois et complétez les éventuels blancs.

La version

Elle consiste à traduire un texte anglais en français.

Les difficultés sont de deux ordres : comprendre le texte anglais, puis rédiger en français correct et compréhensible, tout en restant fidèle au sens.

Évitez le non-sens (= phrase absurde). Un contresens sera moins sanctionné.

Face à des mots inconnus, ne restez pas bloqué(e) ; tenez compte du contexte, de la racine des mots, de l'analyse grammaticale de la phrase pour inférer le sens probable de ces mots.

Un texte anglais traduit en français est souvent plus long à l'arrivée car la langue française est analytique et l'anglais plus synthétique.

Les emprunts à l'anglais en français

Ils sont à éviter lorsqu'il existe un équivalent.

- *a challenge* : un défi
- *fast food* : la restauration rapide
- *sponsoring* : le parrainage

Le thème

Il s'agit de traduire un texte français en anglais.

Dans les examens, cet exercice est destiné à évaluer vos compétences en grammaire et vos connaissances lexicales. Il faut donc veiller à appliquer les règles apprises et à ne pas calquer des structures françaises, le plus souvent différentes :

▸ Quand la nouvelle loi sera votée, les restaurants paieront moins de TVA.

→ *When the new law is voted, restaurants will pay less VAT.*

Dans cet exemple, il faut appliquer la règle de grammaire sur le choix des temps dans les subordonnées de temps.

Un texte anglais est souvent plus court qu'un texte français car l'anglais est une langue synthétique qui ramasse le sens dans des formules courtes :

▸ Quand on les a questionnés, les consommateurs qui étaient criblés de dettes ont reconnu qu'ils avaient contracté plusieurs emprunts. (20 mots)

→ *When questioned, debt-ridden consumers admitted they had several loans.* (9 mots)

Techniques

Le plus souvent, la traduction littérale ne suffit pas ; c'est pourquoi on a recours à des techniques éprouvées.

1 La transposition

On change de catégorie grammaticale.

- *The new manager speaks fluent Japanese.* (adjectif)
  → Le nouveau directeur parle couramment le japonais. (adverbe)

2 La modulation

On change de point de vue.

- *They were sent the invoice in time.* (passif)
  → On leur a envoyé la facture à temps. (actif)

3 L'équivalence

On recherche l'expression exacte.

- *I look forward to your reply.*
  → Dans l'attente de votre réponse. / Merci d'avance de votre réponse.

4 L'étoffement

On utilise plus de mots. Les prépositions anglaises font souvent l'objet d'un étoffement en français.

- *They spent money on training the workers.*
  → Ils ont dépensé de l'argent pour financer la formation des travailleurs.

5 L'effacement

On utilise moins de mots.

- Je suis allé à Bruxelles par avion.
  → *I flew to Brussels.*

Méthodes

Description et analyse de diagrammes et tableaux

Pour l'examen et dans votre vie professionnelle, vous aurez à effectuer des descriptions et analyses de données fournies par :

- des diagrammes (*charts*),
- des tableaux (*tables*),
- des camemberts (*pie charts*),
- des histogrammes (*bar chart*),
- des graphiques (*graphs*),
- des chiffres (*figures*),
- des courbes (*curves/charts*).

Dans votre rapport, écrit ou oral, après avoir bien observé le document, commencez par préciser (*specify*) ses sources (origine et date), et indiquez son sujet en quelques mots introduisant le contexte et l'ensemble. Ensuite dégagez les principales idées et tendances (*trends*). Terminez enfin par une brève conclusion.

CONSEILS

– Faites attention à la ponctuation des chiffres, qui est différente en anglais et en français.

– Utilisez certaines expressions données ci-dessous (p. 221-225).

– Évitez les traductions littérales si vous partez du français.

– Soyez vigilant(e) sur l'emploi des formes verbales et des prépositions.

– Rédigez des phrases courtes et claires. Mettez-vous à la place d'une personne ne connaissant pas le document.

– Explicitez l'implicite.

– À l'examen respectez le nombre de mots indiqués à 10 % près, et indiquez ce nombre à la fin.

1. Débuts

- *This table was published in (name of source) dated … / in the year 202…*
  (si ce n'est pas la même année. Sinon soyez plus précis en donnant le jour et le mois.)

  → Ce tableau a été publié dans (nom de la source) en date du… / en 202….

- *This chart shows the situation of … in… (time and place)*

  → Ce graphique montre la situation de … en … (moment et lieu)

- *According to the World Trade Organisation, …*

  → D'après l'Organisation mondiale du commerce…

- *These findings come from a study by the European Union.*

  → Ces résultats proviennent d'une étude de l'Union européenne.

2. Indications temporelles (*time indications*)

- *As of / from January 202… to / until December 202…*

  → À partir/dater de janvier 202… jusqu'en / à décembre 202…

- *From / Starting from 202…*

  → Depuis 202…

- *Between 202… and 202…, the situation improved noticeably.*

  → Entre 202… et 202…, la situation s'est nettement améliorée.

- *Since the beginning of this year, investors have had a hard time.*

  → Depuis le début de cette année, les investisseurs traversent une période difficile.
  (Notez les différences de temps entre l'anglais et le français.)

- *This table highlights the most important figures year by year.*

  → Ce tableau fait ressortir les principaux chiffres année par année.

- *Mortgage lending has increased by 10% year-on-year/ per year (up) to just £1.1 billion.*

  → Les prêts immobiliers ont augmenté de 30 % sur un an / par an pour atteindre juste 1,1 milliard de livres.

- *In February, industrial investment fell by about 20% from a year ago.*

  → En février, les investissements industriels ont baissé de 20 % environ depuis l'an dernier.

3. Tendances à la hausse (*upward trends*)

- *China's textile exports went up / grew / increased by 5.3% last year to CNY 6.5b.*

  → Les exportations chinoises de textiles ont augmenté de 5,3 % l'an dernier, atteignant 6,5 milliards de yuans.

- *Shares shot up / soared on the stock markets in 202… .*

  → Les actions ont monté en flèche sur les marchés boursiers en 202… .

- *American producers raised their prices significantly on the domestic market.*

  → Les producteurs américains ont augmenté leurs prix de façon significative sur leur marché intérieur.

- *Production rose by less/more than 3% in Brazil.*

  → La production a augmenté de moins/plus de 3 % au Brésil.

- *There was a big rise in commodity prices in 202… .*

  → Il y a eu une forte augmentation/hausse des prix des matières premières en 20… .

- *Real estate prices in Paris began to spiral upwards three years ago.*
  → Les prix de l'immobilier à Paris se sont mis à monter en flèche il y a trois ans.
- *They peaked / reached a peak in the summer of 2020 / last September.*
  → Ils ont atteint un sommet / pic l'été 2020 / en septembre dernier.
- *Last year, trade volumes grew by a sluggish 0.5%.*
  → L'an dernier, le volume des échanges commerciaux a connu une croissance faible limitée à 0,5 %.

4. Tendances à la baisse (*downward trends*)

- *Imports slowly dropped / fell / went down / decreased slightly by 2.4% afterwards.*
  → Les importations ont lentement diminué / connu une légère baisse de 2,4 % ensuite.
- *Oil prices suddenly spiralled downwards / plummeted / collapsed at the end of last summer.*
  → Les prix du pétrole ont soudain dégringolé / se sont effondrés / écroulés à la fin de l'été dernier.
- *They reached their lowest level / point on October 25.*
  → Ils ont atteint leur plus bas niveau / leur point bas le 25 octobre.
- *There has been a 4% drop / fall / decrease of 4% in oil consumption.*
  → Il y a eu une baisse de 4 % de la consommation de pétrole (et elle continue).
- *It is the biggest one-year decline in trade since the Second World War.*
  → C'est la plus forte baisse d'échanges commerciaux sur une année depuis la Seconde Guerre mondiale.
- *Tanzania's GDP shrank at an annualised rate of 1.2 % in the last quarter.*
  → Le PIB de la Tanzanie est tombé à un taux annualisé de 1,2 % au cours du dernier trimestre.

5. Tendances stables (*stable trends*)

- *House prices have remained stable / unchanged / steady since…*
  → Les prix de l'immobilier sont restés stables / inchangés depuis…
- *The recession has bottomed out…*
  → La récession est à son plus bas niveau (mais va s'améliorer)…

- *There has been no change in this trend since…*
  → La tendance n'a pas changé depuis…
- *Germany maintained its position as the world's number-one exporter in the first quarter.*
  → L'Allemagne a préservé sa position de premier exportateur mondial / de numéro un mondial pour les exportations au premier trimestre.
- *Their sales figures are stagnant / disappointing.*
  → Leurs chiffres de ventes stagnent / sont décevants.

6. Comparaisons (*comparisons*)

- *The situation in the USA is better / worse than in the EU.*
  → La situation aux États-Unis est meilleure / pire que dans l'Union européenne.
- *There are more / fewer company failures now than in…*
  → On observe davantage de fermetures / moins de fermetures d'entreprises aujourd'hui qu'en…
- *These results are comparable to those of two years ago.*
  → Ces résultats sont comparables à ceux d'il ya deux ans.
- *Dublin's population, compared to / with London's, is much smaller.*
  → La population de Dublin, comparée / par rapport à celle de Londres, est bien plus petite.
- *Unlike Indians, few Chinese people speak English well.*
  → À la différence des Indiens, peu de Chinois parlent bien anglais.
- *Things are much the same as they were last year.*
  → La situation est très semblable à ce qu'elle était l'an dernier.
- *This product is twice / three times as expensive in … as in …*
  → Ce produit coûte deux fois plus / trois fois plus cher en … qu'en …
- *Office rents in this district are half as high as in that one.*
  → Les loyers de bureaux dans ce quartier-ci sont 50 % moins chers que dans celui-là.

7. Prévisions (*Forecasts*)

- *If present trends continue, the top three exporters may / will soon account for 25% of world trade.*
  → Si les tendances actuelles continuent, les trois premiers exportateurs représenteront (peut-être) bientôt 25 % des échanges mondiaux.

- *Banks are not likely to change their policy for a long time yet.*
  → Les banques ne sont pas susceptibles de changer de politique avant longtemps.
- *Some drastic changes are bound to occur soon.*
  → Des changements drastiques ne manqueront pas de se produire bientôt.
- *A gradual improvement in car sales is expected soon.*
  → On s'attend à une amélioration graduelle des ventes pour bientôt.

8. Conclusion

- *To conclude / In conclusion / In short, this chart clearly shows that…*
  → En conclusion / En bref, ce graphique montre clairement que…

Présentation d'une lettre commerciale (*layout of a business letter*)

La disposition en bloc (*fully blocked display/layout*) est la plus simple et la plus courante. Toutes les lignes commencent à gauche, sauf le nom de la société expéditrice (*sender*) généralement pré-imprimée sur la feuille, et la ponctuation (très importante) est utilisée seulement dans le corps de la lettre.

Rédigez des lettres courtes, idéalement sur une seule page, ne traitant qu'un sujet à la fois.

1 Date

Elle est généralement mentionnée en premier juste au-dessus ou au-dessous de la référence (*"Our ref/Your ref"*). La présentation diffère entre l'anglais et l'américain :

- En américain *"9/4/20…"* veut dire *"September 4, 20…"*.
- En anglais britannique, la même indication signifie *"9 April 20…"*.

Pour éviter toute confusion, n'écrivez jamais de simples chiffres mais : *"September the fourth"*, ou *"2 April 20…"* (prononcé *"the second of April"*).

Pour éviter les erreurs, écrivez simplement le chiffre du jour sans *th/st/nd* qui est facultatif. Mettez une majuscule au nom du mois (*April, May*, etc.)

2 Nom du destinataire (*addressee*)

Si vous ne le connaissez pas parce que c'est la première fois que vous écrivez à une entreprise ou un organisme, n'en mettez pas. Si vous le connaissez, mettez-le avec le titre (inchangé) suivi de la fonction et/ou du service (*department*) où le destinataire travaille.

- *Mr Pinkerton, General Manager*
- *Ms Farrow, Accounting Department*

De plus en plus souvent, on appelle une femme Ms (prononcé *"miz"*, condensé de *Mrs et Miss)*.

3 Adresse et code postal (*post code* en Grande-Bretagne et Irlande et *zip code* aux États-Unis)

– En Grande-Bretagne, le code postal vient juste après le nom de la ville, mais avant le nom du comté :

- *Marlborough SN81JA, Wiltshire, Great Britain*

– Aux États-Unis, il est placé après le nom de l'État écrit en abrégé.

- *CA 94708-1544, USA (CA= California)*

4 Formule d'appel (*opening salutation*)

– Si vous ne connaissez pas le nom de la personne, écrivez :

- *Dear Sir* ou *Dear Madam*, ou *Dear Sirs* si vous écrivez à un service.

– Si vous connaissez le nom du destinataire, employez-le :

- *Dear Mr Hayley / Dear Mrs Fretter*

– Très rapidement votre correspondant anglophone utilisera votre prénom. Répondez-lui avec le sien.

- *Dear Bill / Dear Nicky*

5 Objet (*subject*)

S'il y en a un, il est généralement placé juste au-dessus ou au-dessous de la formule d'appel, et souvent écrit en majuscules (*capital / block letters*) ou souligné (*underlined*).

- *Request for information*
- *APPLICATION FOR A JOB OFFER* (= lettre de candidature à un emploi ou lettre de motivation)

6 Corps de la lettre (*content / contents*)

N'employez pas de formes contractées (par exemple : *we'll*) considérées comme familières, mais le style doit rester simple et direct avec des phrases courtes.

a) Introduction

Si possible, référez-vous à une lettre reçue, à une annonce publicitaire, une brochure, etc.

- *Thank you for your letter dated 7 August 202... .*
- *We have received your letter / order / complaint dated June 3, 202...*

- *Following this morning's telephone conversation, we are pleased to confirm…*
- *I am interested in your job offer published in* The Economist *of May 30.*

b) Faits

Commencez par le principal, et traitez les suivants par ordre logique ou chronologique :

- *We wish to order 100 boxes of envelopes …*

  → Je vous prie de noter ma commande de 100 boîtes d'enveloppes.

- *Your product is exactly what we need, so we would like to meet you to discuss details …*

  → Votre produit correspond exactement à ce que nous recherchons, nous souhaitons donc vous rencontrer pour en discuter dans les détails…

- *Your order will be dispatched today, so you should receive the articles in time for your exhibition.*

  → Votre commande va vous être expédiée ce jour même ; vous devriez donc la recevoir à temps pour votre exposition.

c) Conclusion

Terminez sur une note positive et courtoise :

- *Thank you very much for your help / your offer.*

  → Je vous remercie vivement de votre aide / offre.

- *May we apologize once more for this incident."*

  → Je tiens à vous renouveler mes excuses pour cet incident.

- *Please confirm my booking as soon as possible* (ou *ASAP*).

  → Veuillez (avoir l'obligeance de) confirmer ma réservation dès que possible.

- *I look forward to your reply / hearing from you / seeing you / working with you.*

  → Je vous remercie d'avance de votre réponse. / Je serai très heureux/se de vous rencontrer / de collaborer avec vous.

7 Salutation finale (*closing salutation*)

Elle est bien plus simple et courte qu'en français :

- *Yours faithfully / Faithfully yours* (si vous ne connaissez pas le destinatare)

  → Veuillez agréer mes salutations distinguées / meilleurs sentiments

- *Yours sincerely* (la plus courante)

  → Cordialement

- *Yours / Best wishes / Kindest regards* (si vous connaissez bien le destinataire)

  → Amitiés / Amicalement

8 Signature

Manuscrite, elle est suivie du nom imprimé (pour la lisibilité) souvent suivi du rappel de la fonction *("Sales Manager")*, et de *Mrs* ou *Ms* pour une femme.
– Ms Helen Gifford / GIFFORD

Chief accountant

9 Pièce jointe (*enclosure*)

P.J. = Enc.

Cette indication se note en bas de la lettre à gauche.

REMARQUES Les mails ou courriels *(emails)* tendent de plus en plus à remplacer les courriers. À l'examen, on vous demandera l'un ou l'autre.

La date et les adresses s'affichent souvent automatiquement. Le style en est le plus simple et bref possible. Les questions sont au style direct. De nombreuses formules indiquées ci-dessus sont moins importantes et plus courtes et les formes contractées sont assez fréquentes.

Mais politesse et courtoisie restent de rigueur, et une réponse rapide est généralement attendue, sans précipitation toutefois.

N'oubliez pas d'indiquer l'objet *(subject)* et s'il y a une piece jointe *(attachment)*.

Formules utiles :

I am going to email you the necessary documents ASAP.

Please send your order by tomorrow.

▶ Réponse à une demande de renseignements

ACTION INTERNATIONALE
12 rue du Moulin Bleu
24 000 Périgueux
FRANCE

18 March 202…

Mr Thomas TRIMMAN
QUALITY EQUIPMENT
10 Hewell Street
Bedford BE8 OPD
GREAT BRITAIN

Dear Mr Trimman

Request for information

Thank you for your letter dated 15 March 20… in which you ask for information about the French market. We are willing to offer you our services as sole agents for your products which, in our opinion, would sell very well in France. More and more people are joining walking clubs, walking further and further, and in need therefore of the right equipment. Your high-quality products would attract a wide range of walkers who would be happy to improve the conditions in which they pursue their leisure activities.

We suggest meeting as soon as possible to discuss the matter further. Over the next few weeks, our chief representative in Britain, Charles Leroger will be visiting several firms with whom we do business. He would be delighted to call on you, at your convenience, to give you all the information you need about the market and about our company, methods, terms and prices, etc.

You will find enclosed a document that will give you a good idea of the international activities of our company. We look forward to hearing from you and to doing business with you.

Yours sincerely

Pauline DUVAL
Marketing Manager

Enc: Brochure

▸ Lettre avec facture

Institut Framotard
18 avenue Mariaud
69 006 Lyon FRANCE

25 April 202…

Ms Lucy O'Connor
Sales Manager
Rodell & Lewis
Roxboro Road
Limerick
Irlande

Dear Ms O'Connor

Order ref.55/LV

Thank you for your letter dated 17 April 202… . We enclose our pro forma invoice amounting to €15,450 for your order ref. 55/LV, together with the bill of exchange, nb. 559. We will instruct our agent to forward your order as soon as we receive confirmation of credit transfer from your bank.

The invoice includes extra charge for air freight and special packing in insulated boxes. It also shows the 10% trade discount we have granted you as this is a trial order.

We hope these arrangements are satisfactory, and we look forward to doing further business with you.

Yours sincerely

Fabien Lebreton
Chief Accountant

Enc

Lettre d'excuses

STATIONERY SUPPLIES LTD
5 Whiteladies Road
Reading
ENGLAND RG3 5WW

12 February 202…

Mr Jean Thomas
Manager
TOUS CADEAUX
9 rue Sylvain Delaterre
14 000 CAEN
FRANCE

Dear Mr Thomas

We thank you once again for your order nb 2003 which we had agreed to deliver by 1 April. Unfortunately, we have been informed that the manufacturer is unable to provide a certain number of the products in your order. He is confronted by a shortage of raw materials, particularly paper where there has been a cutback in supplies of imported pulp.

Thus, we will be unable to deliver the gift wrapping, gift boxes and paper bags in time, as we had promised, for the Stationery Fair. They will not be available until June.

We apologize profusely for this delay, and would ask you to let us know if you wish to maintain or cancel your order.

We look forward to hearing from you and to continuing our business activities.

Yours sincerely

Carolyn Ladley
Sales Manager

Comment lire et utiliser un document efficacement

1 Prenez connaissance du document de manière synthétique pour le cadrer, en répondant aux questions suivantes :

- Quel type de document est présenté ici ?
  → *This is an article from the press / Document 4 is a diagram published by …*
- De quoi s'agit-il?
  → *This text is about … / Document 1 deals with …*
- D'où ce document a-t-il été extrait et quand a-t-il été produit ?
  → *It comes from* The Guardian *published in 2020. / It is an extract from a report written on October 12, 202…*
- De quel pays ?
  → *The UK, the USA, India, etc.*
- Que savez-vous déjà sur la question ? (Si possible, car cela vous aidera à mieux comprendre.)

2 Lisez le document une première fois rapidement

1. Que dit le titre, et éventuellement, que dit le sous-titre (*subtitle)* ? Ce dernier, s'il y en a, peut aider à la compréhension mieux que le titre qui n'est parfois qu'une accroche (*catchword*) ou un jeu de mots (*pun*).

2. Pour avoir une vision d'ensemble, vous pouvez commencer par lire le premier et le dernier paragraphes, ainsi que les première et dernière phrases de chaque paragraphe. Cette technique peut vous être utile si votre temps est limité.

Lisez le document jusqu'au bout, ne vous arrêtez pas sur les passages difficiles ou que vous ne comprenez pas bien. D'autant plus que la fin peut vous aider à comprendre l'ensemble du document.

Lors de cette première lecture, vous pouvez repérer les mots importants en les soulignant ou en les surlignant.

3. Évitez d'utiliser le dictionnaire (si vous en avez un). Il est normal de ne pas tout comprendre à ce stade. Le contexte doit vous aider à comprendre, et les mots difficiles ne doivent pas vous empêcher de comprendre l'ensemble.

4. Au cours de la lecture, ne revenez en arrière que si c'est absolument nécessaire. Sinon, cela peut vous faire perdre du temps. Sautez (*skip*) les passages trop longs et qui ne semblent guère essentiels.

3 Relisez le document plus lentement pour le comprendre plus en profondeur.

Une seconde lecture vous aidera à mieux comprendre le document. Lisez le document plus lentement en pensant aux questions posées. Repérez la structure du texte en vous appuyant sur les idées principales et à leur articulation. Les articles de presse suivent généralement le plan ci-dessous :

a. Introduction au problème

b. Causes et consequences
ou Avantages et inconvénients des faits décrits

c. Solution donnée
ou Conclusion

Généralement, les exemples donnés ne sont pas essentiels ; vous pouvez les ignorer.

Certains textes proposés à l'examen sont abrégés et donc incomplets. Mais ils sont toujours cohérents et assez riches pour donner matière à réfléchir.

Repérer la structure du texte vous permettra ensuite de structurer le résumé (s'il est demandé).

4 Mots ou expressions difficiles

Vous pouvez souvent inférer le sens des mots et expressions en vous aidant du contexte. Vous pouvez aussi analyser le mot à partir de sa racine, du préfixe et du suffixe.

Lorsque vous vous aidez d'un dictionnaire, recherchez le mot à partir de la classe grammaticale (verbe, nom, adjectif, etc.). Ne vous arrêtez pas à la première traduction donnée s'il y en a plusieurs, et lisez les exemples en cherchant celui qui correspond au contexte de votre document. Attention aux faux amis (voir p. 216)

Profitez-en pour vous constituer des listes de mots ou expressions pour enrichir votre anglais.

5 Chiffres et nombres (*figures and numbers*)

Le plus souvent, il n'est pas nécessaire de reprendre tels quels les chiffres mentionnés dans les articles de presse. Ces chiffres doivent vous permettre d'indiquer un ordre de grandeur, des faits généraux. Vous pouvez donc les simplifier, ce qui permettra de les mémoriser plus facilement et montrera que vous avez bien compris l'idée générale.

- *"395"* peut devenir *"almost/nearly 400"* ou *"about 400"* ou simplement *"a lot/many".*
- *"1,022"* peut être remplacé par *"over 1,000"* ou par *"about 1,000"*.

6 Comprendre et utiliser un document iconographique

Le document peut être ambigu ou avoir plusieurs sens. C'est très souvent le cas pour les dessins humoristiques (*cartoons*), dont l'humour n'est pas toujours évident pour un Français. Il y en a souvent à l'examen. Retrouvez les points communs entre le document iconographique et le ou les textes qu'il accompagne, repérez en quoi ce document complète les textes ou leur répond.

Vous pouvez prendre appui sur la question posée afin de vous aider à mieux comprendre et exploiter le document.

Rédaction d'un rapport, d'un résumé, d'un document administratif ou d'un mémo

"KISS" = Keep It Short and Simple! Autrement dit, faites court et simple si vous voulez être lu et compris.

1 La page titre (essentiel)

Elle annonce le sujet central, les noms de l'expéditeur et du ou des destinataire(s) (si possible), date et références.

2 Introduction

Votre document doit commencer par une introduction. Elle doit être brève si votre texte doit comporter un nombre de mots très limité, et doit amener rapidement le lecteur dans le vif du sujet.

3 Contenu

Votre document doit être divisé en paragraphes. Ceux-ci doivent rester courts et ne développer qu'une idée principale. Ils doivent être structurés en suivant une ligne directrice qui amène logiquement à la conclusion. Si vous devez rédiger un compte rendu ou un résumé, n'ajoutez pas d'idées ou de commentaires personnels.

4 Conclusion

Elle doit reprendre en quelques mots l'ensemble du texte, éventuellement en renvoyant à l'introduction, ce qui montre que le sujet a été bien cerné.

Synthèse de documents

Un corpus est un ensemble de documents abordant une même thématique ou problématique sous des angles variés se complétant ou se répondant. À l'examen, celui-ci est suivi d'une question qui vous guidera dans la synthèse demandée : on vous demande généralement non pas de résumer chacun des textes l'un après l'autre (comme dans ce manuel) mais de trouver des réponses à la question posée dans l'ensemble des textes montrant que vous les avez tous compris globalement, ainsi que leur articulation. Et aussi que vous avez un esprit de synthèse capable de dominer un sujet développé en anglais.

1 Repérez la thématique ou la problématique

Faites une lecture rapide de tous les documents pour repérer la thématique ou problématique commune de l'ensemble du corpus, généralement indiquée par la question.

2 Assurez-vous d'avoir compris l'énoncé et les textes en profondeur

Notez ce qui est à dégager. Puis soulignez ou surlignez les mots ou passages importants, repérez les points communs et les différences importantes entre les textes sur la thématique définie. Trouvez la ligne directrice.

3 Rédigez la synthèse

Écrivez d'abord un brouillon. Ne recopiez pas de phrases du texte, surtout si vous le faites dans la même langue que les textes. Ne les traduisez pas non plus. Mais réutilisez les mots ou expressions importants. Faites un plan. Votre rédaction finale reposera alors sur cette trame. Quand vous citerez une idée, précisez de quel document elle vient. Autant que possible n'oubliez pas de point important. En conclusion, reprenez brièvement et clairement les points principaux. N'ajoutez pas de commentaire personnel. Soignez votre écriture. Relisez-vous. Supprimez toute trace de comptage. Vérifiez votre nombre de mots et indiquez-le.

Annexes

Countries and nationalities

Country	Language and/or nationality	One person	Peoples *(= les peuples)*
England	English	an Englishman an Englishwoman	the English
Great Britain	British	a Briton	(the) Britons / the British
Scotland	Scottish	a Scot / a Scotsman a Scotswoman	the Scots
Wales	Welsh	a Welshman a Welshwoman	the Welsh
Ireland / Eire the Republic of Ireland	Irish	an Irishman an Irishwoman	the Irish
the USA	American	an American	the Americans
Austria	Austrian	an Austrian	the Austrians
Belgium	Belgian	a Belgian	the Belgians
the Czech Republic	Czech	a Czech	the Czechs
Denmark	Danish	a Dane	the Danish
France	French	a Frenchman a Frenchwoman	the French
Germany	German	a German	the Germans
Greece	Greek	a Greek	the Greeks
Hungary	Hungarian	a Hungarian	the Hungarians
Italy	Italian	an Italian	the Italians
the Netherlands	Dutch	a Dutchman a Dutchwoman	The Dutch
Norway	Norwegian	a Norwegian	the Norwegians
Poland	Polish	a Pole	the Polish
Portugal	Portuguese	a Portuguese	the Portuguese
Spain	Spanish	a Spaniard	the Spaniards / the Spanish
Sweden	Swedish	a Swede	the Swedes
Switzerland	Swiss	a Swiss	the Swiss
Cambodia	Cambodian	a Cambodian	the Cambodians
China	Chinese	a Chinese	the Chinese
Iraq	Iraqi	an Iraqi	the Iraqis
Israel	Israeli	an Israeli	the Israelis
Japan	Japanese	a Japanese	the Japanese
Pakistan	Pakistani	a Pakistani	the Pakistanis
Saudi Arabia	Arabic	a Saudi Arabian	the Saudi Arabians
Turkey	Turk	a Turk	the Turks

Cities

French name	English name
Abou Dhabi	Abu Dhabi
Alger	Algiers
Anvers	Antwerp
Athènes	Athens
Bagdad	Baghdad
Barcelone	Barcelona
Beyrouth	Beirut
Bombay	Mumbai / Bombay
Bruxelles	Brussels
Bucarest	Bucharest
Copenhague	Copenhagen
Damas	Damascus
Douvres	Dover
Dresde	Dresden
Édimbourg	Edinburgh
Francfort	Frankfurt
Gênes	Genoa
Genève	Geneva
Gand	Ghent
Hambourg	Hamburg
Hanovre	Hanover
La Haye	The Hague
La Havane	Havana
La Nouvelle-Orléans	New Orleans
Le Caire	Cairo
Le Cap	Capetown
Kaboul	Kabul
Londres	London
Lisbonne	Lisbon
Manille	Manila
Marseille	Marseilles
Lyon	Lyons
Mexico	Mexico City
Moscou	Moscow
Pékin	Peking / Beijing
Saint-Pétersbourg	Saint Petersburg
Singapour	Singapore
La Valette	Valletta
Varsovie	Warsaw
Venise	Venice
Vienne	Vienna

THE BRITISH ISLES
Great Britain → England + Wales + Scotland
The United Kingdom → Great Britain + Northern Ireland
The British Isles → The United Kingdom + Republic of Ireland
National capital
Capital
International boundary
Shetland Islands
Lerwick
Orkney Islands
Kirkwall
Thurso
Wick
Lewis
Stornoway
Hebrides
Harris
Little Minch
Skye
Inverness
Aberdeen
Glen More
Spey
Ben Nevis
1 343 m
Dundee
Mull
Oban
Tay
Perth
SCOTLAND
Jura
Islay
Glasgow
EDINBURGH
NORTH SEA
Arran
Tweed
North Channel
Londonderry
NORTHERN IRELAND (Ulster)
BELFAST
Dumfries
Hadrian's Wall
Newcastle-upon-Tyne
Tyne
Sunderland
Carlisle
Middlesbrough
Ouse
Isle of Man
Lancaster
York
Bradford
Leeds
Hull
Blackpool
Irish Sea
REPUBLIC OF IRELAND (Eire)
Manchester
Liverpool
Sheffield
Galway
DUBLIN
Anglesey
Caernavon
ENGLAND
Nottingham
Leicester
Trent
Norwich
Limerick
Great Ouse
Aberystwyth
Birmingham
Coventry
Worcester
Stratford-upon-Avon
Cambridge
WALES
Gloucester
Oxford
Cork
St George's Channel
CARDIFF
LONDON
Swansea
Bristol
Thames
Bath
Canterbury
Dover
Stonehenge
Folkestone
Barnstaple
Southampton
Brighton
Calais
Channel Tunnel
Bournemouth
Portsmouth
Boulogne-sur-Mer
Tintagel
Plymouth
Isle of Wight
St. Ives
English Channel
Isle of Scilly
Scale
100 km
100 miles

The European Union

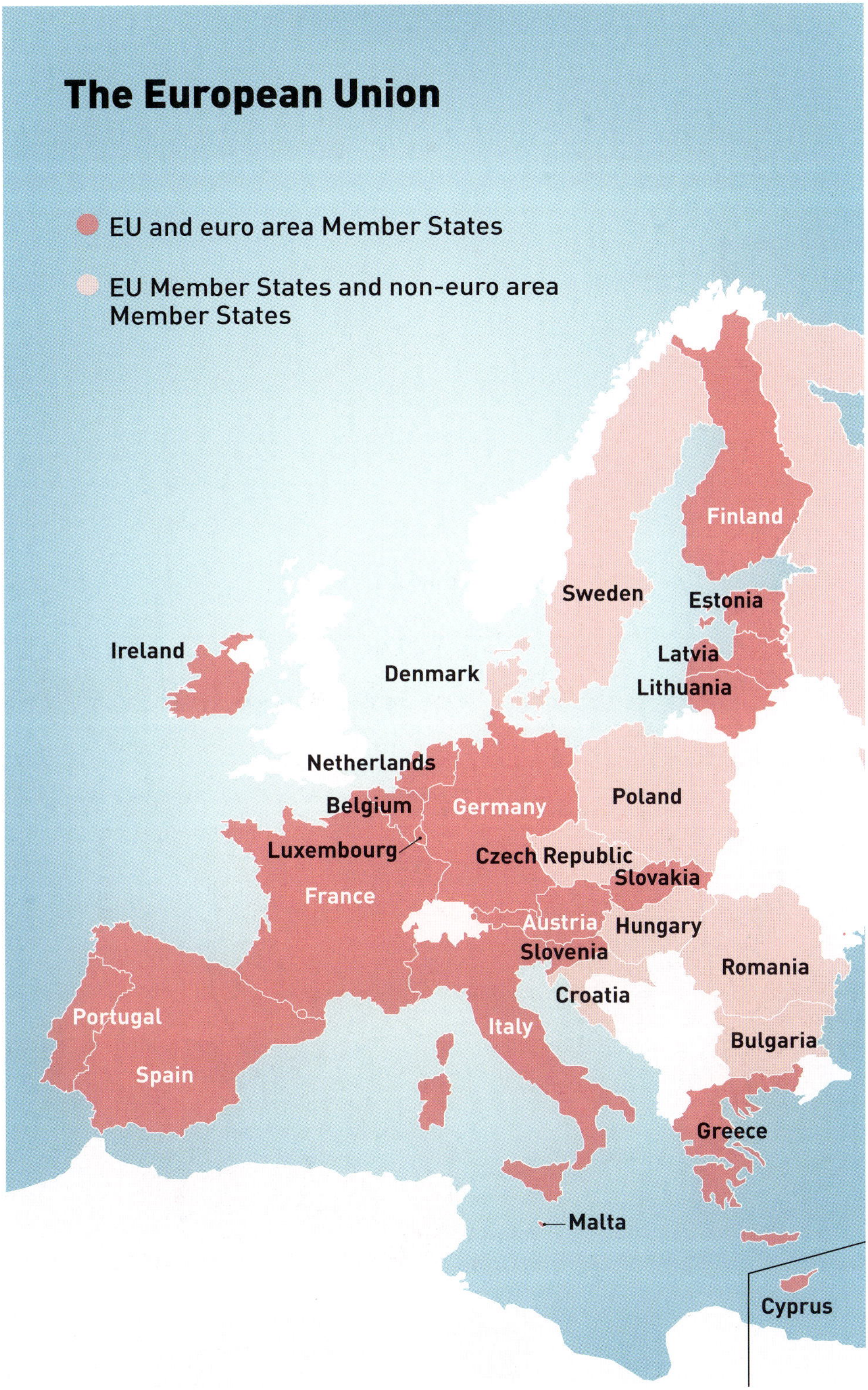

MIXTE
Papier issu de sources responsables
FSC® C022030
www.fsc.org

Achevé d'imprimer en avril 2020 par L.E.G.O. S.p.A. Lavis (TN), ITALIE
N° de project : 10262495 – Dépôt légal : mai 2020